Legal Needs Surveys and Access to Justice

This work is published under the responsibility of the Secretary-General of the OECD. The opinions expressed and arguments employed herein do not necessarily reflect the official views of the member countries of the OECD or the Open Society Foundations.

This document, as well as any data and any map included herein, are without prejudice to the status of or sovereignty over any territory, to the delimitation of international frontiers and boundaries and to the name of any territory, city or area.

Please cite this publication as:
OECD/Open Society Foundations (2019), *Legal Needs Surveys and Access to Justice*, OECD Publishing, Paris.
https://doi.org/10.1787/g2g9a36c-en

ISBN 978-92-64-30952-4 (print)
ISBN 978-92-64-30953-1 (pdf)
ISBN 978-92-64-30954-8 (HTML)
ISBN 978-92-64-30955-5 (epub)

The statistical data for Israel are supplied by and under the responsibility of the relevant Israeli authorities. The use of such data by the OECD is without prejudice to the status of the Golan Heights, East Jerusalem and Israeli settlements in the West Bank under the terms of international law.

Photo credits: Cover © Image courtesy of the Earth Science and Remote Sensing Unit, NASA Johnson Space Center, http://eol.jsc.nasa.gov.

Corrigenda to OECD publications may be found on line at: *www.oecd.org/about/publishing/corrigenda.htm*.

Foreword

Access to justice and legal empowerment are foundational values of intrinsic importance that are also crucial for achieving inclusive and sustainable growth. Governments and civil society organisations (CSOs) alike recognise access to justice as both a fundamental right and a means of guaranteeing opportunities for all. Without it, the most vulnerable groups and people are left behind.

People and businesses regularly face "legal problems"; difficulties in addressing these civil and administrative issues may have significant impact on their ability to participate fully in the economy and society, as well as on their productivity, and relationships. Yet, tools and indicators to measure access to justice are under-developed. While research and measurement methodologies exist for the criminal justice sector, they are less developed in areas of civil justice.

In 2016 the Open Society Justice Initiative ("the Justice Initiative") and the Organisation for Economic Cooperation and Development (OECD), under the auspices of its Public Governance Committee, joined forces to support a better understanding of justice needs and promote effective access to justice and legal empowerment. To do so, our institutions convened representatives from OECD member and partner countries from various links of the justice chain as well CSO and academic experts.

This *Guide on Legal Needs Surveys and Access to Justice* is a result of these efforts. The Guide brings together the experience gained through more than 55 national surveys conducted by governments and civil society organisations in more than 30 jurisdictions in the last 25 years. The approach to legal needs surveys detailed in the Guide reflects a wide array of legal traditions and political and cultural environments, as it has benefitted from measurement initiatives in Korea, Nepal, South Africa, Ukraine and other countries.

The Guide provides a framework for understanding and measuring legal needs as well as methodological guidance and model questions to capture three core components of effective access to justice:

1. The nature and extent of unmet legal and justice needs;
2. The impact of unmet legal and justice needs on individuals, the community and the state; and
3. How specific models of legal assistance and dispute resolution are utilised to meet needs.

The Guide seeks to support countries in better understanding, measuring and gauging their progress in implementing people-centred legal and justice services. It is also designed to support the effective implementation of target 16.3 of the 2030 Agenda ("to promote the rule of law at the national and international levels and to ensure equal access to justice for all') and the OECD Policy Framework for Policy Action on Inclusive Growth.

Finally, the Guide puts forward the concept of a legal needs-based indicator that focuses on access to civil justice. In doing so, it contributes to the work of Praia City Group on Governance Statistics (established by the United Nations Statistical Commission), whose goal is to "encourage countries to produce governance statistics based on sound and documented methodologies and to address the conceptualisation, methodology and instruments needed to produce such statistics."

It is our hope that this pioneering exercise will help us improve access to justice. Understanding people's justice experiences and needs will help countries deliver more effective public policies, not only in the area of justice and legal empowerment, but also in sectors such as health, housing, employment, education.

James Goldston

Executive Director

Open Society Justice Initiative
Open Society Foundations

Marcos Bonturi

Director

Public Governance Directorate

Organisation for Economic Cooperation and Development

Acknowledgements

The Guide is a joint production of the Open Society Justice Initiative ("the Justice Initiative") and the Organisation for Economic Cooperation and Development (OECD) under synergy work on people-focused approaches to measurement of access to justice.

The form and content benefitted from inputs provided by the OECD Public Governance Directorate under the direction of Marcos Bonturi and by the Open Society Foundations' Justice Initiative under the direction of James Goldston and Zaza Namoradze. The OECD work on Equal Access to Justice is led by Tatyana Teplova, Head of Unit, Gender and Justice for Inclusiveness, OECD Public Governance Directorate; coordinated by Chloé Lelievre, Policy Analyst and; under the guidance of Martin Forst, Head of Division, Governance Reviews and Partnerships. The document also draws on the input from Marco Mira d'Ercole, Head of Division, Household Statistics and Progress Measurement. Numerous Justice Initiative staff contributed to the development of this Guide including David Berry, Senior Communications Officer, Matthew Burnett, Policy Officer, Sumaiya Islam, Senior Program Manager, Zaza Namoradze, Director of the Justice Initiative's Berlin Office and Robert O. Varenik, Director of Programs.

Principal authors of the Guide are Professors Pascoe Pleasence and Nigel Balmer, Co-directors of the Centre for Empirical Legal Studies, University College London, with additional content provided by Peter Chapman, Senior Policy Officer, Justice Initiative.

Special thanks are due to the advisory stream of country and expert stakeholders who provided valuable inputs. These include:

1. Statistics South Africa (Raphael Kasonga, Solly Molayi and Isabel Schmidt)
2. Ministerio de Justicia y Derechos Humanos, Argentina (Gustavo Maurino)
3. Law and Justice Foundation of New South Wales, Australia (Geoff Mulherin)
4. Instituto Nacional de Estatística, Cabo Verde (Celso Soares)
5. Departamento Nacional de Planeación, Colombia (Eduardo Freire Delgado, Manuel Felipe Diaz Rangel)
6. Hague Institute for Innovation of Law (HiiL) (Martin Gramatikov)
7. Instituto Nacional de Estadística y Geografía, Mexico (Adrian Franco Barrios)
8. United Nations Development Programme (Aparna Basnyat and Alexandra Wilde)
9. Department of Justice, United States (Allen Beck)
10. World Bank (Paul Prettitore and Bilal Siddiqi)
11. World Justice Project (Alejandro Ponce and Sarah Chamness Long)

In particular, comments and details were provided by authors and expert in the field of legal needs surveys, including Cleber Alvez, Public Defender, State of Rio de Janeiro;

Ab Currie, Canadian Forum on Civil Justice; Hazel Genn, University College London; Gillian Hadfield, University of Toronto; Kuo-Chang Huang, Academia Sinica; Masayuki Murayama, Meiji University; Shruthi Naik; Alan Paterson, University of Strathclyde; Rebecca L. Sandefur, University of Illinois at Urbana-Champaign; Marijke ter Voert, Ministry of Justice, The Netherlands; and Jan Winczorek, University of Warsaw. Numerous representatives from national governmental and civil society organisations also provided valuable feedback on the approach and content of this document, including colleagues from Argentina, Colombia, Indonesia, Kenya, Mongolia, Nepal, Philippines, Sierra Leone, South Africa, Ukraine and the United Kingdom. Colleagues in Korea, Nepal and South Africa experimented with the legal needs methodology presented in the Guide.

Editorial and logistical assistance was made possible by Charlotte Dubald, Roxana Glavanov, Amelia Godber, Myron Manns, Andrea Uhrhammer, Martyna Wanat, Cicely Dupont-Nivore, Lyndon Thompson, Andrew Esson, Meral Gedik and Eleonore Morena.

Table of contents

Tables

Figures

Box

Executive summary

Access to justice underpins inclusive growth and is central to advancing well-being and sustainable development. Effective access to justice helps resolve disputes at the heart of people's lives, promotes government accountability and gives people and businesses confidence to enter into and enforce contracts. In 2008, the United Nations Commission on Legal Empowerment of the Poor estimated that 4 billion people live outside the protection of the law. As part of the 2030 Sustainable Development Agenda, all countries agreed to "promote the rule of law at the national and international levels, and ensure equal access to justice for all" under the Sustainable Development Goal (SDG) 16. Access to justice is both a standalone target and enabler of other development priorities including health and social development.

Access to justice concerns the ability of people to obtain just resolution of justiciable problems (a problem that raises legal issues) and enforce their rights, in compliance with human rights standards; if necessary, through impartial formal or informal institutions and with appropriate legal support. An important component of access to justice is the concept of legal need. Legal need arises whenever a deficit of legal capability requires legal support to appropriately address a justiciable problem to be appropriately dealt with.

According to the broad sample of legal needs surveys used to develop this Guide, justiciable problems are ubiquitous, although people often do not identify their legal dimensions. Common problems include those concerning consumer issues, money, neighbours, family matters, housing and land, employment, social safety net assistance, and access to public services. While there are some differences, patterns of problem experience are remarkably similar across the globe.

Justiciable problems are not randomly distributed across populations. They disproportionally affect disadvantaged groups, and can create and exacerbate disadvantage. One reason for this is that they often bring about or follow from one another, or link to broader socioeconomic problems. Disadvantaged people can draw on fewer resources and have less capability to avoid or mitigate problems. Importantly, the experience of problems increases the likelihood of further problems being experienced.

Why legal needs surveys?

Meaningful understanding of access to justice is crucial for the development of effective civil justice policies, models and financing. Legal needs surveys provide an empirical basis for understanding how peoples' justice issues arise, are experienced and affect a broad range of development priorities. Governments and civil society organisations in diverse countries have conceptualised and implemented legal needs surveys to develop shared understanding, help improve justice services and strengthening linkages across policy sectors.

Legal needs surveys investigate the experience of justiciable problems from the perspective of those who face them (a 'bottom-up' perspective), rather than from that of justice professionals and institutions (a 'top-down' perspective). They seek to identify and explore the full range of responses to problems and, within this, all the sources of help and institutions that are utilised in pursuing problem resolution. They provide a uniquely comprehensive overview that is impossible to achieve by other means.

A framework for conducting legal needs surveys

This Guide builds upon the lessons and experience of 25 years of experience across a range of countries with very different legal traditions. It discusses common pitfalls, key lessons, and effective practice in the implementation of legal needs surveys. It answers common questions in developing, deploying and using legal needs surveys, detailing:

- The essential elements of legal needs survey approaches
- The potential scope of surveys
- How to identify the support that people seek in resolving problems, and their success in doing so
- How to identify processes and institutions involved in problem resolution
- The outcomes and impacts of problems that can be measured
- Common elements of surveys that can be used across jurisdictions and in different contexts
- The contribution surveys can make to creating access to justice indicators

The Guide sets out a framework for the design, implementation and analysis of legal needs surveys. It provides tools in a modular way so that they can be applied in different types of surveys. The Guide examines the concepts, framing, scope and units of measurement used in legal needs surveys. It also proposes taxonomies of justiciable problems, sources of help and dispute resolution processes, to support greater consistency and opportunity for comparison between surveys, as well as reviewing how legal need has been measured through surveys. The Guide further notes that meaningful collaboration between government, civil society and affected communities is critical in developing, implementing and analysing legal needs surveys. Such partnerships are similarly essential for identifying and driving policy reforms.

The Guide proposes model survey questions concerning: problem identification; problem seriousness; problem impact; sources of help; problem resolving behaviour; process; if and how problems have concluded; strategy decisions; perceptions of dispute resolution processes and outcomes; the cost of problem resolution; legal capability; and duration. It also incorporates these into illustrative questionnaires, to provide resources for survey planners.

The proposed taxonomies are built upon eight primary justiciable problem categories, eight distinct categories of sources of help and five process categories.

Towards meaningful access to justice indicators

Finally, the Guide suggests strategies for measuring access to justice with legal needs surveys. The UN 2030 Agenda provides an opportunity to define critical global dimensions of access to justice under SDG target 16.3, going beyond the criminal justice system. National and global policy and measurement frameworks often fail to account meaningfully for the prevalence of civil justice issues and the substantive costs they impose on society.

Access to civil justice indicators built from legal needs surveys can increase the visibility of civil justice barriers and highlight the experiences of particular populations. A global legal needs-based indicator focused on access to civil justice could also complement work towards other SDGs by enabling policy makers to better identify how justice systems interact with other developmental priorities.

In accordance with the SDG framework, civil justice measures need to be capable of "timely and reliable" disaggregation in order to highlight the experience of different vulnerable groups.

Overview of legal needs surveys and access to justice

Inclusive development and access to justice

Access to justice and the rule of law contribute to inclusive development in numerous ways. Effective access to justice helps, for example, to resolve employment and land disputes, promotes government accountability and allows businesses, large and small, to confidently enter into and enforce contracts. Enforcing legal entitlements and effectively and equitably resolving disputes are not just issues of law and rights; effective enforcement of legal entitlements are enablers and outcomes of inclusive development.

In September 2015, United Nations (UN) member states adopted a global development framework that recognises access to justice as both a development goal as well as an enabler of other development priorities such as health, the environment, and social development. In Sustainable Development Goal (SDG) target 16.3, member states agreed to "promote the rule of law at the national and international levels, and ensure equal access to justice for all,"[1] thereby highlighting the need for more effective measures of civil justice.

The addition of access to justice into the SDGs reflects an emerging consensus that access to justice is central to inclusive development.

For example, the World Bank's 2011 *World Development Report: Conflict, Security, and Development* found that politically fragile or conflict-affected countries failed to achieve even a single Millennium Development Goal (The World Bank, 2011, p. 1). The report argued that injustice and barriers to access to justice were critical obstacles to a population and country's overall development and stated "strengthening legitimate institutions and governance to provide citizen security, justice, and jobs is crucial to break cycles of violence" (The World Bank, 2011, p. 2). Similarly, the UN Women's 2011 report *Progress of the World's Women: In Pursuit of Justice* found that even with the global trend of expanding women's rights and legal entitlements across development sectors, there was an urgent need to invest in women's access to justice. Investing in access to justice will serve to "accelerat[e] progress on gender equality and ensur[e] that excluded women and girls are not left behind" (UN Women, 2011, p. 121). The Human Rights Council's *Expert Mechanism on the Rights of Indigenous Peoples* declared that access to justice is "essential for the protection and promotion of all other human rights" for indigenous peoples.[2] The Council recommendations suggest that "family law, child protection law and civil law" are critical to address socioeconomic disadvantage."[3]

Problems of access to justice and inclusive development are not just limited to developing countries and fragile socio-political contexts; legal problems and disputes are pervasive in many contexts. We live in an increasingly "law-thick" world (Hadfield, 2010, p. 133), where processes of "juridification" (Habermas, 1987). have "institutionalised in civil law a large share of the routine stuff of life" (Sandefur, 2016, p. 445). Legal rights, responsibilities and protections provide frameworks for behaviour in the spheres of, for example, consumerism, education, employment, children and families, health, housing, land, access to natural resources and welfare.

As legal entitlements and responsibilities expand, so too does the need for access to justice. Cappelletti and Garth famously argued "the possession of rights is meaningless without mechanisms for their effective vindication" (Cappelletti and Garth, 1978, p. 185). Thus, alongside this growth of national and supranational law there has arisen a great interest in whether populations have effective access to justice; both in terms of the means available to people, and obstacles they face in seeking to resolve "justiciable" problems (i.e. problems raising legal issues, whether or not these are recognised as such by individuals facing them, and whether or not action taken to deal with them involves lawyers or legal process) (Genn, 1999, p. 12).[4]

In 2008, the United Nations Commission on Legal Empowerment of the Poor estimated that four billion people live outside the protection of the law, and that "the majority of humanity is on the outside looking in [...] on the law's protection" (UN Commission on Legal Empowerment of the Poor, 2008, p. 3). In the face of these challenges, the United Nations Development Programme (UNDP) argues that access to justice is "a basic human right as well as an indispensable means to combat poverty, prevent and resolve conflicts" (United Nations Development Programme, 2004, p. 3). The Organisation for Economic Cooperation and Development (OECD) speaks of the inability of significant proportions of the population to resolve appropriately disputes and problems, which "diminishes access to economic opportunity, reinforces the poverty trap, and undermines human potential and inclusive growth" (OECD, 2016, p. 1). According to the OECD:

> *"Many legal and justice services remain fragmented, uncoordinated, underdeveloped thus limiting justice sector productivity, sustainability and value for money." (OECD, 2016, p. 1)*

As attention to access to justice has increased, those responsible for planning and budgeting have focused primarily on criminal justice processes. Although the SDGs adopt a broad articulation of the linkages between access to justice and development, the global indicators selected to measure progress are restricted to criminal justice. These indicators measure access to justice through the reduction of "unsentenced detainees as proportion of overall prison population"[5] and increases in the "proportion of victims of violence in the previous 12 months who reported their victimisation to competent authorities or other officially recognised conflict resolution mechanisms."[6]

When civil legal issues are explored in planning and budgeting, it is primarily through a focus on administrative data, such as total numbers of cases and time required to resolve particular legal issues. Such administrative data generated in courts and justice sector institutions provides a narrow perspective of access to justice. People and organisations seek justice from a range of judicial, legislative, executive, customary and civil society organisations (Figure 1). Yet, current national and global measures privilege administrative data within the court system.

This is beginning to shift. Numerous countries have begun to bring broader planning for access to justice into their development and strategic plans. In Colombia, the Department of National Planning has developed an access to justice index (*Índice de Acceso Efectivo a la Justicia*), making it another element of inclusive development.[7] In South Africa, Statistics South Africa has adapted their victims of crime survey into a broader Governance, Peace, Security and Justice Survey that aims to improve understanding of the scope of legal needs, sources of information and advice and strategies that people rely on to resolve them. In 2017, the Inter-Agency and Expert Group (IAEG), the UN-body responsible for developing global indicators to measure progress towards the SDGs, recognised a global need to supplement criminal indicators with an indicator focused on "access to civil justice".[8]

Figure 1. Components of justice system

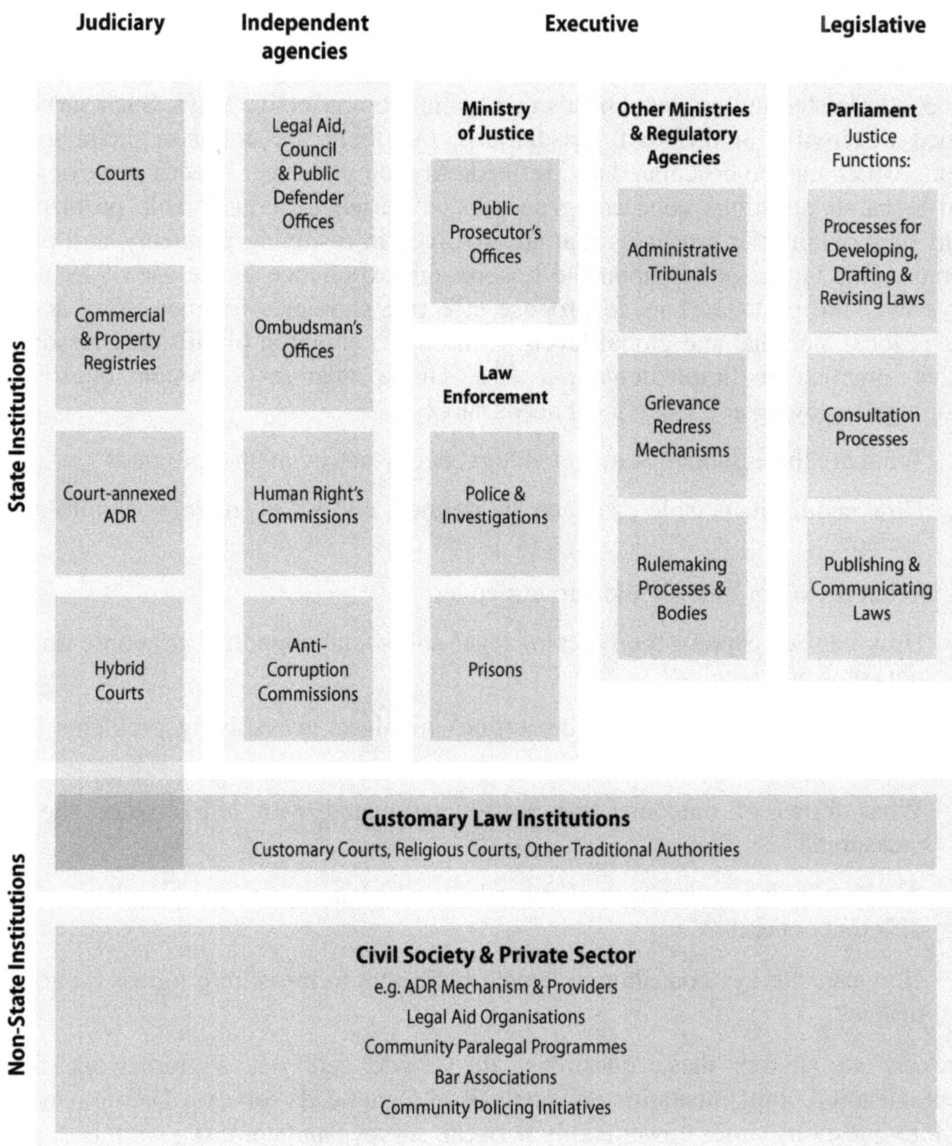

Source: Adapted from World Bank (2012).

Legal needs surveys are a critical way for planners, policymakers and advocates to understand meaningful progress towards access to justice. In the same way that victimisation surveys promote understanding of crime and violence from the perspective of people as opposed to institutions,[9] legal needs surveys reveal the frequency and diversity of legal problems, as well as the range of official and unofficial institutions people use to seek resolution. Such surveys cut across and go beyond the plethora of government and other administrative data, to provide a multidimensional picture of the ways in which access to justice can be secured, and so help to improve development outcomes.

This Guide offers a strategy and methodological framework for justice and development policymakers to understand progress towards greater access to justice.

Purpose of this document

This document seeks to assist planners, statisticians, policymakers and advocates to develop, administer and use legal needs surveys in more effective ways. Such surveys are designed differently in different jurisdictions, but there are common methodological elements which can be articulated and refined. At their core, legal needs surveys address shared research questions concerning peoples' experience of justiciable problems, the support they obtain, the processes that are involved in resolving problems, and problem outcomes. This Guide builds upon the lessons and experience in the use of legal needs surveys over the past 25 years to propose effective strategies for measuring access to justice at local, national and global levels. It discusses common pitfalls, key lessons, and effective practice in implementation. The Guide answers common questions in developing, deploying and using legal needs surveys:

1. What are the essential elements of legal needs survey methodologies?
2. How should justiciable problems be defined, and what problems should surveys include?
3. What period of time should surveys cover?
4. How can we capture the types of legal and social support that people do (or do not) seek and receive?
5. How can the processes and institutions involved in resolving problems be best identified?
6. What forms of outcome and impact associated with legal issues should be measured?
7. Are there common elements that can be used in surveys across jurisdictions and in different contexts?
8. How can surveys contribute to create indicators to measure progress on access to justice?

In seeking to answer these questions, the Guide sets out a framework for the conceptualisation, implementation and analysis of legal needs surveys. The time available to explore questions varies considerably between surveys and contexts; so, this document approaches issues in a modular way, providing guidance that could be incorporated into different types of surveys.

This Guide does not seek to prescribe a template for measuring access to justice. A narrow template approach would constrain assessments, which should be "tailor[ed …] to the specific contexts of each country, the diversity of needs and uniqueness of each individual case" (United Nations Development Programme, 2012, p. 2, p. 9). However, legal needs surveys are a distinct form of access to justice assessment, grounded in a very particular approach and set of concepts that will benefit from greater collaboration and consistency. While unique approaches and survey questions will be necessary in relation to unique research questions, there are good reasons for fostering greater coherence in relation to shared legal needs research questions. Many surveys continue to ignore and overlook important lessons learned from the last 25 years of experience, and the methodological framework offered by this document will help improve the quality and replicability of legal needs surveys.

In addition to supporting local and national planners, statisticians, policymakers and advocates, this Guide seeks to contribute to global discourse on measuring access to justice. As noted previously, the IAEG is committed to developing broader global indicators on "access to civil justice", and legal needs surveys can be a powerful tool for meaningful measurement. Similarly, the UN Statistical Commission's Praia City Group on Governance Statistics is evaluating the status of global governance statistics, and legal needs surveys will be an important source of data for access to justice.

Structure of this document

Chapter 1 defines access to justice and legal needs, and then explores the nature, history, purpose, limitations and impact of legal needs surveys. In doing this, Chapter 1 describes how legal needs surveys are a unique and essential tool for understanding access to justice, reviews the general scope of surveys, and illustrates how legal needs surveys have shaped policy to improve outcomes.

Chapter 2 establishes a methodological and conceptual framework for the conduct of legal needs surveys, and offers illustrative taxonomies of legal problems, sources of help and dispute resolution processes with multiple levels of detail. Chapter 2 also addresses how surveys can be used to measure legal needs.

Chapter 3 provides a series of models containing core questions, along with explanations of their form. It then situates these model questions within an illustrative short-form questionnaire, explaining its contents and format.

Chapter 4 describes how the methodologies of legal needs surveys can contribute to indicators of access to justice, including their use in the SDG framework.

Annexes provide an annotated summary of model survey questions, an illustrative long-form questionnaire, expanding upon the short-form questionnaire in Chapter 3, and a list of topics addressed by legal needs surveys conducted in the past 25 years.

Notes

[1] Target 16.3, as detailed in Resolution 70/1 of the UN General Assembly, 25 September 2015, entitled "Transforming our World: The 2030 Agenda for Sustainable Development".

[2] United Nations A/HRC/24/50, "Access to justice in the promotion and protection of the rights of indigenous peoples: Study by the Expert Mechanism on the Rights of Indigenous Peoples" (2013), Para 3, available at http://undocs.org/A/HRC/24/50.

[3] United Nations A/HRC/24/50, Access to justice in the promotion and protection of the rights of indigenous peoples: Study by the Expert Mechanism on the Rights of Indigenous Peoples (2013), Annex. Expert Mechanism advice No. 5 (2013), available at http://undocs.org/A/HRC/24/50 notes that: "Historical injustices contribute to multiple contemporary disadvantages for indigenous peoples, which in turn increase the likelihood of indigenous peoples coming into contact with the justice system. The relationship of indigenous peoples with domestic criminal justice systems cannot, therefore, be considered in isolation from historical factors or the current economic, social and cultural status of indigenous peoples. Moreover, there are other areas of law, including family law, child protection law and civil law that have an impact on this relationship. Solutions include not only reforms to criminal justice systems themselves but also measures addressing the socioeconomic situation of indigenous peoples and all human rights of indigenous peoples which are interrelated, interdependent and indivisible".

[4] Genn's definition reflects her focus on the United Kingdom's national legal framework. In a global context, a definition of "justiciable" problems might include explicit reference to issues of international law and situate the definition, as with access to justice, in a broader context of international human rights law. See also n. 25 below.

[5] SDG 16.3.2 available at https://unstats.un.org/sdgs/indicators/indicators-list/.

[6] SDG 16.3.1 available at https://unstats.un.org/sdgs/indicators/indicators-list/.

[7] See Colombia's Department of National Planning: http://dnpsig.maps.arcgis.com/apps/Cascade/index.html?appid=b92a7ab2fe6f4a06a6aec88581d6873e.

[8] See Report of the Inter-agency and Expert Group on Sustainable Development Goal Indicators, E/CN.3/2017/2 (2016) annex V available at https://unstats.un.org/unsd/statcom/48th-session/documents/2017-2-IAEG-SDGs-E.pdf.

[9] The UNODC-UNECE Manual on Victimization Surveys (2009) available at: https://www.unodc.org/documents/data-and-analysis/Crime-statistics/Manual_on_Victimization_surveys_2009_web.pdf.

References

Cappelletti, M. and B. Garth (1978), "Access to justice: The newest wave in the worldwide movement to make rights effective", *Buffalo Law Review*, pp. 181-292.

Genn, G. (1999), *Paths to Justice: What People Do and Think About Going to Law*, Oxford.

Habermas, J. (1987), *The Theory of Communicative Action, Volume 2: Lifeworld and System*, Polity Press, Cambridge.

Hadfield, G. (2010), "Higher demand, lower supply? A comparative assessment of the legal resource landscape for ordinary Americans", *Fordham Urban Law Journal*, pp. 129-156.

OECD (2016), *Towards Inclusive Growth – Access to Justice: Supporting People Focused Justice Services*, OECD, Paris.

Sandefur, R. (2016), "What we know and need to know about the legal needs of the public", *Carolina Law Review*, pp. 443-459.

UN Women (2011), *Progress of the World's Women: In Pursuit of Justice*, UN Women, New York.

United Nations Commission on Legal Empowerment of the Poor (2008), *Making the Law Work for Everyone: Report of the Commission on Legal Empowerment of the Poor*, United Nations Development Programme, New York.

United Nations Development Programme (2012), *Access to Justice Assessments in the Asia Pacific: A Review of Experiences and Tools from the Region*, United Nations Development Programme, Bangkok.

United Nations Development Programme (2004), *Access to Justice: Practice Note*, New York: United Nations.

United Nations Human Rights Council (2013), *Access to Justice in the Promotion and Protection of the Rights of Indigenous Peoples: Study by the Expert Mechanism on the Rights of Indigenous Peoples*, United Nations Human Rights Council, New York.

World Bank (2011), *World Development Report 2011: Conflict, Security, and Development*, The World Bank, Washington, DC.

Chapter 1. Access to Justice and Legal Needs Surveys

This Chapter establishes a methodological and conceptual framework for the conduct of legal needs surveys, and offers illustrative taxonomies of legal problems, sources of help and dispute resolution processes, with multiple levels of detail. This chapter also addresses how surveys can be used to measure legal needs

Defining access to justice and legal needs

Although the definition is contested (Schetzer et al., 2002, p. 5),[1] access to justice is broadly concerned with the ability of people to obtain just resolution of justiciable problems and enforce their rights, in compliance with human rights standards (United Nations Development Programme, 2005, p. 5);[2] if necessary, through impartial formal or informal institutions of justice and with appropriate legal support.[3] In its "descriptive aspect", access to justice "denotes the general subject of the extent to which citizens are able to gain access to the legal services necessary to protect and vindicate their legal rights" (Cornford, 2016, p. 28). In functional terms, this does not mean that use of legal services is necessary to ensure access to justice, only that appropriate services are available for those who are unable to achieve otherwise appropriate solutions to justiciable problems.

The concept of access to justice is thus closely linked to the constituent concept of legal need. In broad terms, legal need arises whenever a deficit of legal capability[4] necessitates legal support to enable a justiciable issue to be appropriately dealt with. A legal need is unmet if a justiciable issue is inappropriately dealt with as a consequence of effective legal support not having been available when necessary to make good a deficit of legal capability. If a legal need is unmet, there is no access to justice.

Beyond this, legal need is an "elusive" concept, difficult to "pin down" (Engel, 1998, p. 124);[5] largely due to the nature of the concept's constituent components. Views differ on the constitution of legal capability, the arbiters of necessity (whether those facing problems, experts, or others), the forms of support necessitated (whether, for example, capability building, informational, relieving, etc.) and the appropriateness of how justiciable problems are dealt with (which can attach to decision making, processes or outcomes, and again in relation to which there are multiple potential arbiters).

Understanding the dimensions of access to justice and legal needs

Understanding access to justice and legal needs requires a multidimensional approach to research and data management within the justice system. Access to justice extends beyond formal process to informal dispute resolution and, ultimately, to social justice and the distribution of welfare, resources and opportunity. The above definition of access to justice incorporates at least seven distinct dimensions:

- The substance of law
- The availability of formal or informal institutions to secure justice
- The quality of formal or informal institutions of justice
- The availability of legal assistance
- The quality of legal assistance
- The quality of outcomes
- Legal capability

Understanding progress towards each of these dimensions requires a range of tools and techniques. Chapter 4. discusses sources of data in more detail and this Guide provides an in-depth exploration of a specific tool: legal needs surveys.

What are legal needs surveys?

Legal needs surveys investigate the experience of justiciable problems from the perspective of those who face them, rather than the professions and institutions that may play a role in their resolution. Thus, legal needs surveys can identify and explore the full range of responses to problems and, within this, the full range of sources of help and institutions available. Problems may be personal, organisational or shared (within households, communities, etc.); and while most legal needs surveys have focused on personal experience, some have focused on the experience of businesses or defined social units (such as households).

Legal needs surveys are distinct from crime victimisation or offending surveys, as their focus is on civil legal issues (family, commercial, administrative, etc.);[6] although many stand-alone legal needs surveys also enquire into the experience of matters relating to criminal law (beyond those that are counterparts of civil law). Legal needs surveys are distinct from other forms of access to justice assessment survey[7] in their comprehensive approach to identifying a range of justiciable problems, and their primary focus on experience, rather than perceptions and attitudes.[8]

Legal needs surveys have a long history; the first were conducted in the 1930s.[9] The use of such surveys has increased in recent decades, and they are now relatively commonplace across the globe.[10] Over the past 25 years, more than 55 large-scale (i.e. 1,000 respondents or more) stand-alone national legal needs surveys of individuals have been conducted in more than 30 separate jurisdictions.[11] Legal needs modules have also been incorporated into seven large-scale government run national surveys,[12] along with the World Justice Project's *General Population Poll,* which is routinely implemented in over 100 countries (Adams et al., 2017; Adams et al., 2018).

As shown in Table 1.1, in addition to the *General Population Poll,* in the 25 years to 31 December 2017 national legal needs surveys have been conducted in Argentina, Australia, Bangladesh, Brazil (module), Bulgaria, Canada, Colombia, England and Wales, Georgia, Hong Kong, India, Japan, Jordan, Kenya, Kyrgyzstan, Lebanon, Macedonia, Mali, Mexico (module), Moldova, Mongolia, Nepal, the Netherlands, New Zealand, Northern Ireland, Poland, Scotland, Sierra Leone, Slovakia, Taiwan, Tajikistan, Tunisia, Uganda, Ukraine, the United Arab Emirates and the United States. Extensive sub-national surveys have also been carried out, for example, in China,[13] Ecuador,[14] Russia,[15] Indonesia[16] and Yemen,[17] along with smaller surveys in countries including Azerbaijan, Rwanda and Egypt.[18]

Table 1.1. National legal needs surveys conducted in the last 25 years (to 31 December 2017)

Country	Study	Date	Size	Mode	Funder	Scope
United States	Comprehensive Legal Needs Study	1993	3 087	Mixed	Legal Profession	Low/mid-income
England & Wales	Paths to Justice	1997	4 125	Face-to-face	Research grant	General population
New Zealand	Legal Advice & Assistance Survey	1997	5 431	Face-to-face	Legal aid agency	General population
Scotland	Paths to Justice Scotland	1998	2 684	Face-to-face	Research grant	General population
England & Wales	English & Welsh Civil & Social Justice Survey	2001	5 611	Face-to-face	Legal aid agency	General population
Netherlands	Paths to Justice in the Netherlands	2003	3 516	Online	Government	General population
Canada	National Survey of Civil Justice Problems	2004	4 501	Telephone	Government	Low-income
England & Wales	English & Welsh Civil & Social Justice Survey	2004	5 015	Face-to-face	Legal aid agency	General population
Slovakia	Legal Needs in Slovakia	2004	1 085	Face-to-face	World Bank	General population
Japan	National Survey of Everyday Life & the Law	2005	12 408	Face-to-face	Research grant	General population
Northern Ireland	Northern Ireland Legal Needs Survey	2005	3 361	Face-to-face	Government	General population
Canada	National Survey of Civil Justice Problems	2006	6 665	Telephone	Government	General population
England & Wales	English & Welsh Civil & Social Justice Survey	2006-9	10 537	Face-to-face	Legal aid agency	General population
Hong Kong	Demand & Supply of Legal & Related Services	2006	10 385	Mixed	Government	General population
Japan	Access to Legal Advice: National Survey	2006	5 330	Face-to-face	Research grant	General population
New Zealand	Unmet Legal Needs & Access to Services	2006	7 200	Telephone	Legal aid agency	General population
Bulgaria	Access to Justice & Legal Needs in Bulgaria	2007	2 730	Face-to-face	Open Society Foundations	General population
Japan	Everyday Life & Law	2007	5 500	Online	Research grant	General population
Australia	Legal Australia-Wide Survey	2008	20 716	Telephone	Legal aid agency	General population
Canada	National Survey of Civil Justice Problems	2008	7 002	Telephone	Government	General population
Bangladesh	Survey of citizens' experiences of crimes and civil wrongs	2009	9 753	Face-to-face	World Bank/DfID	General population
Netherlands	Paths to Justice in the Netherlands	2009	5 166	Online	Government	General population
England & Wales	English & Welsh Civil & Social Justice Panel Survey	2010	3 806	Face-to-face	Legal aid agency	General population
Ukraine	Legal Capacity of the Ukrainian Population	2010	2 463	Face-to-face	Open Society Foundations	General population
Jordan	Legal Aid Survey	2011	8 968	Face-to-face	World Bank	General population
Moldova	Met and Unmet Legal Needs in Moldova	2011	2 489	Face-to-face	Open Society Foundations	General population
Taiwan	Legal Dispute Settlement Behaviour	2011	5 601	Face-to-face	Research sector	General population
Colombia	National Legal Needs Survey	2012	3 321	Face-to-face	World Bank/Government	General population

England & Wales	English & Welsh Civil & Social Justice Panel Survey	2012	3 911	Face-to-face	Legal aid agency	General population
England & Wales	Legal Services Benchmarking Survey	2012	4 017	Online	Regulator	General population
Georgia	KAP Survey Concerning Justiciable Events	2012	4 206	Face-to-face	Open Society Foundations	General population
Kyrgyzstan	Access to Legal Services for Low Income People	2012	2 424	Face-to-face	Open Society Foundations	Low-income
Macedonia	Macedonian Legal Needs Survey	2012	2 858	Telephone	Open Society Foundations	General population
Tajikistan	Demand for Legal Aid	2012	1 200	Face-to-face	Open Society Foundations	General population
Netherlands	Justice Needs and Satisfaction Survey	2013	4 228	Online	HiiL	General population
Netherlands	Paths to Justice in the Netherlands	2014	5 773	Online	Government	General population
Canada	National Survey of Everyday Legal Problems	2014	3 263	Telephone	Research grant	General population
England & Wales	Legal Problem Resolution Survey	2014	10 058	Telephone	Government	General population
Mali	Justice Needs and Satisfaction Survey	2014	8 400	Face-to-face	Int. Dev. (Netherlands)	General population
England & Wales	Survey of Individuals' Handling of Legal Issues	2015	8 192	Online	Regulator	General population
Poland	Barriers to Access to Legal Services	2015	3 500	Face-to-face	Legal Profession	General population
Uganda	Justice Needs and Satisfaction Survey	2015	6 202	Face-to-face	Int. Dev. (Sweden)/NGO	General population
Argentina	Unmet Legal Needs and Access to Justice	2016	2 800	Telephone	Government	General population
Moldova	Legal Empowerment Needs Survey	2016	1 112	Face-to-face	Open Society Foundations	Young people
Mongolia	Legal Needs Survey	2016	1 630	Face-to-face	Open Society Foundations	General population
Tunisia	Justice Needs and Satisfaction Survey	2016	~7 500	Face-to-face	Int. Dev. (Netherlands)	General population
Ukraine	Justice Needs and Satisfaction Survey	2016	6 559	Face-to-face	Int. Dev. (Netherlands)	General population
United Arab Emirates	Justice Needs and Satisfaction Survey	2016	3 924	Face-to-face	Government	General population
Bangladesh	Justice Needs and Satisfaction Survey	2017	6 000	Face-to-face	Int. Dev. (N'/lands)/BRAC	General population
India	Access to Justice Survey	2017	45 551	Face-to-face	DAKSH	General population
Jordan	Justice Needs and Satisfaction Survey	2017	6 001	Face-to-face	Int. Dev. (Netherlands)	General population
Kenya	Justice Needs and Satisfaction Survey	2017	~6 000	Face-to-face	World Bank/Judiciary	General population
Lebanon	Justice Needs and Satisfaction Survey	2017	6 000	Face-to-face	Int. Dev. (Netherlands)	General population
New Zealand	Unmet Legal Needs Survey	2017	~1 000	Telephone	Government	Low-income
Sierra Leone	Needs Assessment for Provision of Non-Criminal Justice Services	2017	1 057	Face-to-face	Open Society Foundations	General population
Nepal	Legal Need Survey Nepal	2017-2018	3 000	Face-to-face	Open Society Foundations	General population

Note: On the 2012 the Legal Services Benchmarking Survey in England and Wales: Number represents respondents who had experienced at least one legal problem, identified through an initial screening survey.

Many sub-national surveys have also been undertaken in jurisdictions in which national surveys have been undertaken;[19] sometimes targeting specific population groups, such as those living in disadvantaged urban settlements in Argentina (Bercovich et al., 2013). In addition, eight dedicated large-scale national legal needs surveys of businesses have been conducted in recent years (Table 1.2).[20]

Table 1.2. Legal needs survey modules within larger national surveys

Country/Institution	Study	Date	Size	Mode	Funder	Scope
Scotland	Crime and Justice Survey	2008 →	6-12 000	Face-to-face	Government	General population
Brazil	National Household Sample Survey	2009	399 387	Face-to-face	Government	General population
Kenya	Kenya Integrated Household Budget Survey	2015-2016	21 773	Face-to-face	Government	General population
Colombia	National Quality of Life Survey	2016	51 492	Face-to-face	Government	General population
World Justice Project	General Population Poll	2016 →	~ 1 000	Mixed	Various	General population
Mexico	General Population Poll	2017	25 600	Face-to-face	Government	General population

Since 31st December 2017, further surveys have been undertaken and more are planned to be undertaken. For example, adding to the list of jurisdictions below, a stand-alone survey was undertaken in South Korea early in 2018, a similar survey is planned for Italy and Statistics South Africa is incorporating a legal needs module into its large-scale Governance, Public Safety and Justice Survey from 2018. These have substantially drawn, or will draw, on drafts of this Guide.

Why conduct legal needs surveys?

Legal needs surveys provide a uniquely comprehensive overview of the justice system and people's experience of resolving justiciable problems. It is an overview that is impossible to achieve by other means and, as such, legal needs surveys provide vital data concerning access to justice. Such surveys provide an empirical basis for understanding how people's justice issues arise and how they affect numerous development sectors. At a national level, they are increasingly viewed as an important tool for policymakers and civil society. From Argentina to Ukraine, Mongolia to Sierra Leone, governments and civil society organisations have conceptualised and implemented legal needs surveys with a goal towards improving justice sector services and strengthening linkages across sectors.

Administrative data – collected by courts, legal service providers, civil society legal assistance programmes, etc. – is essential for programming and assessment. However, they cannot provide policymakers with the information necessary to assess the true scope of needs, as they do not encompass problems that parties deal with only informally or ignore. Moreover, fragmented responsibility for administrative data, a lack of standardisation and data duplication across government agencies and organisations makes it extremely difficult, and in some cases impossible, to piece together different administrative data to create even a limited aggregate picture. The same limitations attach to data collected from professionals working both within the legal system and outside it.

Legal needs surveys can look across and beyond institutions and the experience of professionals. They are unique in that they enable the collection of data concerning problems involving no legal services or processes, in addition to those that do. Legal needs surveys thus provide the "big picture" of people's efforts to access justice. They enable the quantification of justiciable problem experience across populations, mapping of patterns of problem resolving behaviour, and illuminate changes in experience and behaviour over time. They can also identify obstacles to accessing legal services and processes, such as poor service delivery, from individual and community perspectives. They also provide insight into levels of legal capability (including legal understanding, awareness of services, legal confidence, etc.), attitudes towards and trust in the justice system, and the relation of justiciable problems to wider social and economic problems and morbidity.

Legal needs surveys are not an alternative to analyses of administrative data and data derived from professionals working in the legal system. Rather, they are an essential complement. Legal needs surveys contextualise administrative data and provide an overview of a population's perspective on access to justice. As Mahamane Maïga, Director of Mali's Justice, Planning and Statistics Unit, stated during a strategic workshop following the 2014 Malian legal needs survey:

> *"Normally, we are the ones who judge. This time, it is the citizens who are judging us." (Barendrecht et al., 2014a, p. 101)*

The triangulation of administrative and survey data is common across other sectors. In health, for example, administrative data is supplemented in some jurisdictions by the standardised, nationally representative *Demographic and Health Surveys* (DHS), which "provide data for a wide range of monitoring and impact evaluation indicators in the areas of population, health, and nutrition."[21] Concerning food security, the UN's Food and Agriculture Organisation supplements more orthodox approaches to assessing food security (for example food availability or nutritional status) with the *Food Insecurity Experience Scale*,[22] a survey module based on respondents' experiences. With regard to land tenure, the global community has recently agreed to a core set of household survey questions to measure the strength of tenure from the perspective of the population as opposed to legal assessments.[23]

As Table 1.1 and Table 1.2 show, legal needs surveys to date (particularly stand-alone national surveys) have historically tended to be undertaken in upper and middle-income jurisdictions, with relatively few stand-alone surveys conducted in low income jurisdictions. This is changing, however. Earlier legal needs surveys tended to be conducted in jurisdictions with well-established and relatively well-funded legal infrastructures (in particular, public legal assistance services and legal aid schemes). Interest tended to focus on patterns of vulnerability, problem clustering, problem impact, advice seeking behaviour, obstacles to resolving problems, and individual capability. This interest was generally set in the context of efforts to better target and develop established services and processes. In more recent years, interest in legal needs surveys has spread to a far broader range of jurisdictions. This has included jurisdictions with emerging legal infrastructures (or legal infrastructures undergoing fundamental reform following socio-political transformation) where there is increasing recognition of the value of such surveys to explore the reach of law, legal empowerment (Golub and McQuay, 2001),[24] the nature and role of customary dispute resolution processes, microjustice,[25] and appropriate forms of legal services infrastructure (in particular, public legal assistance services and legal aid schemes). In these jurisdictions, interest is often set within the context of the rule of law.

As will be discussed, the choice of the location and purpose of a survey has an impact on how it can and should be undertaken. Correspondingly, this document attempts to provide, for the first time, comprehensive guidance appropriate to all jurisdictions.

Limits of legal needs surveys

While legal needs surveys provide a unique overview of the experience of justiciable problems across populations, they have limits. As pointed out above, they complement and situate, rather than supplant, other core sources of justice data. Administrative data, in particular, remains vital in assessing the impact of specific interventions. Owing to their quantitative form, they are less effective in equipping policymakers with detailed accounts and explanations underlying particular decisions. Here, in-depth qualitative methods are generally more insightful. Also, while repeated cross-sectional and longitudinal[26] surveys can clearly demonstrate changes in behaviour and justice outcomes over time, and highlight the impact of broad reform programmes, they are – owing to the fact that correlation is distinct from causation – less suited to isolating the impact of particular interventions or service reforms, whether at an individual or societal level. Experiments and quasi-experiments employing different data collection methods are generally more insightful.[27] And, while legal needs surveys provide valuable insight into the relative use of particular legal services or processes, they can be – because of the technical nature of certain aspects[28] – ill-suited to exposing the details of some service or process use. This is particularly so in the case of general population surveys which seek to capture details of rare service or process use, as these surveys inefficiently capture data concerning phenomena experienced by only a small proportion of respondents.[29] Again, observation or administrative data is generally more insightful. Table 1.3 summarises the relative strengths and weaknesses of legal needs surveys.

Table 1.3. Utility of legal needs surveys

Ideally suited to	Incidence/patterns of justiciable problem experience, including for specific population groups
	Prevalence/patterns of problem resolving behaviour
	Sources of help
	Obstacles to access
	Awareness (of law and services)
	The cost of legal services to individuals
	Individuals' perspectives
Reasonably suited to	Nature of help obtained
	Perceived causes/consequences of justiciable problems
	Perceived impact of legal services
	Rationales for/objectives of behaviour
	Manner of dispute resolution
	The cost of legal services to individuals
	Impact of broad reform programmes
Less suited to	Technical aspects of service delivery/formal legal processes
	Rare problem types and behaviours (unless appropriate sample frame)
	Causes/consequences of justiciable problems (beyond perceptions)
	Impact of specific legal services (beyond perceptions)
	Impact of specific reforms

The above limitations do not detract from the core utility of legal needs surveys, nor take away from the fact that legal needs surveys are flexible tools. Surveys can be used within a variety of research design frameworks and alongside other forms of data collection as part of a "triangulated" research design, in which multiple methods are used to obtain "a more detailed and balanced picture of the situation" (Altrichter et al., 2008, p. 147).[30]

What have we learned from legal needs surveys?

Prevalence of justiciable problems

Despite significant variation in the design of the legal needs surveys conducted over the past 25 years, a remarkably consistent big picture has emerged across diverse national contexts. First and foremost, it is evident that justiciable problems are ubiquitous across the globe.[31] The lowest estimate from the surveys detailed in Table 1.1 was that 10% of adults experienced one or more problems over a two-year period (2016 Colombian survey); while the highest was that 90% of adults experienced problems over a four-year period (2015 Ugandan survey).[32] Most commonly, estimates fell in the range of 30% to 60% over a three or four-year period.

The ubiquity of legal problems is not surprising, given the extent of law in contemporary life. Nor is it surprising that the nature of justiciable problems is somewhat similar across jurisdictions, as people engage in many of the same activities.[33] Thus consumer problems are routinely found to be among the three most prevalent justiciable problems, along with those concerning neighbours and money.[34] Problems relating to families, housing, employment, social safety net assistance, public services and nationality are also commonly experienced. Obtaining formal identification is also common among some population groups. However, important exceptions are found in some countries. For example, in Mali and Uganda – predominantly agricultural jurisdictions – common justiciable problems concerned land: expropriation, land grabbing, water and nationalisation. These problems were rare elsewhere (Barendrecht et al., 2014a; Piest et al., 2016).[35] In contrast, in both jurisdictions consumer problems were relatively rare.[36] In Mali, for instance, the next five most common problems concerned (in descending order) employment, family, neighbours, housing and money (Barendrecht et al., 2014a). Similarly, in Uganda they were family, neighbours, money, employment and public services (Piest et al., 2016). However, in Yemen, Mongolia and Sierra Leone, countries in which problems concerning land were common, consumer problems were also common (Coumarelos et al., 2012, p. 5).

Inequality of problem experience

Justiciable problems are not randomly distributed across populations. Particular problems are associated with particular social groups or stages of life. It appears that "socioeconomic disadvantage is pivotal" (Coumarelos et al., 2012, p. 5) to the social patterning of problems. Surveys have repeatedly demonstrated associations between disadvantage and justiciable problem experience.[37]

Disadvantaged groups associated with elevated experience of justiciable problems include those receiving social safety net assistance, those with long-term health problems or a disability (particularly mental health problems), [38] single parents,[39] victims of crime[40] and displaced persons.[41] For example, findings from the 2008 Australian LAW Survey indicated that people "with combined mental and physical illness/disability of a high severity were more than 10 times as likely to report legal problems as those with no illness/ disability" (Coumarelos et al., 2013, p. 8).

While patterns of vulnerability vary between jurisdictions – owing to differences in social structures and behaviour – a systematic review of findings concluded that "patterns are fairly similar across jurisdictions, with few conflicts" (Pleasence et al., 2013a, p. 30).[42] However, the picture as regards gender is less uniform. In some jurisdictions "women's weaker agency and lower social and economic participation" (Prettitore, 2014, p. 2) results in very different patterns of justiciable problem reporting. For example, in Jordan, 75% of those who reported problems were men. Significant differences in reporting patterns were also identified in Mali, where men were associated with problems concerning such issues as employment, land and public services, while women were associated with problems concerning family, children, neighbours and social safety net assistance (Barendrecht, 2014a).[43]

There are various reasons for the link between justiciable problem experience and disadvantage. Certain problems are a feature of disadvantage, such as those concerning social safety net assistance. Disadvantaged people draw on fewer resources and are less able to avoid or mitigate problems.[44] Moreover, justiciable problems have an additive effect, meaning that the experience of problems increases the likelihood of further problem experience,[45] exacerbating disadvantage.

Impact of justiciable problems and problem clustering

Justiciable problems often bring about or follow on from one another, or broader social, health or economic problems. They have been repeatedly found to have a substantial impact on the lives of those facing them.[46] For example, the 2015 Ugandan *Justice Needs and Satisfaction Survey* found that 54% of problems resulted in stress-related illness, 52% in loss of income, 42% in loss of time and 28% in problems with relationships (Piest et al., 2016, p. 55). The impact of justiciable problems can provoke and/or worsen broader social problems, including poverty:

> *"There is a relationship between legal problems and poverty. Legal problems, left unaddressed, can cause an economic or social shock that pushes vulnerable persons into poverty. For example, [...] wrongful termination of employment, financial debt or denial of social safety net benefits can cause vulnerable persons to fall into poverty. Unresolved legal problems can also prevent an individual in poverty from escaping it." (Prettitore, 2015, p. 1)*

Figure 1.1 illustrates an example vicious cycle of poverty involving justiciable, health, labour, financial and housing problems.

On the basis of the 2004 *English and Welsh Civil and Social Justice Survey*, the economic cost of the impact of justiciable problems on individuals and public services was estimated to exceed US$ 5 billion per year (Pleasence, 2006, p. i). Similarly, on the basis of the 2014 Canadian *National Survey of Everyday Legal Problems,* the annual cost to public services was estimated to be "approximately $800 million (and perhaps significantly more)" (Farrow et al., 2016, p. 16).

The impact of justiciable problems also contributes to the phenomenon of problem clustering; which is the increased tendency of particular justiciable problems to co-occur when more than one problem type is experienced.[47] As noted following the 2011 Moldovan survey, "it is easy to see how domestic violence can cause relationship breakdown, unemployment, tenant-landlord and debt problems" (Gramatikov, 2012,

p. 19). Problem clustering also occurs when some problem types arise from similar sets of circumstances or are associated with the same demographic factors.

Figure 1.1. Vicious cycle involving justiciable and wider socioeconomic problems

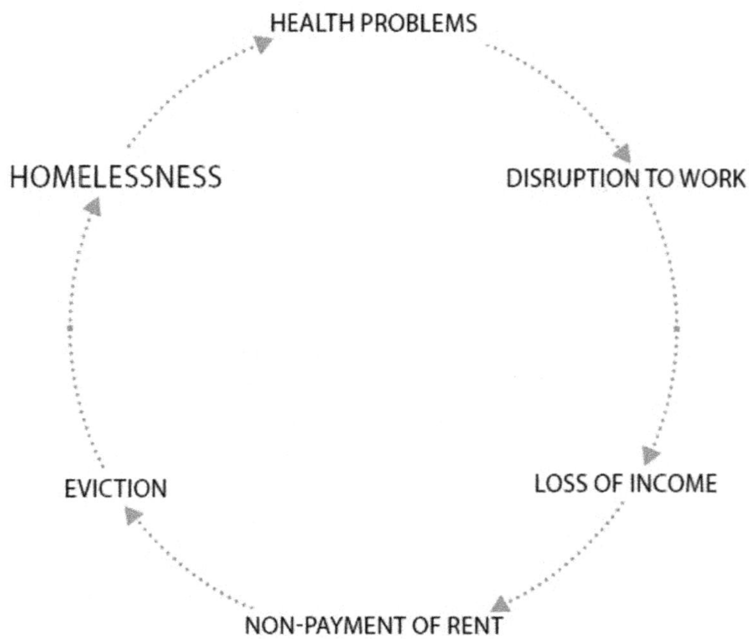

Source: Adapted from Tobin Tyler et al. (2011).

Problem resolution and barriers to justice

People facing justiciable problems take many different paths to justice, often involving little or no reference to law. A consistent finding of legal needs surveys has been that "the formal judicial system is marginal to the experience of justice" (Piest et al., 2016, p. 81).[48] Although the use of formal process can be difficult to identify, and reporting is inconsistent, only a minority of surveys have found that courts or tribunals resolved more than 10% of justiciable problems[49] with some suggesting a rate of 5% or lower.[50] And where formal process is used, it tends to be used in relation to particular problem types, such as those concerning family breakdown.

In developing and some middle-income jurisdictions, traditional dispute resolution processes are more common than court processes.[51] For example, in Bangladesh, people turn to the *Shalish* more often than to the courts.[52] However, the general picture is that most problems are addressed through informal methods, often directly between the parties.

The global picture of lawyer use is similar to that of court use. Only a minority of people facing justiciable problems obtain assistance from a lawyer, with a median reported rate of around 12%.[53] The 2016 Ugandan *Justice Needs and Satisfaction Survey* put the figure at just 2%.[54] As with court use, lawyer use is strongly linked to problem type. Family problems are typically associated with high levels of lawyer use, and consumer problems with low levels.[55] Between countries, however, notable differences exist between problem type and the use of lawyers.[56] Other factors associated with lawyer use include the availability of legal services,[57] people's understanding and characterisation of their problems,[58] awareness and proximity of legal services,[59] legal confidence (sometimes referred to as "subjective legal empowerment"),[60] cost,[61] problem seriousness and value.[62] It should be noted that the majority of these factors are aspects of legal capability.

In addition to statistical associations, frequently mentioned barriers to accessing legal services include language, social convention/etiquette, expectation and, physical obstacles to accessibility (beyond geography) - such as opening hours, waiting times, etc. – and cost.[63]

Lawyers are only one potential source of advice for resolving legal problems and enforcing entitlements. When acting to resolve justiciable problems, people seek help from a wide range of sources, both formal and informal, promising and "unpromising" (Pleasence, 2006, p. 108).[64] Aside from lawyers, common sources of formal help include independent advice organisations (including civil society organisations), unions, community leaders, justice institutions and other government bodies; along with public service workers, such as doctors and social workers. The range of sources varies between jurisdictions, reflecting differences in the socio-political structure and available services. In Tajikistan, for example, the Mahalya and house committees are notable sources of information and support (Social Research Center, 2012). In England and Wales, independent Citizens Advice Bureaux;[65] in Uganda, Local Council Courts; in Japan, insurance companies;[66] in Moldova, the police;[67] and in Yemen, Sheikhs.[68] Also, these "different sources [are] helpful for different types of problem" (Piest et al., 2016, p. 71). Moreover, specialised forms of paralegal assistance and advice are becoming more prevalent in countries seeking to expand access to justice, such as Argentina,[69] South Africa,[70] Indonesia[71] and the United States.[72]

Relatives, friends and colleagues often inform people's choices. For example, in Macedonia, almost half of all consultations with "most essential advisers" followed suggestions by those within survey respondents' social networks (Srbijanko et al, 2013). Previous experience and personal understanding of options also influence choice.

When individuals fail to find help at their first port of call and are signposted or referred[73] to another source, some abandon the effort. The more frequently people are directed elsewhere, the more they are likely to drop out of the formal advice system. This process is known as "referral fatigue" (Pleasence et al., 2004, p. 77).

As with court and lawyer use, individuals seek advice depending on the type of problem. They are more likely to seek advice for problems pertaining to family breakdown, employment,[74] personal injury and housing than they are for consumer problems.[75] Women are more likely to seek help, and help seeking appears to increase with age (although in some countries it appears to tail off in later years) and the reported seriousness and value of problems. There is also good evidence that language, socio-cultural factors, geography, available technology and other physical access and service infrastructure issues influence advice seeking behaviour.[76]

However, there are dangers in assuming that behaviour will be similar in different situations or countries. For example, women in Mali are particularly "reluctant to approach formal institutions" in the context of family disputes for "fear of the consequences" (Barendrecht et al., 2014a, p. 70). People in Bulgaria are unusual in that they routinely turn to public authorities to resolve justiciable problems of all types (Gramatikov, 2008). In a few countries, a small but significant number of respondents report that criminal connections are sometimes relied on to resolve justiciable problems.[77]

Beyond the sources noted above, a growing number of individuals are looking to the Internet for help.[78] For example, the 2015 Ukrainian *Justice Needs and Satisfaction Survey* indicated that people turned to the Internet for 23% of problems, up from just 12% five years earlier (HiiL, 2016a). However, "people who use the Internet to help resolve legal problems are not representative of the public as a whole" (Pleasence et al., 2015, p. xi),.[79] and success in using the Internet is related to legal capability (as is success in using legal assistance services more generally).[80]

Finally, legal needs surveys repeatedly find that a significant proportion of people fail to take any action whatsoever to resolve problems. Estimates for inaction from stand-alone legal needs surveys range up to 44% (Ukrainian *Legal Needs and Satisfaction Survey*).[81] Evidently there are good and bad reasons for inaction (Pleasence and Balmer, 2014). However, across jurisdictions, many reasons for inaction provided by respondents to legal needs surveys convey "a rather negative and powerless quality" (Genn, 1999, p. 70).[82]

People often believe that action would make no difference to the outcome of their problem. Indeed, this was so for a majority of respondents to the 2012 Australian, 2012 Georgian and 2015 Ukrainian surveys who took no action;[83] despite their "making this judgement without the benefit of any advice" (Genn, 1999, p. 71). Additionally, individuals may avoid taking action for fear of the consequences on relationships and sometimes personal safety. For example, the most recent Ukrainian legal needs survey indicated that 12% of internally displaced persons took no action to resolve justiciable problems because they were scared to do so (along with 3% of other survey respondents). Individuals may be also ignorant of their rights or options,[84] sources of help, or dispute resolution processes. In some jurisdictions, people also worry about the fairness of processes and, in some jurisdictions, corruption.[85]

Multivariate statistical analysis of factors associated with inaction, as reported for nine national surveys,[86] suggests reasonably consistent associations between inaction and problem type. Inaction was found to be particularly associated with problems concerning anti-social neighbours (and, to a lesser extent, problems concerning employment).[87] The reverse was the case for family problems (and, to a lesser extent, consumer problems). Inaction has also been found to be more common among men, and among individuals who faced language obstacles or regarded problems as the product of "bad luck"; and to become less common with age (although perhaps more common again in later years), education level, income, awareness of legal rights and legal services, legal confidence, problem value and problem seriousness. "This suggests an association between elements of social disadvantage and basic problem resolution strategy that sits on top of the association between social disadvantage and vulnerability to problems" (Pleasence et al., 2014, p. 15).

Thus, legal needs surveys have demonstrated that different population groups have different attitudes to problem resolution,[88] face different obstacles to action,[89] and have different needs in relation to the help and processes available.[90] As well as the broad global picture set out above, policy and service development must therefore also be guided by proper understanding of the experience and needs of those they serve.

Building a global picture

Opportunities for detailed comparison of experience between jurisdictions are limited by the different methods adopted by the many legal needs surveys detailed in Table 1.1 and Table 1.2. The repeated British and Dutch *Paths to Justice* surveys, the *English and Welsh Civil and Social Justice Surveys* and the Hague Institute for Innovation of Law's

(HiiL) *Justice Needs and Satisfaction Surveys* have allowed for some confidence in comparisons. However, despite many similarities, significant and important differences among surveys in different countries have tended to undermine efforts to compare findings.[91] Thus, initiatives such as the World Justice Project's *General Population Poll* – which ask the same questions across many countries and has now adopted many of the methodological recommendations set out in this document – have the potential to provide a valuable comparative picture of experience across the globe. Moreover, several members of the OECD-Justice InitiativeAdvisory Stream guiding the development of this document, as well as others working with the OECD, have initiated processes to translate this global Guide into national surveys to support policy, such as the new surveys in South Korea (Kim and Choi, 2018).

Inclusive process

Legal needs surveys are most effective when those defining and supporting the research, whether from government or civil society organisations, bring other groups into the process. As described throughout this Guide, defining and contextualising the legal problems people experience, as well as possible mechanisms for resolution, is a challenging exercise. Meaningful engagement with frontline service providers and community groups enables the development of a better, more responsive survey. Such interaction equips frontline organisations with a deeper understanding of the survey process, which will, in turn, generate trust and enable those organisations to engage with the findings.

When incorporating civil legal needs questions into government surveys, the previous experiences of independent civil society in conducting surveys have proven to be a valuable guide for government policymakers. In Colombia, for example, when the Department of National Planning sought to integrate a national civil justice module they looked to the experiences of the civil society organisation Dejusticia, which had previously conducted an urban legal needs survey. By working in partnership, the government was able to learn from Dejusticia's experience, while Dejusticia in turn was better prepared to make use of the survey's findings. In Nepal, the National Judicial Academy partnered with the Social Science Baha, a civil society think tank, to develop and implement a nationwide legal needs survey.

Conducting the survey through an inclusive process both provides the best results and enables the most effective use of the findings by different stakeholders. In both government-led and independent surveys, civil society groups can serve as important partners for connecting with hard-to-reach groups. In Nepal, for example, legal service providers are working with a research team to better account for the range of civil justice problems and active justice institutions at the local level. In Kenya, a legal assistance and advocacy organisation helped introduce the research team to a marginalised community where there was deep suspicion of external and government representatives. In South Africa organisations supporting community advice offices have participated in testing and refining civil legal needs related questions being developed by Statistics South Africa. Greater inclusivity will enable policymakers and advocates to understand how the survey generates particular types of information and strengthens possibilities for policy impact.

Finally, inclusive processes can enhance the value of survey findings. A wide range of government agencies and civil society organisations may be affected by legal needs survey findings. Each agency or organisation can play a role to play in interpreting findings and driving programmatic and policy reform. Governments and civil society organisations have used a number of public dissemination techniques to discuss the findings, their dissemination, and the strategic use of media. Guaranteeing the availability of data is also a key consideration. Surveys are costly undertakings and lead agencies are often unable to conduct the numerous types of analyses that are relevant to particular constituencies. It is critical that independent organisations and government institutions make anonymised survey data available for researchers and advocates. This approach ensures that the survey exercise has broader use and applicability and can be combined with other sources of justice data to inform policy in a multitude of ways.

Impacts of legal needs surveys

Legal needs surveys have proved effective in helping to identify areas for policy reform. They also serve as a mechanism for monitoring changes in experience and behaviour against a backdrop of legal services reform.[92] They form part of a broad evidence base upon which policymakers, service designers and practitioners can draw. Research can affect the policy process in "diffuse ways" (Weiss, 1980, p. 318). Research "provides a background of empirical generalisations and ideas that *creep* into policy deliberations" (Weiss, 1980, p. 318).

Thus, the more than 55 national legal needs surveys, along with many more sub-national surveys, conducted over the past 25 years, have gently contributed to "transform[ing] thinking about legal aid and advice" (Pleasence et al., 2013a, p. 43) globally and within an increasing number of jurisdictions. Professor Hazel Genn, author of the seminal *Paths to Justice* surveys in the United Kingdom, has characterised this transformation as having distinct phases (Genn, 2017). The first – arguably the most important – sees findings concerning the ubiquity of justiciable problems and the relatively rare use of formal legal systems bring about a "policy 'flip' [from] system to citizen-focus," which leads to policy and design of services "with <u>needs</u> and <u>behaviour</u> in mind, rather than funder convenience or policy assumptions" (Genn, 2017).

This policy-flip is evident in numerous policy documents across jurisdictions in which legal needs surveys have been prominent, such as Australia, Canada, England and Wales, and Ukraine.[93] Indeed, the English and Welsh Legal Services Commission's 2005 strategy document *Making Legal Rights a Reality* has been described as "entirely based" on legal needs survey findings that were used "to try and reconfigure how services were organised" and have "had a very great impact" (Pleasence, Balmer and Sandefur, 2013, p. 43-44). The policy flip was also a central theme of the findings of a survey of governmental stakeholders in Australia, Canada, England and Wales, New Zealand, Northern Ireland and Scotland. The survey investigated the perceived impact of legal needs surveys in those jurisdictions. The findings, as one respondent put it, highlighted the role of legal needs surveys in helping policy officials "learn about both the substance of civil legal needs and the client perspective on access to justice more generally" (Pleasence, Balmer and Sandefur, 2013, p. 54).[94] At the most basic level, the survey findings made clear to those in the formal justice system that experience of justiciable problems occurs largely outside their purview. As one respondent noted: "The incidence of legal problems is not what lawyers and judges think" (Pleasence, Balmer and Sandefur, 2013, p. 56).

Respondents also identified key legal needs survey findings that have been instrumental in the reformulation of access to justice policy in broader social and instrumentalist terms. Most frequently highlighted were "findings that certain groups [are] disproportionately exposed to a higher problem incidence by virtue of their demographic characteristics"

(Pleasence, Balmer and Sandefur, 2013, p. 67), so-called problem clustering, and "the health and social costs of legal problems" (Pleasence, Balmer and Sandefur, 2013, p. 56). Findings concerning service gaps and factors influencing service use, and factors that might influence demand for particular services also had an impact. Such findings were described as having led to, in Genn's words, "smarter approaches" (Genn, 2017) to legal service delivery, and service transformation centred on targeting, accessibility and the integration of legal services (and, beyond this, the integration of legal and other public services). More than four in five respondents "were able to set out specific policies that legal needs survey findings had influenced," and, in all, respondents suggested that 28 separate policies or initiatives were impacted by legal needs surveys (Pleasence et al., 2013a, p. 54).

A series of interviews with officials in the United Kingdom public, private and NGO sectors revealed that they "attributed the policy response of 'joined-up services' to assist the public to the research discovery of 'joined-up' problems" (Pleasence et al., 2013a, p. 43). For example, the introduction of Community Legal Advice Centres (CLACs) was described as "a 'research-based policy' designed to respond to the discovery that problems cluster" (Pleasence et al., 2013a, p. 43). More generally, officials saw legal needs surveys as "persuasive and influential," and described them as "having transformed understanding of public justice needs, of not-for-profit service provision, and of market service provision" (Pleasence et al., 2013a, p. 44).

There have been differences between jurisdictions in the purposes for commissioning surveys, and thus their impact on policy. The above examples of impact concern jurisdictions with well-established legal infrastructures, including public legal assistance services, in which the focus of policy interest is in refining established processes and services. In contrast, in jurisdictions with emerging or transitional legal infrastructures, there is a greater policy focus on the reach and use of law, and the appropriate form of legal services infrastructure. For example, the 2011 *Met and Unmet Legal Needs in Moldova* survey was part of efforts that enabled the Soros Foundation-Moldova (the survey's sponsor) to inform and be a part of the working group created by Ministry of Justice to develop the Strategy for Justice Sector Reform for 2011 – 2016.

However, across jurisdictions, law-centred interests are now commonly conjoined with broader interest in the relationship between justiciable problems and wider social health and economic problems. Linked to this is the utility of legal services in addressing wider social policy goals.[95] At a national level, this has seen survey findings used "in building a case for legal advice and funding in addition to general policy development" (Pleasence et al., 2013a, p. 53). Legal needs surveys have further situated the legal problem experience into a far broader policy context. Justice sectors need to consider how they engage with other sectors, just as other sectors[96] need to consider how legal problems and services may be important to their concerns and goals.

Internationally, this has recently manifested in an agreement to pursue U.N. Sustainable Development Goal 16.[97] Goal 16 is "dedicated to the promotion of peaceful and inclusive societies for sustainable development, the provision of access to justice for all, and building effective, accountable institutions at all levels."[98] The SDG agenda is predicated in part on the notion that "the rule of law and development have a significant interrelation and are mutually reinforcing, making it essential for sustainable development at the national and international level."[99]

Target populations and methodological variations among past legal needs surveys

Target populations of past legal needs surveys

Legal needs surveys have mostly focused on nationally representative samples. However, some of the surveys in Table 1.1 and Table 1.2 have focused on specific target populations – such as those focused on low incomes or young people[100] – and some have involved oversampling of defined population groups, such as Indigenous people in Australia and Syrian refugees in Jordan.[101] These surveys focus on generating information about the experiences of sections of the population of particular interest to policymakers. However, all the surveys in Table 1.1 and Table 1.2 have utilised broad population sample frames and, for the most part, probability samples.[102] Such sample frames may yield only small numbers of especially vulnerable populations and may even exclude some vulnerable populations altogether (i.e. where there is a gap between the target population and the sample frame (coverage error)). The report of the 2006-2009 *English and Welsh Civil and Social Justice Survey* noted that its address-based sample frame[103] excluded "around 2% of the population" (Pleasence et al., 2010, p. 6). The report went on to state that:

> *"While the experience of people who share many of the characteristics of such 'out of sample' populations will be captured ... and will cast good light on what the experience of 'out of sample' populations is likely to be like, it is important to bear this limitation of the survey in mind when considering its findings." (Pleasence et al., 2010, p. 6)*

Sections of the populations identified as missing from the survey's sample frame included people living in residential care homes, students living in education establishments, prisoners, military personnel living in defence establishments, Roma/travellers, people living in local authority provided temporary accommodation (other than in local authority housing stock), people in immigration detention centres and the street homeless. Some of these groups are among the most marginalised and vulnerable groups in society. The methodological report of the 2011 Colombian *National Legal Needs Survey* similarly highlighted that its sample frame excluded groups such as prisoners, service personnel, people in nursing homes and the street homeless (Uprimny et al., 2013).

Accordingly, parallel and complementary surveys of specific vulnerable populations can, and sometimes should, be used to complement standard sample frames, especially where there is clear potential for coverage bias. The 2001 *English and Welsh Civil and Social Justice Survey* and the 2011 Colombian *National Legal Needs Survey*, for example, were supplemented by separate surveys of specific vulnerable populations. In England and Wales, a separate survey was conducted of people living in local authority temporary accommodation (Pleasence et al., 2004). In Colombia, separate surveys were conducted of individuals living in extreme poverty and those with a disability (Uprimny et al., 2013).[104]

The experience of discrete vulnerable populations has been more often separately investigated using methods other than surveys. For example, the experience of older people,[105] homeless people,[106] those with mental illness,[107] and prisoners[108] have been investigated through qualitative projects undertaken within the Law and Justice Foundation of New South Wales's *Access to Justice and Legal Needs* research programme. Also, more recently, focus groups have been used to investigate the experience of young drug users, young people of Roma origin and commercial sex workers in Moldova, in parallel with the 2011 *Legal Empowerment Needs Survey*.

Methodological features and variations

As illustrated in Table 1.1 and Table 1.2, despite being part of the same tradition, the scale and methods of legal needs surveys vary considerably. In terms of scale, the surveys in Table 1.1 and Table 1.2 have drawn on a broad range of sample sizes, and utilised questionnaires of very different lengths. The median sample size of stand-alone legal needs surveys was around 5,000. However, while the 2004 *Legal Needs in Slovakia Survey* had a sample size of just over 1,085, the 2008 *Legal Australia-Wide Survey* had a sample size of over 20,716, the 2017 Indian *Access to Justice Survey* had a sample size of 45,551 and the 2009 Brazilian *National Household Sample Survey* had a sample size of 399,387.

Evidently, required sample size directly links to the prevalence of principal objects of study.[109] If interest is primarily in justiciable problem prevalence, then modest sample sizes may suffice (with sample size needing to increase along with levels of accuracy and confidence).[110] However, if interest is primarily in the rate or patterning of use of different sources of help or dispute resolution processes, then sample sizes need to increase; particularly if behaviour relating to specific types of problem is of interest.

The length of legal needs surveys has also varied considerably. The median questionnaire length of the surveys in Table 1.1 and Table 1.2 was around 6,000 words; but, the 2011 Jordanian *Volume of Demand for Legal Aid Services Survey* ran to fewer than 1,000 words, the various iterations of the *Justice Needs and Satisfaction Survey* ran to around 6,000 words, and the *English and Welsh Civil and Social Justice Panel Survey* ran to over 20,000 words (excluding repeated sections).

As would be expected, given the very different lengths of questionnaires used, the range of topics investigated by legal needs surveys has varied considerably, as has the degree of detail and sophistication of questions. The content of legal needs surveys is discussed further in Chapter 2. and Chapter 3.

Two-thirds of the Table 1.1 and Table 1.2 surveys were conducted face-to-face, with the remainder conducted by telephone, by post, online or using a combination of modes.[111] Differences in mode of conduct help to explain the broad range of reported response rates (as well as some differences in findings[112]). Response rates tend to link to mode of conduct, with face-to-face surveys generally delivering higher response rates that other surveys.[113] So, while the three iterations of the Canadian telephone *National Survey of Civil Justice Problems* had response rates of 17% (2004), 23% (2006) and 21% (2008), the original face-to-face *Paths to Justice* surveys had response rates of 64% in England and Wales and 61% in Scotland.

Large government backed face-to-face surveys can have even higher response rates. For example, the face-to-face 2016 Colombian *National Quality of Life Survey* had a response rate of 96%. However, comparing response rates between surveys conducted in different ways is problematic, particularly between probability and non-probability samples. The 2008 Australian telephone survey was reported to have a 60% response rate, yet “the calculation of this response rate might be considered more forgiving than for the face-to-face surveys” (Pleasence, Balmer and Sandefur, p. 11). In excess of half a million phone calls were required to obtain the sample of 20,716; including 74,802 “unknown other” calls incorporating refusals before screening. The authors of the survey acknowledged that:

"There are several methods for calculating response rate, and response rate estimates can vary dramatically depending on the particular method used." (Coumarelos et al., 2012, p. 12)

High reported response rates of the online surveys in the Netherlands (reaching 83% in the case of the 2003 *Paths to Justice in the Netherlands Survey*) are similarly misleading; and explained "by the sample being drawn from an opt-in panel, meaning that participants had already been filtered for amenability during previous exercises" (Pleasence et al., 2013, p. 11).[114] Opt-in processes mask as well as compound nonresponse bias.

Notes

[1] The concept of access to justice "defies precise definition".

[2] A reference to conformity with human rights standards is necessary to both extend the concept beyond local legal frameworks (which may conflict with accepted international norms) and indicate standards for independent adjudication. Although there is broad agreement on the focus of the concept of access to justice, the concept is fluid. For illustration, a detailed account of the broadening of the concept in the context of justice system reform in Canada is provided by Macdonald (2005).

[3] The debate around access to justice "has many strands" (Paterson 2012, p.60) (including citizens' behaviour in resolving justiciable problems, the availability and accessibility of legal services and state-sanctioned dispute resolution processes, the sustainable provision of legal aid, and the role of non-legal services in delivering justice outcomes) and ideological dimensions. While the concept of access to justice is generally discussed in relation to access to legal services and processes, debates frequently also extend to other human services that have utility in addressing problems existing within such frameworks.

[4] Legal capability refers to the capabilities necessary for a person – or, at a higher level, a household or community – "to resolve legal problems effectively" (Coumarelos et al. 2012, p. 29). The concept of legal capability links to Sen's (1980, 1999) capability approach to disadvantage. For a discussion of legal needs within the context of the concept of legal capability, see Pleasence & Balmer (2019).

[5] Referring to frustration felt among researchers studying legal need in the 1970s that accompanied a period of contraction in the field.

[6] Civil law refers to all law that can be applied to or by individual citizens (or, in a business context, businesses) other than criminal law.

[7] See, for example, United Nations Development Programme (2012).

[8] Many access to justice assessment surveys also include legal needs survey style questions concerning particular problem types. For example, the Vietnamese Provincial Justice Index Questionnaire has included detailed questions concerning land disputes (reported in United Nations Development Programme (2012).

[9] The first legal needs survey is accredited to Clark and Corstvet (1938), who separately surveyed citizens and businesses in Connecticut, United States, to explore "how the needs of the community for legal service were being met" during the 1930s recession at the U.S. Bar.

[10] Landmark legal needs surveys in the 1980s and 1990s – the *Civil Litigation Research Project* (Trubek et al. 1983) and *Comprehensive Legal Needs Study* (Reece & Eldred 1994) in the United States, the *legal Adivce and Assistance Survey* in New Zealand (Maxwell et al. 1999) and the *Paths to Justice* surveys in the United Kingdom (Genn 1999, Genn & Paterson 2001) – introduced "considerable momentum" (Coumarelos et al. 2012, p. 1) to the conduct of such surveys.

[11] Including near national surveys (i.e. those covering the great majority of the population, such as the 2012 Colombian and 2016 United Arab Emirates surveys). Published findings of the stand-alone surveys are available in, in order of listing in Table 1.1, Reese & Eldred (1994), Genn (1999), Maxwell et al. (1999), Genn & Paterson (2001), Pleasence et al. (2004), Van Velthoven & ter Voert (2004), Currie (2005), Pleasence (2006), GfK Slovakia (2004), Murayama (2007), Dignan (2006), Currie (2007), Pleasence et al. (2010), Asia Consulting Group Limited & Policy 21 Limited (2008), Sato et al. (2007), Ignite Research (2006), Gramatikov (2008), Tamaki, T. (2009), Coumeralos et al. (2012), Akmeemana, S. (2011), Currie (2009), Van Velthoven & Haarhuis (2010), Pleasence et al. (2011a), Kobzin et al. (2011), Prettitore (2013), Gramatikov (2012), Huang et al. (2014), La Rota et al. (2013), Pleasence & Balmer (2013a), BDRC Continental (2012), Institute of Social Studies and Analysis (2012), ACSSC (2012), Srbijanko et al. (2013), Social Research Center (2012), ter Voert & Haarhuis (2015), Farrow et al. (2016), Franklyn et al. (2017), Barendrecht et al. (2014a), Ipsos MORI (2012), Winczorek (2018), Piest et al. (2016), Subsecretaría de Acceso a la Justicia Ministerio de Justicia y Derechos Humanos (2017), Heijstek-Ziemann et al. (2017), Open Society Forum (2018), HiiL (2016a), HiiL (2016b), Kind et al. (2018), Baruah et al. (2018), Núñez et al. (2017), Kind et al. (2017). Details of the 2013 Netherlands survey, 2016 Moldovan survey and 2017 Kenyan, New Zealand, Sierra Leone and Nepal surveys have not been published, as of 1st August 2018.

[12] Details of the Scottish Crime and Justice Survey can be found at: http://www.gov.scot/Topics/Statistics/Browse/Crime-Justice/crime-and-justice-survey/publications. See also, in order of listing in Table 1.1, Subsecretaría de Acceso a la Justicia Ministerio de Justicia y Derechos Humanos (2017), Kenya National Bureau of Statistics (2018), Departamento Nacional de Planeación (2017), Adams et al. (2017, 2018). Indonesia's National Socio-Economic Survey 2017 also included a short series of questions concerning justiciable problems (including those related to compensation, employment, family, harassment, housing, inheritance and land) "which involved law enforcement bodies."

[13] See Michelson (2008).

[14] See ECOLEX (2014).

[15] Details of the Russian survey kindly provided by Martin Gramatikov.

[16] See Gramatikov et al. (2014).

[17] See Barendrecht et al. (2014b).

[18] See Gramatikov and Verdonschot (2010).

[19] For example, surveys have recently been conducted in more than one-quarter of all U.S. states.

[20] In Hong Kong, the Netherlands, Australia, Colombia, and England and Wales. See Asia Consulting Group Limited & Policy 21 Limited (2008), Croes and Maas (2009), Orima Research (2010), Croes (2012), Uprimny et al. (2012), Pleasence & Balmer (2013b) and Blackburn et al. (2015), Larkin et al. (2018).

[21] https://dhsprogram.com/What-We-Do/Survey-Types/DHS.cfm.

[22] http://www.fao.org/in-action/voices-of-the-hungry/fies/en/.

[23] https://unhabitat.org/experts-reach-important-consensus-on-critical-land-indicator/.

[24] The concept of legal empowerment emerged in the field of law and development and now refers to the focus of developmental justice programmes on "empowering individuals to realise their rights and voice their demands more actively" (Kolisetty 2014, p. 9).

[25] See Barendrecht & van Nipsen (2008).

[26] A cross-sectional survey investigates a sample of a population at a single point in time. A longitudinal survey investigates the same sample of a population across time.

[27] See, for example, http://a2jlab.org/.

[28] Lay understanding of the phenomena and concepts involved can be extremely limited in relation to technical matters (such as technical aspects of litigation).

[29] Surveys of users of particular services or processes are not be problematic in this regard. Similarly, general population surveys are inefficient in capturing data concerning rare justiciable problem types. For example, justiciable problems concerning compulsory hospitalisation for mental health issues were removed from the English and Welsh Civil and Social Justice Survey. Their rarity entailed population estimates were unreliable

and it was recognised that surveys of people in hospital, or after discharge from hospital, would be more efficient and insightful.

[30] In the context of the social sciences, the concept of triangulation is generally attributed to Denzin (1978), who also distinguished between methodological triangulation and data, investigator and theoretical triangulation. In this context, it is notable that many surveys capture qualitative data alongside quantitative data; albeit often in the hope of being able to code and quantify such data.

[31] Although the impact of even small methodological differences on results precludes definitive incidence rates being determined across or within individual jurisdictions (Pleasence et al. 2016). Also see Chapters 2 and 3.

[32] Demonstrating further the variation in estimates, and the impact of methodological differences on survey findings, the World Justice Project's 2016 *General Population Poll* put the figure for Colombia at 26% over one year, while the 2012 *Colombian National Legal Needs Survey* put the figure at 43% over 4 years. Similarly, the World Justice Project's 2016 *General Population Poll* put the Ugandan figure at 56% over one year. As is made evident in Chapter 3, great caution should be exercised in comparing estimates between surveys that have utilised different methodologies. Even small methodological differences can bring about substantial changes in response patterns.

[33] Pleasence et al. (2004, p. 28) refer to these circumstances as the "defining circumstances" of problems. See, also, van Velthoven and ter Voert's (2005) application of participation theory in this context.

[34] Consumer problems have been found to be among the three most common justiciable problems by 27 of 37 surveys for which relevant findings are available, excluding crime victimisation, if reported, and, in the case of the English and Welsh online surveys, excluding non-contentious legal issues (such as conveyancing). The figures for problems concerning neighbours and money are 20 of 28 and 22 of 35, respectively.

[35] For citizens of countries such as Mali and Uganda, "land is the most important economic, social and legal asset" (Piest 2016, p. 131). The 2017 Indian survey, which found problems concerning land to be second most common after those concerning money, also found that 71% of disputes concerned agricultural land (Baruah et al. 2018). Other notable differences in patterns of problem reporting include the high level of "elections" related problems reported in Kyrgyzstan (ACSSC 2012) and of religious/witchcraft related issues in Kenya (Kenya National Bureau of Statistics 2018).

[36] Similar findings have also emerged in Indonesia, rural China and rural Taiwan (Gramatikov et al. 2014, Michelson (2007), Chen et al. (2012a). Although, demonstrating the complexity of social and problem patternation, consumer problems were found to be relatively prominent in Yemen (Barendrecht et al. 2014b).

[37] While broadly accurate, in a global context it should be noted that factors of vulnerability to justiciable problems can be diametrically opposed, and vary (sometimes considerably) by problem type. Both elevated socio-economic activity and depressed socio-economic status may fuel problem experience – but in different ways. As Gramatikov (2012, p. 20) explained "On the one hand, poor people are more vulnerable because they have fewer resources to mitigate and cope with legal problems. On the other hand, those who are more affluent participate more in the economic, social and political life".

[38] See, for example, Balmer and Pleasence (2012a) and Coumarelos et al. (2013).

[39] See, for example, Buck et al. (2004) and Pleasence et al. (2013a).

[40] Crime victimisation has commonly been identified as associated with the experience of justiciable problems. For example, this was identified through multivariate analysis in Moldova (Gramatikov 2012). Less often reported is the strong association between experience of justiciable problems and criminal offending. See, for example, Kemp et al. (2007) and Pleasence & McDonald (2013).

[41] Piest et al. (2016) identified internally displaced persons (as a result of partition and civil war) as being associated with much higher problem prevalence. Related to this, Pleasence et al. (2004) found those living in local council temporary accommodation to be associated with high problem prevalence.

[42] Excluding domestic violence, that is consistently gendered across jurisdictions, significant gender based differences in justiciable problem experience have been found in only a minority of jurisdictions. However, some differences are notable.

[43] In addition to the globally consistent gendered reporting of domestic violence, some gender differences have been reported in richer jurisdictions. For example, men in Slovakia were found to be more likely to have

experienced employment or personal injury problems but less likely to have experienced family problems (GfK Slovakia, 2004).

[44] One aspect of this is that problems can have a different character for disadvantaged people. For example, what an affluent person might regard as a trivial consumer issue – such as the purchase of food that is unwholesome – might be highly problematic for someone living in poverty.

[45] This was first described and quantified by Pleasence et al. (2004). Findings are consistent across jurisdictions. For example, in Moldova, 16.7% of respondents reported one problem, 3.5% reported two, 1.3% reported three and 0.6% reported 4 (Gramatikov, 2012).

[46] For example, in Macedonia, 32% of survey respondents described non-trivial problems as "destroying my life" (Srbijanko et al. 2013, p. 82).

[47] The most commonly identified problem clusters have been observed in the context of family breakdown, where domestic violence, divorce, ancillary issues and problems concerning children link closely. Other identified clusters include clusters centred on economic activity (e.g. problems concerning employment, money, consumer transactions, welfare benefits and housing), and problems centred on poor quality housing. See, for example, Pleasence (2006), Gramatikov (2008), Currie (2009), Coumarelos (2012).

[48] Referring to the situation in Uganda.

[49] The World Justice Project's 2016 *General Population Poll* suggested that in about one-third of jurisdictions courts were selected as the mechanism for resolving disputes on more than 10% and sometimes as few as 1% of occasions. (China, Myanmar and Thailand) (Adams et al. 2017). The 2017 *General Population Poll* suggested that in only a few jurisdictions did respondents report turning to an authority or third party to help resolve problems on more than 20% of occasions (Afghanistan, Ethiopia, Greece, Panama, Slovenia and the United States), while in Mongolia the figure was just 4% (Adams et al. 2018). Separately, findings from the 2017 Indian survey suggested that a significant majority of respondents would like to have resolved disputes through courts (Baruah et al. 2018).

[50] For example, Argentina 2016, Australia 2012, England and Wales 2010, 2012, Japan 2005, Uganda 2015 and Ukraine 2015. Figures have been made available for fewer than half of the surveys, and the precise nature of figures has not always been clear.

[51] The World Justice Project's 2016 *General Population Poll* found this to be the case in Bangladesh, Thailand and Uganda (Adams et al. 2017).

[52] The 2009 Bangladesh survey found that a "modest" 16% of disputes involved courts, while 18% involved a village *Shalish* and 41% involved consultation with a political leader/chairman (Akmeemana 2011). The 2017 Bangladesh survey similarly found that courts were used less frequently for dispute resolution (8%) than the *Shalish* (23%) (Kind et al. 2018).

[53] On the basis of 36 surveys for which details were provided.

[54] Although, while court use was also low, local council courts were found to be a popular source of information.

[55] For example, in Georgia, 60% of family problems involved legal consultation, while the figure was just 5% in the case of problems related to social assistance (Institute of Social Studies and Analysis 2012). Similarly, in Japan, where the help of lawyers is rarely sought, the *National Survey of Everyday Life and the Law* found that almost 40% of family problems involve lawyer consultation (Murayama, 2007, p. 31).

[56] For example, personal injury problems are strongly associated with lawyers in the United Kingdom and Canada (e.g. Pleasence et al. 2004, Currie 2009), while the opposite is true in countries such as Japan, New Zealand and Hong Kong (e.g. Murayama 2007, Ignite Research 2006, Asia Consulting Group and Policy 21 Ltd, 2008).

[57] It has been argued, for example, that the "remarkably small population of lawyers" in Japan is the reason for the relatively low level of lawyer use in that country (Sato et al. 2007, p. 11) and that the different levels of lawyer use for different problem types in England and Wales is partly a reflection of patterns of legal services supply (Pleasence & Balmer 2009).

[58] It has been found that whether or not people characterise problems as "legal" is associated with whether or not lawyers are used. Characterisation has been found to substantially affect lawyer use both across and within problem types (Pleasence et al. 2011b). In fact, after controlling for other factors, lawyer use was

found to be 169% higher when problems were "characterised as legal" (Pleasence & Balmer 2014, p. 42). Murayama (2010) also reported a link between people's consciousness of problems being "related to law" and the use of lawyers, though the association was much weaker than that between problem type and lawyer use. More recently, surveys in Argentina and Canada have explored this issue, although results have not yet been published. Murayama (2009, 2010) also found personal connections to the legal profession to be a key predictor of lawyer use.

[59] In Australia, for example, people living in very remote areas and unaware of legal services tended to report very low levels of lawyer use (Pleasence et al. 2014). Even in relatively densely populated England and Wales, Patel et al. (2008) found that people without personal transport who lived five or more miles from a specialist advisor were the least likely to seek advice. Similarly, uneven regional availability and awareness of legal services was found to impact on problem resolving behaviour in Ecuador and Georgia ECOLEX (2014), Institute of Social Studies and Analysis (2012).

[60] In England and Wales, citizens with the highest levels of legal confidence have been found to be 43% more likely to seek help from a lawyer than those with the lowest levels (Pleasence et al. 2015).

[61] Many legal needs surveys have suggested a relationship between income and lawyer use, including surveys in Canada, Colombia, Jordan, Macedonia, the Netherlands, New Zealand, Scotland, Taiwan (Currie 2009, Prettitore 2014, van Velthoven & ter Voert 2005, Ignite Research 2006, Pleasence & Balmer 2009, Huang et al. 2014). Some of these find were U-shaped in form. For example, analyses of data from the 2008 *Legal Australia-Wide Survey*[61] and 2010 *English and Welsh Civil and Social Justice Panel Survey* point to a subtle relationship between income and lawyer use mediated by subsidy and payment mechanisms. Illustrating this mediated relationship, findings from the Australian survey suggested a U-shaped association in the case of family problems (where no cost or low cost legal assistance is available for those on a low income), no association in the case of personal injury (where no-win no-fee arrangements are available) and a positive association in other cases. Additionally, patterns of use of private lawyers and legal services aimed at those with low incomes provided a coherent structure for the findings overall (Pleasence & Macourt 2013). These findings conflict with those of an earlier review of survey findings from seven countries, which suggested that "income has relatively little relationship with the decision to use a legal professional to deal with a dispute or other legal need." However, this earlier review "did not account for the relatively good availability of legal aid in some of the jurisdictions under study" (Pleasence & Balmer 2012a, p. 38).

[62] With lawyer use increasing along with seriousness/value. See, for example, Huang et al. (2014), Pleasence & Balmer (2014). Evidently, "cost-benefit calculations" are applied in people's choices about whether to use lawyers (Kritzer 2008).

[63] For example, Genn (1999), Pleasence (2006), Murayama (2007), Gramatikov (2008), Coumeralos et al. (2012), Barendrecht et al. (2014a, 2014b), Gramatikov et al. (2014).

[64] Pleasence argued that the unpromising nature of many sources of help indicated "real uncertainty as to the most effective way of responding to [legal] problems".

[65] See, for example, Pleasence & Balmer (2013a)

[66] See, for example, Murayama (2007).

[67] See Gramatikov (2012).

[68] Social Research Center (2012), Pleasence (2006), Piest (2016), Murayama (2007), Barendrecht (2014b), respectively. Importantly, in terms of the value of legal needs surveys, in Tajikistan it was found that "Despite the widespread opinion that religious leaders (Mullo/Bibiotun) are popular sources of information, data shows that they are the least popular sources" (Social Research Center 2012, p. 155).

[69] See, for example, the Presidential announcement of the Federal Network for Legal Sponsorship available at http://www.vocesporlajusticia.gob.ar/actualidad/brindaran-asesoria-legal-gratuita-traves-los-caj/.

[70] Address by the Deputy Minister of Justice and Constitutional Development, the Hon JH Jeffery, MP, at the National Symposium of Community Advice Offices, held at the Reef Hotel, Johannesburg, 24 November 2014, available at http://www.justice.gov.za/m_speeches/2014/20141124_CAO.html

[71] See Indonesia's Law on Legal Aid (Law No. 16/2011) available at http://www.ilo.org/dyn/natlex/natlex4.detail?p_lang=en&p_isn=91046.

[72] For example, the Court Navigators Program in New York City Housing Courts https://www.nycourts.gov/courts/nyc/SSI/pdfs/AO-42-14.pdf.

[73] "Signposting" and "referral" are distinguished on the basis of the extent to which the signposting/referring source liaises with the receiving source. Signposting generally refers to the process of providing a client with the details of a more appropriate (or further) source of help, but does not liaise with the other source to facilitate contact. Referral generally refers to the process of actively arranging contact with the other source.

[74] Although the contrary was found in Taiwan (Chen et al. 2012b), and findings were mixed in the case of the 2008 *Legal Australia-Wide Survey.* Initial analysis suggested employment problems were associated with increased advice seeking (Coumarelos et al. 2012), but later analysis – incorporating a different and broader set of explanatory variables suggested employment problems were associated with less legal and non-legal advice (Pleasence et al. 2013b).

[75] And, to a lesser extent, problems concerning debt.

[76] See, for example, Pleasence & Balmer (2014) and Pleasence et al. (2015).

[77] See, for example, Kobzin et al. (2011) and Institute of Social Studies and Analysis (2012).

[78] Legal needs surveys suggest that people often struggle to find what they are looking for online (which generally goes beyond the details of offline sources of help), although it appears that most people obtain *some* useful information through their efforts (Pleasence et al. 2015).

[79] In addition to "the first digital divide" (which relates to the ability of individuals to physically access the Internet), the second digital divide" (which relates to the capability of individuals to use Internet resources – see, for example, Attewell (2001)) acts to distort the profile of those who look to the Internet for help resolving problems. For example, Internet use increases along with educational attainment (Pleasence et al. 2015). Also, there is evidence that younger people, while having relatively high levels of Internet access, use the Internet to help resolve problems "to a lesser degree than similarly connected age cohorts, and are less successful when doing so" Denvir et al. (2011, p. 96).

[80] See, for example, Pearson & Davis (2002), Legal Services Commission (2004), etc.

[81] This is similar to the estimate of 41% from the 2010 *Legal Capacity of the Ukrainian Population Survey.* Other Eastern European surveys have also uncovered high levels of inaction; for example, 36% in Macedonia in 2012, 29% in Georgia in 2012 and 21% in Moldova in 2011. High rates of inaction in Africa include 38% in Uganda in 2015 and 28% in Tunisia in 2016. In contrast, estimates as low as 4% have come from England and Wales in 2014, and 5% in Canada in 2014. Some of the difference is due to differences in what actions are asked about and the form of questions. In both these last jurisdictions, estimates have been higher in other surveys; and the World Justice Project's 2016 *General Population Poll* included dozens of country estimates, the lowest of which was 42%, for Liberia. The estimate for the United Kingdom was 57%.

[82] The report of the 2012 Georgian *KAP Survey Concerning Justiciable Events* referred to this as "a nihilistic approach to the legal system" (Institute of Social Studies and Analysis 2012, p. 96).

[83] See Coumarelos et al. (2012), Institute of Social Studies and Analysis (2012), HiiL (2016a), respectively.

[84] Recent legal needs survey findings from England and Wales indicate that levels of understanding of legal rights and responsibilities are low (Pleasence and Balmer 2012b, Pleasence et al. 2015, 2017).

[85] For example, in the case of Indonesia, Gramatikov et al. (2014, p. 89) reported that "a deeper look at three of the most frequent and serious categories of problems - land disputes, crimes and money related disputes - reveal that people are concerned about the time it takes, the stress and negative emotions as well as the fairness of the process." And in Ukraine, Kobzin et al. (2011, pp. 57-61) have categorised the broad barriers to access to justice as including emotional, informational, physical, financial, effectiveness, bureaucratic, corruption, and secondary victimisation barriers.

[86] See Australia (2008), England and Wales (2001, 2004, 2010, 2012), Moldova (2011), the Netherlands (2003, 2009) and Taiwan (2011).

[87] And personal injury, although the picture was slightly mixed, with the Australian survey indicating the reverse.

[88] For example, Barendrecht et al. (2014a, p. 82) report that some justice preferences in Mali differ from norms elsewhere, such as putting more weight on "obedience to the heads of families."

[89] For example, geography and language issues affect diverse population groups differently (e.g. Pleasence et al. 2014).

[90] See, for example, Pleasence et al. (2014, 2015).

[91] See, for example, Pleasence et al. (2013a).

[92] This monitoring function lies behind the repetition of surveys in, for example, the Netherlands (2003, 2009, 2013) and the United Kingdom (2001, 2004, 2006-9, 2010, 2012, 2014, 2015), and the ambition to do the same in Argentina in future.

[93] See, for example, Pleasence et al. (2013a) and Pleasence et al. (2014).

[94] It was also observed that findings connected policy with real people, and thus could "inspire staff."

[95] See, further, the *Impact of Legal Needs Surveys* section below.

[96] For example, the Legal Aid Interagency Round Table in the United States is working to raise consciousness of how legal problems affect federal agency objectives, from employment issues to homelessness. For more information, see, for example, White House Legal Aid Interagency Round Table (2016) or the Legal Aid Interagency Roundtable website: https://www.justice.gov/lair.

[97] At a supranational level interest in the socio-economic aspects of is evident in the recent activities and outputs of organisations such as the OECD and World Bank. For example, the OECD (2015, p. 3), in exploring economic dimensions of access to justice, has observed that "improving access to justice is increasingly recognised as a critical dimension of inclusive growth and as a means for tackling inequality." Similar sentiments have also emanated from the World Bank: "Legal problems, left unaddressed, can cause an economic or social shock that pushes vulnerable persons into poverty. For example, ... wrongful termination of employment, financial debt or denial of social safety net benefits can cause vulnerable persons to fall into poverty ... [Legal services] can protect the vulnerable from falling into poverty because of the economic shocks caused by legal problems" (Prettimore, 2015, p. 1).

[98] Furthermore, Goal 16.3 is to "promote the rule of law at national and international level and ensure equal access to justice for all."

[99] http://www.un.org/sustainabledevelopment/peace-justice/.

[100] The 2016 Moldovan Legal Empowerment Needs Survey was of young people, aged 14 to 23 years old.

[101] The 2008 *Legal Australia Wide Survey* included a boost of indigenous people to allow comparisons to be made with the general population. The survey was also stratified by state to allow state by state comparisons to be made (Coumarelos et al. 2012). The 2017 *Justice Needs and Satisfaction Survey* in Jordan included an oversample of Syrian refugees living in Jordanian cities. For security reasons, residents of refugee camps were not surveyed (Nunez et al. 2017). In the context of the 2017 *Justice Needs and Satisfaction Survey* in Jordan, simple random sampling naturally yielded a sub-sample of 20% Syrian refugees (Kind et al. 2017a).

[102] Examples of non-probability samples include those of the four online Dutch surveys – which utilised opt-in panels – and of the 2008 *Law Australia-Wide Survey* can also be distinguished from others in its use of quota sampling, as opposed to probability sampling. Probability sampling can also be problematic in jurisdictions in which comprehensive sample frames are not available. As Kondo et al. (2014) observe, "random sampling of rural populations in developing nations can be challenged by incomplete enumeration of the base population." This has affected sample designs in, for example, the recent surveys in Sierra Leone and Nepal. Various sample designs are used within the context of the World Justice Project's *General Population Poll.*

[103] The survey utilised the small user Postcode Address File (PAF), which represents the standard sample frame for face-to-face general population surveys in England and Wales.

[104] The coverage limitations of telephone and online surveys are generally greater than those of face-to-face surveys such as the *English and Welsh Civil and Social Justice Survey* and Colombian *National Legal Needs Survey*. Although the proportion of the world's population with personal telephone and Internet access continues to grow, significant numbers of people still do not have such access, particularly in lower gross domestic product (GDP) per capita countries and among the most vulnerable population groups. Moreover, coverage problems are compounded for telephone and online surveys by the disruption of landline penetration by mobile phone services and the lack of comprehensive registers of telephone or Internet users. Thus, as is detailed in Chapter 2, dual-frame sampling (incorporating overlapping landline and mobile telephone sample frames) is increasingly used for telephone surveys, and "contact phase" mixed mode surveying (in which, for example, letters invite people to participate in online surveys) is being trialed for online surveys, despite their introduction of additional (practical and theoretical) complexity and cost to the survey process.

[105] See Edwards & Fontana (2004).

[106] See Forell et al. (2005).

[107] See Karras et al. (2006).

[108] See Grunseit et al. (2008).

[109] Sample size must be considered in combination with survey reference period. A sample size can be smaller, if a reference period is longer. However, longer reference periods can be problematic, as is discussed in Chapter 2.

[110] To maintain absolute levels of accuracy, sample size also needs to increase with prevalence. For example, based on an alpha level of 0.05 (which equates to a Z value of 1.96) – and referencing problem prevalence as reported through the 2008 Australian *LAW Survey* – an (absolute) margin of error of 1% would necessitate a sample size of 827 in relation to clinical negligence, 6,283 in relation to consumer problems and 9,604 in relation to any problem. If the margin of error were 2%, then the figures would change to 207, 1,571 and 2,401 respectively.

[111] While different modes of conduct allow for different lengths of questionnaire – with face-to-face surveys having the potential to be much longer than telephone or online surveys – differences in mode are not the primary driver of the questionnaire length of Table 1.1 surveys. Many of the shorter surveys were conducted face-to-face, particularly in low GDP per capita countries where other modes are impractical.

[112] As Pleasence et al. (2013) noted, differences in the mode of conduct of legal needs surveys are associated with differences in response rate, coverage, formulation of questions, interviewer effects, levels of satisficing behaviour and expectations as to the nature and importance of the subject matter of questions. An illustration of the impact of methodological differences on survey findings comes from the 2018 *Nationwide Legal Needs and Access to Justice Survey* in South Korea. This was conducted both in person and online, with the two modes of conduct delivering problem incidence rates of 15 per cent and 56 per cent, respectively (Kim & Choi, 2018).

[113] See, for example, Sykes and Collins (1988), Bowling (2005) and Groves et al. (2009).

[114] The authors went on, "Actual nonresponse is far greater than whether panel members respond to an invitation for a study (i.e. at the specific survey sampling point). Not surprisingly, studies comparing results from nonprobability samples and traditional methods almost always find major differences, though it can be difficult to determine whether sample bias (due to major undercoverage/nonresponse) or mode is the greater cause (Baker et al., 2010)".

References

ACSSC (2012), *Access to Legal Services for Low-Income People in the Kyrgyz Republic,* ACSSC, Bishkek.

Adams, K., J.C. Botero, A. Coto, A. Evangelides, A. Gryskiewicz, C. Gutiérrez Patiño, S. Chamness Long, L. McDaniel, M. Mujeeb, A. Ponce and N. Treacy (2017), *Global Insights on Access to Justice,* World Justice Project, Washington, DC.

Adams, K., J.C. Botero, A. Evangelides, A. Gryskiewicz, C. Gutiérrez Patiño, M. Harman, A. Hopkins, S. Chamness Long, R. Martin, A. Ponce and L. Solís Saravia (2018), *Global Insights on Access to Justice,* World Justice Project, Washington, DC.

Akmeemana, S. (2011), *Disputes, Crimes and Pathways of Redress: A Household Survey on Citizens' Perceptions and Experiences of the Justice System in Bangladesh,* World Bank, Washington, DC.

Altrichter, H., A. Feldman, P. Posch and B. Somekh (2008), *Teachers Investigate their Work; An Introduction to Action Research Across the Professions,* 2nd edition, Routledge, London.

Asia Consulting Group and Policy 21 Ltd (2008), *Consultancy Study on the Demand for and Supply of Legal and Related Services,* Department of Justice, Hong Kong.

Attewell, P. (2001), "The first and second digital divides", in *Sociology of Education*, Vol. 74, pp. 252-259.

Baker, R., S.J. Blumberg, J.M. Brick, M.P. Couper, M. Courtright, J.M. Dennis, D. Dillman, M.R. Frankel, P. Garland, R.M. Grovers, C. Kennedy, J. Krosnick, J. and P.J. Lavrakas (2010), "Research synthesis: AAPOR report on online panel", in *Public Opinion Quarterly,* Vol. 74(4), pp. 711-781.

Balmer, N.J. and P. Pleasence (2012), *The Legal Problems and Mental Health Needs of Youth Advice Service Users: The Case for Advice,* Youth Access, London.

Barendrecht, M. and P. van Nispen (2008), "Microjustice", TILEC Discussion Paper No. 2008-010, HiiL, The Hague.

Barendrecht, M., M. Gramatikov, R. El Khoury, G. Motiejunas, S. Muller, D. Osborne, K. Heijstek-Ziemann and J.H. Verdonschot (2014a), *The Need of the Malians for Justice: Towards More Fairness,* HiiL, The Hague.

Barendrecht, M., M. Gramatikov, R. El Khoury, G. Motiejunas, S. Muller, D. Osborne and K. Heijstek-Ziemann (2014b), *Justice Needs of Yemenis: From Problems to Fairness,* HiiL, The Hague.

Baruah, P., S. Naik, S. Prakash and K. Mandyam (2018), *Paths to Justice: Judicial and Non-Judicial Dispute Resolution in India.*

BDRC Continental (2012), *Legal Services Benchmarking: Report,* BDRC Continental, London.

Blackburn, R., J. Kitching and G. Saidakis (2015), *The Legal Needs of Small Businesses: An Analysis of Small Businesses' Experience of Legal Problems, Capacity and Attitudes,* Small Business Research Centre (for the Legal Services Board), Kingston.

Bowling, A. (2005), "Mode of questionnaire administration can have serious effects on data quality", in *Journal of Public Health*, Vol. 27(3), pp. 281-291.

Bradshaw, J. (1972), "Taxonomy of social need", in G. McLachlan (ed.), *Problems and Progress in Medical Care: Essays on Current Research*, 7th series, Oxford University Press, London.

Buck, A. P. Pleasence, N.J. Balmer, A. O'Grady and H. Genn (2004), "Lone parents and civil law: Their experience of problems and their advice-seeking behaviour", in *Social Policy and Administration*, Vol. 38(3), pp. 253-269.

Chen, K.-P., K.-C. Huang, Y.-L. Huang, H.-P. Lai and C.-C. Lin (2012a), "The legal problems of everyday life: The nature, extent and consequences of justiciable problems experienced by Taiwanese", Paper presented at the Law and Society Association Conference, Honolulu, 7 June 2012.

Chen, K.-P., K.-C. Huang, Y.-L. Huang, H.-P. Lai and C.-C. Lin (2012b), "Exploring advice seeking behavior: Findings from the 2011 Taiwan Survey of Justiciable Problems", Paper presented at the Law and Society Association Conference, Honolulu, 7 June 2012.

Chong, D. and J.N. Druckman (2007), "Framing theory," in *Annual Review of Political Science,* Vol. 10, pp. 103-126.

Clark, C.E. and E. Corstvet (1938), "The lawyer and the public: An A.A.L.S. Survey," in *The Yale Law Journal*, Vol. 47(8), pp. 1272-1293.

Cornford, T. (2016), "The meaning of access to justice", in E. Palmer, T. Cornford, A. Guinchard and Y. Marique (eds.), *Access to Justice: Beyond the Policies and Politics of Austerity,* Oxford.

Coumarelos, C., P. Pleasence and Z. Wei (2013), "Law and disorders: Illness/disability and the experience of everyday problems involving the law", *Justice Issues*, Vol. 17, Law and Justice Foundation of New South Wales, Sydney.

Coumarelos, C., D. Macourt, J. People, H.M. McDonald, Z. Wei, R. Iriana and S. Ramsey (2012), *Legal Australia-Wide Survey: Legal Need in Australia,* Law and Justice Foundation of New South Wales, Sydney.

Croes, M.T. (2012), "Companies on their paths to justice: How small and medium-sized enterprises in the Netherlands deal with potential legal problems", in *Utrecht Law* Review, Vol. 8(1), pp. 51-77.

Croes, M.T. and G.C. Maas (2009), *Geschilbeslechtingsdelta Midden-en Kleinbedrijf: Over het Optreden en Afhandelen van (Potentieel), Juridische Problemen in het Midden - en kleinbedrijf,* Ministry of Justice, The Hague.

Currie, A. (2009), "The legal problems of everyday life", in R.L. Sandefur (ed.), *Access to Justice,* Emerald, Bingley.

Currie, A. (2007), *The Legal Problems of Everyday Life: The Nature, Extent and Consequences of Justiciable Problems Experienced by Canadians,* Department of Justice, Ottawa.

Currie, A. (2005), *A National Survey of the Civil Justice Problems of Low and Moderate-Income Canadians: Incidence and Patterns,* Department of Justice, Ottawa.

Denvir, C., N.J. Balmer and P. Pleasence (2011), "Surfing the web – Recreation or resource? Exploring how young people in the UK use the internet as an advice portal for problems with a legal dimension", in *Interacting with Computers*, Vol. 23, pp. 96-104.

Denzin, N.K. (1978), *The Research Act: A Theoretical Introduction to Sociological Methods*, 2nd edition, McGraw-Hill, New York.

Departamento Nacional de Planeación (2017), "Indice de Acceso Afectivo a la Justicia: Discussion on Indicators", Unpublished PowerPoint Presentation.

Dignan, T. (2006), *Northern Ireland Legal Needs Survey,* Northern Ireland Legal Services Commission, Belfast.

ECOLEX (2014), *Effectiveness and Access to Justice in Ecuador,* ECOLEX, Quito.

Edwards, S. and A. Fontana (2004), *The Legal Information Needs of Older People,* Law and Justice Foundation of New South Wales, Sydney.

Engel, D.M. (1998), "How does law matter in the constitution of legal consciousness", in B.G. Garth and A. Sarat, A. (eds.), *How Does Law Matter,* Northwestern University Press, Evanston, IL.

Farrow, T.C.W., A. Currie, N. Aylwin, L. Jacobs, D. Northrup and L. Moore (2016), *Everyday Legal Problems and the Cost of Justice in Canada,* Canadian Forum on Civil Justice, Toronto.

Forell, S., E. McCarron and L. Schetzer (2005), *No Home, No Justice? The Legal Needs of Homeless People in NSW,* Law and Justice Foundation of New South Wales, Sydney.

Franklyn, R., T. Budd, R. Verrill and M. Willoughby (2017), *Findings from the Legal Problem Resolution Survey,* Ministry of Justice, London.

Genn, H. (2017), "Access to justice in the 21st century," Paper presented at the Reshaping Justice: Client-Centred Service Delivery, Technology and Innovation Research Symposium, 20 June 2017, Sydney.

Genn, H. (1999), *Paths to Justice: What People Do and Think About Going to Law,* Oxford.

Genn, H. and A. Paterson (2001), *Paths to Justice Scotland: What People in Scotland Think and Do About Going to Law,* Oxford.

GfK Slovakia (2004), *Legal Needs in Slovakia II,* GfK Slovakia, Bratislava.

Golub, S. and K. McQuay (2001), "Legal empowerment: Advancing good governance and poverty reduction", in *Law and Policy Reform at the Asian Development Bank,* Asian Development Bank, Manila.

Gramatikov, M.A (2012), *Met and Unmet Legal Needs in Moldova,* Soros Foundation – Moldova, Chișinău.

Gramatikov, M.A. (2008), "Multiple justice problems in Bulgaria", *Legal Studies Working Papers,* Vol. 16/2008, Tilburg University, Tilburg.

Gramatikov, M.A. and J.H. Verdonschot (2010), *Legal Needs of Vulnerable People: A Study in Azerbaijan, Mali, Rwanda, Egypt and Bangladesh,* Tilburg Institute for Interdisciplinary Studies of Civil Law and Conflict Resolution Systems, Tilburg.

Gramatikov, M.A., S. Muller, M. Barendrecht, D. Osborne, G. Motiejunas and R. Porter (2014), *Justice Needs in Indonesia 2014: Problems, Processes and Fairness,* HiiL, The Hague.

Groves, R.M., F.J. Fowler, M.P. Couper, J.M. Leprowski, E. Singer and R. Tourangeau (2009), *Survey Methodology,* 2nd edition, John Wiley and Sons, Hoboken, New Jersey.

Grunseit, A., S. Forell and E. McCarron (2008), *Taking Justice into Custody: The Legal Needs of Prisoners,* Law and Justice Foundation of New South Wales, Sydney.

Heijstek-Ziemann, K., M. Gramatikov, S. Muller, J. Piest, N. Balau, J. Sallila and R. El Khoury (2017), *Justice Needs in Tunisia 2017: Legal Problems in Daily Life,* HiiL, The Hague.

HiiL (2016a), *Justice Needs in Ukraine: Legal Problems in Daily Life,* HiiL, The Hague.

HiiL (2016b), *Justice Needs in the United Arab Emirates,* HiiL, The Hague.

Huang, K.-C., C.-C. Lin and K.-P. Chen (2014), "Do rich and poor behave similarly in seeking legal advice? Lessons from Taiwan in comparative perspective", *Law and Society Review,* Vol. 48(1), pp. 193-223.

Ignite Research (2006), *Report on the 2006 National Survey of Unmet Legal Needs and Access to Services,* Legal Services Agency, Wellington.

Institute of Social Studies and Analysis (2012), *KAP Survey Concerning Justiciable Events in Georgia,* Open Society – Georgia Foundation, Tblisi.

Ipsos MORI (2012), *The English and Welsh Civil and Social Justice Panel Survey: Wave Two Technical Report,* Ipsos MORI, London.

Karras, M., E. McCarron, A. Gray and A. Ardasinski (2006), *On the Edge of Justice: The Legal Needs of People with a Mental Illness in NSW*, Law and Justice Foundation of New South Wales, Sydney.

Kemp, V., P. Pleasence and N.J. Balmer (2007), *The Problems of Everyday Life: Crime and the Civil and Social Justice Survey,* Centre for Crime and Justice Studies, London.

Kenya National Bureau of Statistics (2018), *Basic Report: 2015/16 Kenya Integrated Household Budget Survey (KIHBS),* Kenya National Bureau of Statistics, Nairobi.

Kim, S. and S. Choi (2018), "Reflections and lessons from the 2018 Nationwide Legal Needs and Access to Justice Survey in South Korea", unpublished report prepared for the Judiciary of the Republic of Korea.

Kind, M., M. Gramatikov, R. Núñez and N. Kernchen (2018), *Justice Needs and Satisfaction in Bangladesh: Legal Problems in Daily Life,* HiiL, The Hague.

Kind, M., M. Gramatikov, R. Núñez, R. El Khoury, N. Kernchen, G. Astafjevas and R. Lapeira (2017), *Justice Needs and Satisfaction in Lebanon: Legal Problems in Daily Life,* HiiL, The Hague.

Kobzin, D., A. Chernousov, R. Sheiko, M. Budnik, M. Kolokolova and S. Scherban (2011), *The Level of Legal Capacity of the Ukrainian Population: Accessibility and Effectiveness of Legal Services,* International Renaissance Foundation and Kharkov Institute of Social Research, Kharkov.

Kolisetty, A. (2014), "Examining the effectiveness of legal empowerment as a pathway out of poverty: A Case study of BRAC", *Justice and Development Working Paper*, Vol. 26/2014, Washington, DC.

Kondo, M.C., K.D.W. Bream, F.K. Barg and C.C. Branas (2014), "A random spatial sampling method in a rural developing nation", in *BMC Public Health,* Vol. 14(338).

Kritzer, H.M. (2008), "To lawyer or not to lawyer: Is that the question?", *Journal of Empirical Legal Studies,* Vol. 5(4), pp. 875-906.

La Rota, M.E., S. Lalinde and R. Uprimmy (2013), *Encuesta Nacional de Necesidades Jurídicas Análisis General y Comparativo Para Tres Poblaciones*, Dejusticia - Centro de Estudios de Derecho, Justicia y Sociedad, Bogota.

Larkin, K., V. Clarke, C. McDonnell and M. Turner (2018), *The Legal Needs of Small Businesses 2013-2017,* BMG Research, Birmingham.

Legal Services Commission (2004), *Improving Access to Advice in the Community Legal Service: Report on Evaluation Research on Alternative Methods of Delivery*, Legal Services Commission, London.

Macdonald, R.A. (2005), "Access to justice in Canada today: Scope, scale and ambitions", in J. Bass, W.A. Bogart and F.H. Zemans (eds.), *Access to Justice for a New Century: The Way Forward,* Law Society of Upper Canada, Toronto.

Maxwell, G., C. Smith, P. Shepherd and A. Morris (1999), *Meeting Legal Service Needs: Research Report Prepared for the Legal Services Board,* Legal Services Board, Wellington.

McCann, M. (2006), "On legal rights consciousness: A challenging analytical tradition", in B. Fleury-Steiner and L.B. Nielsen (eds.), *The New Civil Rights Research,* Ashgate, Aldershot.

Michelson, E. (2008), *Popular Attitudes towards Dispute Processing in Urban and Rural China,* The Foundation for Law, Justice, and Society, Oxford.

Michelson, E. (2007), "Climbing the dispute pagoda: Grievances and appeals to the official justice system in rural China", in *American Sociological Review*, Vol. 72, pp. 459-485.

Murayama, M. (2010), "Individual behaviour and institutional conditions: How could we measure institutional factors in survey?", Paper presented at the IISJ Workshop Current Socio-Legal Perspectives on Dispute Resolution, Onati, Spain, 15th–16th July 2010.

Murayama, M. (2009), "Expanding access to lawyers: The role of legal advice centres", in R.L. Sandefur (ed.), *Access to Justice,* Emerald, Bingley.

Murayama, M. (2007), "Experiences of problems and disputing behaviour in Japan", in *Meiji Law Journal*, Vol. 14, pp. 1-59.

Núñez, R., M. Gramatikov, S. Muller, K. Heijstek-Ziemann, M. Kind, N. Kernchen, R. El Khoury, N. Balau, G. Astafjevas and R. Lapeira (2017), *Justice Needs and Satisfaction in Jordan 2017: Legal Problems in Daily Life,* HiiL, The Hague.

OECD (2015), *Equal Access to Justice: OECD Expert Roundtable Background Notes*, OECD, Paris.

Open Society Forum (2018), *Current Legal Empowerment Situation in Mongolia,* Open Society Forum, Ulaanbaatar.

Orima Research (2010), *Small Business Dispute Resolution: Summary Report,* Department of Innovation, Industry, Science and Research, Canberra.

Patel, A., N.J. Balmer and P. Pleasence (2008), "Geography of advice seeking," in *Geoforum,* Vol. 39, pp. 2084-2096.

Paterson, A. (2012), *Lawyers and the Public Good: Democracy in Action?,* Cambridge University Press, Cambridge.

Pearson, J. and L. Davis (2002), *The Hotline Outcomes Assessment Study Final Report - Phase III: Full-Scale Telephone Survey*, Center for Policy Research, Denver, CO.

Piest, J., M. Gramatikov, S. Muller, K. Heijstek-Ziemann and J. Sallali (2016), *Justice Needs in Uganda: Legal Problems in Daily Life,* HiiL, The Hague.

Pleasence, P. (2006), *Causes of Action: Civil Law and Social Justice*, 2nd edition, The Stationery Office, Norwich.

Pleasence, P. and N.J. Balmer (2019), "Justice and the capability to function in society", *Daedalus,* Vol. 148(1).

Pleasence, P. and N.J. Balmer (2014), *How People Resolve 'Legal' Problems,* PPSR (for the Legal Services Board), Cambridge.

Pleasence, P. and N.J. Balmer (2013a), *English and Welsh Civil and Social Justice Panel Survey: Wave 2,* Legal Services Commission, London.

Pleasence, P. and N.J. Balmer (2013b), *In Need of Advice: Findings of a Small Business Legal Needs Benchmarking Survey,* PPSR (for the Legal Services Board), Cambridge.

Pleasence, P. and N.J. Balmer (2012a), "Caught in the middle: Justiciable problems and the use of lawyers", in M. Trebilcock, A. Duggan and L. Sossin (eds.), *Middle Income Access to Justice*, Toronto University Press, Toronto.

Pleasence, P. and N.J. Balmer (2012b), "Ignorance in bliss: Modeling knowledge of rights in marriage and cohabitation", in *Law and Society Review,* Vol. 46(2), pp. 297-333.

Pleasence, P. and N.J. Balmer (2009), "Understanding advice seeking behaviour: Findings from New Zealand and England and Wales", in K.-C. Huang (ed.), *Empirical Studies of Judicial Systems*, Academia Sinica, Taipei.

Pleasence, P. and D. Macourt (2013), *What Price Justice? Income and the Use of Lawyers,* Law and Justice Foundation of New South Wales, Sydney.

Pleasence, P. and H. McDonald (2013), *Crime in Context: Criminal Victimisation, Offending, Multiple Disadvantage and the Experience of Civil Law problems,* Law and Justice Foundation of New South Wales, Sydney.

Pleasence, P., N.J. Balmer and C. Denvir (2017), "Wrong about rights: Public knowledge of key areas of consumer, housing and employment law in England and Wales", *Modern Law Review*, Vol. 80(5), pp. 836-859.

Pleasence, P., N.J. Balmer and C. Denvir (2015), *How People Understand and Interact with the Law*, Legal Education Foundation, London.

Pleasence, P., N.J. Balmer and C. Denvir (2014), *Reshaping Legal Services: Building on the Evidence Base,* Law and Justice Foundation of New South Wales, Sydney.

Pleasence, P., N.J. Balmer and S. Reimers (2011b), "What really drives advice seeking behaviour? Looking beyond the subject of legal disputes", *Oñati Socio-Legal Series,* Vol. 1(6).

Pleasence, P., N.J. Balmer and R.L. Sandefur (2016), "Apples and oranges: An international comparison of the public's experience of justiciable problems and the methodological issues affecting comparative study", *Journal of Empirical Legal Studies,* Vol. 13(1), pp. 50-93.

Pleasence, P., N.J. Balmer and R.L. Sandefur (2013a), *Paths to Justice: A Past, Present and Future Roadmap,* Nuffield Foundation, London.

Pleasence, P., Z. Wei and C. Coumarelos (2013b), "Law and disorders: Illness/disability and the response to everyday problems involving the law", *Updating Justice*, Vol. 30, Law and Justice Foundation of New South Wales, Sydney.

Pleasence, P., N.J. Balmer, A. Patel and C. Denvir (2010), *Civil Justice in England and Wales*, Legal Services Commission, London.

Pleasence, P., N.J. Balmer, A. Patel, A. Cleary, T. Huskinson and T. Cotton (2011a), *Civil Justice in England and Wales: Report of Wave 1 of the English and Welsh Civil and Social Justice Survey*, Legal Services Commission, London.

Pleasence, P., A. Buck, N.J. Balmer, A. O'Grady, H. Genn and M. Smith (2004), *Causes of Action: Civil Law and Social Justice,* 1st edition, The Stationery Office, Norwich.

Prettitore, P.S. (2015), "Poverty and legal problems in Jordan: Defining the relationship", *MENA Knowledge and Learning Quick Notes Series*, Vol. 150, World Bank, Washington, DC.

Prettitore, P.S. (2014), "The justice gap and poverty: Learning from household surveys in Jordan and Colombia", *MENA Knowledge and Learning Quick Notes Series*, Vol. 136, World Bank, Washington, DC.

Prettitore, P.S. (2013), "Justice sector services and the poor in Jordan: Determining needs and priorities", *MENA Knowledge and Learning Quick Notes Series*, Vol. 96, World Bank, Washington, DC.

Reese, R.W. and C.A. Eldred (1994), *Findings of the Comprehensive Legal Needs Study*, American Bar Association, Chicago.

Sato, I., H. Takahashi, N. Kanomata and S. Kashimura (2007), "Citizens' Access to legal advice in contemporary Japan: Lumpers, self-helpers and third- party advice seekers", Paper presented at the Joint Annual Meeting of the Law and Society Association and the Research Committee on Sociology of Law, Humboldt University, Berlin, 26 July 2007.

Schetzer, L., J. Mullins and R. Buonamano (2002), *Access to Justice and Legal Needs: A Project to Identify Legal Needs, Pathways and Barriers for Disadvantaged People in New South Wales,* Law and Justice Foundation of New South Wales, Sydney.

Sen, A. (1999), *Development as Freedom,* Oxford University Press, Oxford.

Sen, A. (1980), "Equality of what?", S. McMurrin (ed.), *Tanner Lectures on Human Values,* Volume 1, Cambridge University Press, Cambridge.

Social Research Center (2012), *Legal Issues: Needs of Population of Legal Services and Practiced Ways of Meeting those Needs,* Branch Office of the International Organization of Open Society Institute – Assistance Foundation in Tajikistan, Dushanbe.

Srbijanko, J.K., N. Korunovska and T. Maleska (2013), *Legal Need Survey in the Republic of Macedonia: The Legal Problems People face and the Long Path to Justice,* Open Society Foundation – Macedonia, Skopje.

Subsecretaría de Acceso a la Justicia Ministerio de Justicia y Derechos Humanos (2017), *Diagnosticode Necesidades Jurídicas Insatisfechas y Niveles de Acceso a la Justicia,* Subsecretaría de Acceso a la Justicia Ministerio de Justicia y Derechos Humanos, Buenos Aires.

Sykes, W. and M. Collins (1988), "Effect of mode of interview: Experiments in the UK", in R.M. Groves, P.P. Biemer, L.E. Lyberg, J.T. Massey, W.L. Nichols and J. Waksberg (eds.), *Telephone Survey Methodology*, Wiley, New York.

Tamaki, T. (2009), "Summary tables of the results of an internet survey on dispute resolution", Part 1 and Part 2, in *Niigata University Journal of Law and Politics,* Vol 41(3/4), pp. 205-240, Vol. 42(1), pp. 157-180.

ter Voert, M.J. and C.M. Klein Haarhuis (2015), *Geschilbeslechtingsdelta 2014: Over Verloop en Afloop van (Potentieel), Juridische Problemen van Burgers*, Ministry of Security and Justice, The Hague.

Tobin Tyler, E., E. Lawton, K. Conroy, M. Sandel and B. Zuckerman (2011), *Poverty, Health and Law*, Carolina Academic Press, Durham, North Carolina.

Trubek, D.M., J.B. Grossman, F.L.F. Felstiner, H.M. Kritzer and A. Sarat (1983), *Civil Litigation Research Project Final Report,* University of Wisconsin Law School, Madison, WI.

United Nations Development Programme (2012), *Access to Justice Assessments in the Asia Pacific: A Review of Experiences and Tools from the Region,* United Nations Development Programme, Bangkok.

United Nations Development Programme (2005), *Programming for Justice: Access for All: A Practitioner's Guide to a Human Rights-Based Approach to Access to Justice,* United Nations Development Programme, Bangkok.

Uprimny, R., M.E. La Rota, S. Lalinde and D.E. Lopez (2012), *Encuesta Nacional de Necesidades Jurídicas y Acceso a la Justicia Marco Conceptual y Metodológico*, Bogota, Dejusticia, Colombia.

van den Bos, K., E.A. Lind and H.A.M. Wilke (2001), "The psychology of procedural and distributive justice viewed from the perspective of fairness heuristic theory", in R. Cropanzano (ed.), *Justice in the Workplace: From Theory to Practice*, Lawrence Erlbaum Associates Publishers, Mahwah, NJ.

van Velthoven, B.C.J. and K. Haarhuis (2010), *Geschilbeslechtingsdelta 2009: Over Verloop en Afloop van (Potentieel), Juridische Problemen van Burgers,* Ministry of Justice, The Hague.

van Velthoven, B.C.J. and M.J. ter Voert (2005), "Paths to justice in the Netherlands", Paper presented at the International Legal Aid Group conference, Killarney, Ireland, 8-10 June 2005.

van Velthoven, B.C.J. and M.J. ter Voert (2004), *Paths to Justice in the Netherlands: Looking for Signs of Social Exclusion,* Ministry of Justice, The Hague.

Weiss, C.H. (1980), "Knowledge creep and decision accretion", *Knowledge: Creation, Diffusion, Utilization*, Vol. 1(3), pp. 381-404.

Winczorek, J. (2018), "Uphill paths: Polish research on access to justice", Paper presented at the UCL International Conference on Access to Justice and Legal Services, London, 13 June 2018.

Chapter 2. Framework for Conducting Legal Needs Surveys

This Chapter establishes a methodological and conceptual framework for the conduct of legal needs surveys, and offers illustrative taxonomies of legal problems, sources of help and dispute resolution processes; with multiple levels of detail. This chapter also addresses how surveys can be used to measure legal needs.

Legal needs surveys in context

Legal needs surveys constitute a specialised form of survey research. They should therefore adhere as far as is possible to good practice in the survey research field. Their conduct should involve consideration of the relative benefits of different modes of survey administration, determination of the most appropriate sample frame and sampling method, maximisation of validity and reliability in questionnaire design, review and testing of design elements ahead of full implementation, conduct of suitable forms of analysis, and timely and faithful reporting.

General guidance on survey research, and more particular guidance on its conduct in developing and transitional countries and in the justice sector, is readily available.[1] This chapter complements this existing guidance by identifying and expanding upon a variety of considerations that are unique to legal needs surveys.

Legal needs surveys give rise to unique considerations because they are situated within a unique conceptual framework, at the heart of which is the concept of the "justiciable" problem. Legal needs surveys must therefore be framed appropriately and justiciable problems appropriately defined. There are also unique considerations concerning survey scope, units of measurement, and the operationalisation of other distinct concepts relating to justiciable problem experience, such as forms and sources of help, dispute resolution processes, outcomes, legal capability and legal need.

This chapter examines the concepts, framing, scope and units of measurement used in legal needs surveys and provides taxonomies of justiciable problems, sources of help and dispute resolution processes. These taxonomies can assist in the process of defining the subject matters of legal needs surveys, as well as supporting greater consistency and opportunity for comparison between surveys. This chapter also discusses how legal needs survey questionnaires are best structured.

"Justiciable" problems

The term "justiciable" has been used intermittently since the 15th Century to indicate an issue within the jurisdiction of a court of law, or one liable to be taken to court.[2] However, in the context of legal needs surveys, the term has acquired a more particular meaning (coined in the reporting of the seminal *Paths to Justice* survey [Genn, 1999, p. 12]), arising from the recognition that beyond problems that become "legal" – through use of traditional legal services or processes, or simply through consideration in legal terms – there are many for which law provides a framework, and in which law could potentially be invoked, but for which no (explicit, at least) consideration is given to law (often appropriately and without cause for concern). Accordingly, throughout this document, the term "justiciable" is used to describe problems that raise legal issues, whether or not this is recognised by those facing them, and whether or not lawyers or legal processes are invoked in any action taken to deal with them.

Framing legal needs surveys: Defining the subject matter

The presentation of research and the formulation of questions can have a substantial impact on the nature of responses. This is called the "framing effect", where framing refers to "the process by which people develop a particular conceptualisation of an issue or reorient their thinking about an issue" (Genn, 1999, p. 12). Framing is therefore a key consideration in designing a survey.

Thus, a primary consideration in designing a legal needs survey is how to communicate to respondents the subject matter of the survey. The concept of a justiciable problem, as defined above, is not commonly used or understood. It is also well documented that public understanding of law is generally low[3] and that legal concepts tend to be narrowly conceived (often with an emphasis on criminal justice).[4]

Framing legal needs surveys around the concept of "justiciable" problems is therefore problematic, but so too are references to "legal" problems or even to "law" in general. Such references risk constraining survey responses to problems that have involved the use of legal services or those commonly conceived of as being legal. Thus, around half of the large-scale national legal needs surveys detailed in Table 1.1 have eschewed references to law in their framing.[5] For example, the 2016 Mongolian survey was introduced as being about "problems that citizens commonly face."

The risk of references to 'law' was made evident by an experiment in which a survey was randomly presented to individuals as being about either 'different kinds of legal problems or disputes' or, less technically, about 'different kinds of problems or disputes'. It was found that a single use of the word 'legal' when introducing the survey led to a substantial decrease in the likelihood of problems being reported:

> *"Framing problems as 'legal' [...] was associated with a significant reduction in problem prevalence when compared to introducing problems without any reference to them being legal ... Where problems were introduced as legal, 50.8% reported one or more problem, with this rising to 62.6% where they were not."*

Furthermore, responses may be influenced simply by revealing the name of the survey sponsor if the name is legal in nature (Pleasence et al., 2013).

Good practice in the conduct of legal needs surveys avoids references to law, justiciable problems or other technical concepts, and instead introduces surveys by describing the subject matter in purely lay terms. For example, surveys can begin with generic reference to "common" and/or "everyday" problems, perhaps accompanied by examples (e.g. land grabbing, unfair dismissal by an employer, being injured as a result of someone else's mistake, or being involved in a dispute over money in a divorce settlement). This has the benefit of focusing attention on to the types of issues that are justiciable, but using only lay language. As legal needs surveys are often conducted in different languages, a further benefit of using lay language is that there is less need to translate technical legal terms or the concept of justiciable problems, for which no direct equivalents exist.[6]

The same considerations apply in relation to the drafting of questions seeking to identify justiciable problems. Around two-thirds of the national legal needs surveys detailed in Table 1.1 have sought to exclude references to law in the problem identification process, along with the use of legal terminology.[7] Following this practice, justiciable problems detailed in questionnaires should be carefully described in lay terms to ensure that descriptions are *both* recognisable *and* justiciable. This requires both expert methodological and expert legal input.[8]

As the report of the 2016 Argentinian survey explained:

> *"Instead of referring to problems in legal terms, the circumstances of problems were presented: it was asked whether [respondents] had experienced a problem or situation of a certain kind, in colloquial and descriptive terms, rather than using legal language. This approach reduces underreporting of problems, including problems experienced by people who are not aware they have legal*

consequences." (Subsecretaría de Acceso a la Justicia (Ministerio de Justicia y Derechos Humanos, 2016, p. 14)

The range of justiciable problems

The range of justiciable problems that could be studied is almost as broad as the range of people's activities. While various categories of justiciable problems have been explored in most legal needs surveys, there has been significant variation in the mix of problem categories and types presented. All of the surveys in Table 1.1 and Table 1.2, for which details are available, captured data concerning family, employment and housing related problems; problems central to people's lives and welfare all around the globe.[9] Almost all also collected data concerning consumer and money related problems, and the majority collected data concerning problems relating to discrimination, education, injuries (due to negligence), neighbours, treatment by the police and government services (particularly welfare provision).[10]

Questions about certain problem types are more frequently posed in particular jurisdictions. Historically, for example, problems concerning identity documentation and land (as distinct from housing) have typically been explored in development contexts.[11] In contrast, questions concerning immigration are usually addressed to people living in high income jurisdictions; the same is true of problems concerning the care of others. Some questions have been asked in relatively few jurisdictions, such as questions about defamation, or - in very recent surveys - online harassment (included in the 2017 Sierra Leonean survey).

A number of surveys have included questions about "other" problems once questions about specific categories have been answered. This is not good practice, however, as it introduces uncertainty and ambiguity as to the nature and scope of problems under study. Problems should be defined as clearly as possible. An unspecified "other" category places the onus on respondents to determine the sort of things an "other" category might contain. This leads to frames of reference varying significantly among respondents (e.g. depending on their experience and interpretation of previous questions). It also affects the number of non-justiciable problems reported.

The great amount of time involved in identifying justiciable problems means that there is always pressure to limit the range of problems included in legal needs surveys. Ultimately the range of problems included in legal needs surveys must reflect the concerns and interests of stakeholders and the technical limitations of such surveys. These vary between surveys.

Certain criteria can help determine the range of problems included in surveys. One will be problem prevalence, which links – as was discussed in Chapter 1 – to the efficiency of legal needs surveys as a research tool. Problem prevalence also constitutes one of Barendrecht et al.'s six approaches to determining "priorities in the justice system" (Barendrecht et al., 2008). However, other criteria are likely to be equally or even more influential in the minds of survey sponsors. These include the value, impact and cost of problems (both to those affected and more widely; particularly to public services) – alluded to in Barendrecht et al.'s approaches concerning "severity" and "needs for protection" – and Barendrecht et al.'s other approaches, relating to the costs of self-protection, the cost of leaving a situation, and supply side features, such as specialised courts.

If legal needs survey type questions are incorporated into other types of surveys, then it may be appropriate to ask about only a very limited range of problem types. These might be those directly linked to the subject matter of the host survey (e.g. housing related problems) or, in the case of general surveys, to subjects of particular interest or concern to stakeholders.

Differences in the types of problems and the manner in which they are queried limit the extent to which findings in different jurisdictions can be compared. If comparison is important, particular care should be taken to use consistent problem identification questions, addressing equivalent problem types.

In the absence of any broad international standards for the conduct of legal needs surveys, efforts to achieve consistency among surveys have hitherto been possible only on a partial and ad hoc basis. Drawing on a comprehensive review of past surveys, Table 2.1 therefore sets out a taxonomy of all justiciable problems included in past national legal needs surveys. Eight primary problem categories are central: employment, family, accidental injury/illness, public services and administration, money and debt, consumer, community and natural resources, and land and housing. The use and evolution of such a taxonomy in constructing and analysing legal needs surveys would greatly increase the scope for comparison among future surveys' findings.

Levels of detail

Questions aimed at identifying justiciable problems lie at the heart of legal needs surveys. However, such questions can be – and have been – delivered in many ways. For example, the 2005 Northern Irish survey presented respondents with 110 distinct problem types, while the 2017 Indian survey simply asked respondents whether they "had a dispute in the past 5 years" and followed-up by asking what disputes were about.[12] The most common approach is to present respondents with descriptions of a broad range of problems. Indeed, around half of surveys for which details are available ask questions about 70 or more distinct problems; often – in the case of face-to-face surveys – by presenting them on show-cards.[13] The presentation of distinct problem categories has both advantages and disadvantages.

On the positive side, it increases clarity of purpose, meaning and scope. The more detail provided, the less respondents are left to interpret the scope of questions, and the lower the risk of misinterpretation and/or of relevant memories being neglected.[14] Neglecting areas of memory will reduce problem reporting, affecting accuracy and potentially limiting the prospects of statistical analysis. In the specific context of legal needs surveys, experimental evidence indicates that more detailed questions result in increased reporting of problems, although the experiments were not conclusive, and the impact of varying levels of detail differed depending on the problem type (Pleasence et al., 2016).

An example of misinterpretation resulting from lack of detail is provided by the 2006-2009 *English and Welsh Civil and Social Justice Survey*, in which "discrimination" was often misunderstood as referring to insensitive or unpleasant behaviour, rather than to prejudicial treatment in relation to opportunities and access, as was intended. As a result, later surveys in the series asked about discrimination in the context of other defined problems (Pleasence et al., 2011a). No "discrimination" problem category appears in Table 2.1, reflecting the fact that discrimination (and, separately, harassment) occurs in the context of many of the problems set out in Table 2.1. Discrimination can be easily incorporated into surveys by adopting the innovation of the *English and Welsh Civil and*

Social Justice Survey; namely, by asking about discrimination as a characteristic of the problems set out in Table 2.1.[15]

On the negative side, presenting respondents with numerous problems increases the risk of fatigue and satisficing behaviour.[16] It is also time consuming, making it impractical for shorter surveys or for surveys where time needs to be made available for other questions. Thus, as a compromise between accuracy and brevity, a number of surveys have approached problem identification by presenting respondents with relatively short lists of problem categories, providing examples to increase clarity and assist recall. Similarly, the 2017-2018 pilot of the South African *Governance, Public Safety and Justice Survey* presented respondents with a short list of disputant types (including family/relatives/friends, neighbours, other individuals, community/civic groups, employers, company or business officials, health/education institutions or officials, and government institutions or officials), with some examples to aid recall.[17]

Given the centrality of problem identification, further experimental investigation into the impact of different approaches to problem identification on survey findings would be invaluable.

Exclusion of "trivial" problems

To avoid "being swamped with trivial matters" (Genn, 1999, p. 14), more than half of the national legal needs surveys detailed in Table 1.1[18] have only asked respondents about "difficult to solve" problems (e.g. following the lead of the highly influential *Paths to Justice* surveys[19]). This approach does reduce problem reporting to a significant extent, but such an approach is problematic and not recommended.

Experimental evidence shows that asking about only "difficult to solve" problems can decrease problem reporting by around 30% (Pleasence et al., 2016). This hardly constitutes preventing "the floodgates opening" and is hugely problematic in conceptual terms; as it conflates problem occurrence, problem resolving strategy and legal capability. For example, what is difficult to solve for one person may not be for another. As was noted by the authors of the 2008 Australian survey, some problems will therefore not be captured by surveys using the "difficult to solve" filter, simply "because they were easy to handle" (Coumeralos et al., 2012, p. 11), and this ease of handling may have been a product of an individual's greater legal capability (which is important to understand in relation to need) and/or the availability of more effective problem resolution mechanisms or services (which is also important to understand, and goes to the heart of access to justice policy). Even a problem leading to legal advice or a formal court process could potentially be viewed as "easy to solve" and not reported (e.g. as a result of delegating difficult decisions, good advice and representation). A far better approach to filtering out "trivial" problems is therefore to only follow-up problems that reach a minimum seriousness threshold, after all problems have been identified. This approach is explored further, below.

Table 2.1. Illustrative standard problem categories for legal needs surveys

Problem category	Primary sub-categories	Secondary sub-categories	Tertiary sub-categories	Quaternary sub-categories
Employment	Application and promotion			
	Disciplinary procedures			
	Termination	Unfair dismissal		
		Redundancy		
	Rights at work	Pay, pension, etc. related		
		Working conditions		
		Other rights (e.g. hours, leave, etc.)	Maternity/paternity related	
			Other	
		Contract changes		
	Harassment			
Family	Relationships and care of children	Relationships	Relationship breakdown	Divorce or separation (binary)
				Alimony/division of property
			Other relationship problems	
	Children	Care of children	Child support, custody and contact	
			Public law children	Adoption and guardianship
				Child neglect
		Education		
		Other children problems		
	Domestic violence (victim)			
	Wills and probate			
Accidental injury / illness	Workplace	Industrial disease		
		Workplace accident		
	Traffic related			
	Other	Victim of crime		
		Other		
		Clinical negligence		

Public services and administration	Health	Other quality of medical care		
		Compulsory treatment/discharge		
		Access to health services		
		Disease control		
	Abuse by state officials	Unfair treatment by the police		
		Abuse by other state officials		
	Education (respondent)	Fairness of assessment		
		Suspension/exclusion		
		Access to education		
	Access to public services (excl. health)			
	Citizenship, ID and certification	Immigration		
		Obtaining ID		
		Other state registration/certification		
	Money and government	Government payments, loans and allowances	Social safety net payments/loans	Excluding pensions
				State pension
			Disability payments/loans	
			Educational payments/loans	
			Other payments/loans	
			Social safety net tax allowances	
		Tax		
Money and debt	Debt	Problems paying bills/repaying loans (excluding creditor action)		
		Creditors taking action	Legal action (or threat of)	
			Harassment / intimidation	
			Loss of collateral (excluding land)	Pawnshop related
				Other (excluding land)
	Money	Problems recovering money owed (loans and insurance)	Problem collecting money owed to you (loans (category excludes tenants))	
			Problem obtaining insurance pay-out	

		Financial services	Inaccurate credit rating	
			Problems concerning banks, financial advisors, etc.	Misrepresentation / mis-selling
				Mismanagement (financial loss)
				Incorrect / disputed fees
Consumer	Services (excluding utilities)	Other services (excluding utilities)	Other professional services (e.g. accountants, mechanics, plumbers, etc.)	
			Other services (e.g. transport services, leisure services, etc.)	Non-delivery or inadequacy of service
				Incorrect / disputed fees
	Goods	Non-delivery of goods		
		Defective / unsafe goods		
	Utilities	Incorrect / disputed billing		
		Non-delivery of contracted quality		
		Access to utilities		
Community and natural resources	Access to natural resources		Water	Location
				Other
			Other utilities	
		Access to forest, waterways, etc.	Access (e.g. rights of way)	
			Hunting, fishing, foraging	
		Grazing		
	Maintenance and protection	Maintenance		
		Security		
		Environmental damage		
	Governance of community groups			
Land and housing	Land	Land grabbing, expropriation		
		Use of	Subsistence farming	
			Other	
		Building, conveyancing and boundaries	Building permissions, permits	
			Conveyancing	
				Boundaries

	Housing	Home ownership	Neighbours (excl. anti-social)	Other
			Foreclosure/repossession	
		Tenancy	Neighbours (excl. anti-social)	Strata related
				Other
			Condition of housing	
			Terms of lease	
			Eviction	
			Harassment	
			Other	
		Homelessness		
	Neighbours (anti-social)			
	Problems as a landlord	Rent related		
		Property damage		
		Other		
Other	Care (excl. children)	Residential care		
		Care of adults		
	Environmental (other)			
	Development project related			
	Internet related	Abuse, harassment, bullying		
		Other		
	Other			
Business	Trading	Suppliers/purchases		
		Clients/sales		
	Regulation, permits, etc.			
	Employment (of others)			
	Land, business premises, etc.	Use/expropriation of land		
		Acquisition, development, sale, etc.		
		Rented business premises		
	Money			
	Business structure			
	Tax			

	Corruption, bribes, protection		
	Other		
Crime	Victim of crime	Violence (excl. domestic violence)	Non-sexual
			Sexual
		Theft, burglary, dishonesty	
	Accusation / Offending	Arrested / detained	
		Fines / outstanding fines	
		Offending	Road traffic
			Other offending

Business related problems

As with individuals acting in a private capacity, businesses – both individuals acting in a business capacity and distinct organisations – face justiciable problems, which impact on business functioning and sustainability, the wellbeing of workers, and the wider economy.[20] As noted in Chapter 1. , a number of dedicated legal needs surveys of businesses have been undertaken in recent years. Moreover, around one-third of past surveys of individuals have incorporated questions about problems faced by respondents in a business, as well as in a personal, capacity. For many self-employed persons, the two capacities can feel, and be, difficult to distinguish.[21] This raises the significance of business-related problems in many people's lives. It is particularly relevant in countries in which a significant proportion of the population work on their "own account".[22] In general, in low income countries around half of all workers work on their own account.[23]

The significance of business-related problems in people's lives poses methodological challenges to ensuring that the nature of the universe of problems recorded by surveys is distinct and defined.

If business problems are in a general population legal needs survey's scope, then – as business capacity is a distinct functional capacity and can have a distinct legal capacity, and as problems related to running a business generally have distinctive characteristics, - questions should ideally be formulated to distinguish business and personal problems and enable samples of "individuals" and "businesses" to be separately identified. However, clear distinctions will not always be straightforward, or even possible, owing to the capacity-ambiguity inherent in some aspects of working on one's own account (e.g. relating to finance where there is no separate business entity in law). The most coherent approach may therefore be to draw a distinction between problems that are solely an aspect of respondents' work and problems that are at least to some extent personal.

In considering how business and personal problems can be distinguished, three basic approaches have been adopted in the past. The first has been to exclude all business-related problems from the scope of surveys. This was the approach of the *Paths to Justice* surveys of the late 1990s, which made it clear that problems experienced in a business capacity should not be reported. The second approach has been to ask questions about business related problems separately (as in, for example, the 2008 Australian *LAW* survey). If this approach is adopted, it should be made clear that questions about personal problems exclude problems experienced in a business capacity (although this has rarely been the case). The third approach has been to ask, on follow-up after selection for detailed questioning, whether problems relate to business activities (as in, for example, the 2017 iteration of the World Justice Project's *General Population Poll* and the 2017-18 Nepalese survey).[24] Provided that problems selected for follow-up are randomly selected from those identified, reasonable estimates of the total incidence of personal and business related problems may be possible – provided sufficient problems are followed up – but a limitation of this approach is that data are not available across the full sample of identified problems.[25]

Distinguishing business from personal problems provides conceptual coherence, provides greater flexibility in relation to analysis and facilitates the comparison of survey findings. However, in some – particularly low income – countries and social contexts, it may be difficult to draw the distinction and perhaps, in any event, valuable to include problems experienced by individuals working on their own account. A case in point is the 2017-18 Nepalese survey, in which respondents were asked to include only problems that they had faced themselves, but this was defined to include "problems experienced through a business that provides you with self-employment (but not an enterprise providing employment to others)."

Crime victimisation and offending

While not a primary focus of legal needs surveys, the majority of past legal needs surveys have asked about one or more aspects of respondents' experience of crime. This is in addition to questions concerning civil dimensions of criminal behaviours (such as domestic violence, corruption, crime compensation, etc.). As with business related problems, the experience of crime is conceptually quite distinct from the experience of justiciable problems. However, there are commonalities between the criminal and civil justice system and associated sources of help. Furthermore, strong associations have been found between the social patterning of crime victimisation, offending and justiciable problem experience.[26]

Aside from illuminating access to criminal justice issues, the primary benefit of including questions on crime in legal needs surveys is that it allows the investigation of overlapping service needs. If there is little survey sponsor interest in such matters, then questions concerning crime can be limited or excluded, as appropriate. This is particularly so in jurisdictions in which separate victimisation surveys are conducted. Currently, Statistics South Africa is exploring ways to gather victimisation data and legal needs data in rotating years to provide a more comprehensive picture of access to justice.[27]

For reference, detailed guidance on the conduct of victimisation surveys has been produced elsewhere, including by the United Nations Office on Drugs and Crime and the United Nations Economic Commission for Europe.[28]

Problem seriousness

Justiciable problems vary in their seriousness; a matter relevant to prioritisation and action, both by individuals and public services. Accordingly, the great majority of surveys detailed in Table 1.1 and Table 1.2, for which details are available,[29] have investigated relative seriousness in some way. However, conceptualisations of seriousness diverge.

Past surveys have variously sought to measure seriousness with reference to perceptions, economic value and impact; all of which are connected, but distinct. Problems perceived as serious do not necessarily concern matters of high value and are not necessarily impactful; although they will often have substantial perceived value and potential impact.

The 2011 Moldovan and 2016 Mongolian surveys, for example, asked (respectively) about perceived problem "importance" and "seriousness" in the abstract; while the 2012 Georgian survey, for example, asked about the perceived importance of resolving problems. The 2011 Taiwanese survey, which asked about both seriousness and importance of resolution, identified significant differences in reporting patterns between perceptions of seriousness in the abstract and of the importance of resolving problems (Chen et al., 2012b). Turning to economic value, the 2012 Macedonian and Taiwanese surveys asked about the monetary value of matters in dispute; while the 2006 English and Welsh survey adopted the approach of contingent valuation in asking about willingness to pay for problems to be resolved. As for impact, the 2004 Dutch survey, for example, asked about the extent to which respondents became preoccupied with problems; and the 2012 Tajik survey asked about the impact of problems on life in general. Increasingly, surveys are also following the lead of the *English and Welsh Civil and Social Justice Survey* and investigating specific life-impacts (in various degrees of detail).

The broader impact of justiciable problems

Questions about the impact of justiciable problems on a wide range of life circumstances are important if there is interest in justiciable problems' broader social and economic impact. This line of inquiry enables policymakers to connect legal problems to broader social and economic development policies and outcomes.

The principal life-impact question developed for the 2004 *English and Welsh Civil and Social Justice Survey* included nine impact areas: physical health, stress, relationships, violence (aimed at the respondent), property damage, the need to move home, loss of employment, loss of income, and loss of confidence. The form of the question has been widely adopted, with most surveys asking about a similar range of impacts.

However, some surveys have looked at a broader range of impacts. The 2010 *English and Welsh Civil and Social Justice Panel Survey* and 2012 Georgian survey both covered 18 impact areas, with questions extending to alcohol and drug abuse, fear, and problems related to documentation. The 2017-8 Nepalese survey went further still. It asked about more than 50 impact areas, tailored to particular problem types. These extended to stigmatisation, denial of public and community services, and problems concerning documentation. However, there may be limited value to such detailed data if there are relatively few problems of relevant types or instances of particular impacts.

A small number of surveys have included follow-up questions designed to obtain further details of life changes, upon which estimates of the economic impact of problems on individuals and public services were based. For example, the 2004 survey included 23 follow-up questions, to establish, for example, the extent of lost income, receipt of state support (e.g. as a consequence of unemployment) and use of public services (e.g. medical services). On the basis of responses to these questions, the economic cost of justiciable problems to individuals and public services was estimated to be around US$5 billion per year (Pleasence, 2006, p. i). In the most recent exercise of this type, the 2014 Canadian survey incorporated 30 detailed follow-up impact questions. Here, the annual cost to public services was estimated to be "approximately $800 million (and perhaps significantly more)" (Farrow et al., 2016 p. 16).

Building on life-impact questions, some surveys – following the lead of the 2006 New Zealand survey – have also similarly asked about factors leading to the experience of reported justiciable problems (e.g. the 2016 Argentinian survey).

Abstract problem seriousness scales

A variety of abstract problem seriousness scale questions have been used in legal needs surveys in recent years.

Following a major methodological review, the 2010 *English and Welsh Civil and Social Justice Panel Survey* introduced a simple visual analogue scale (VAS)[30] (a technique used extensively in medicine[31]) to assess problem seriousness. This involved presenting respondents with a single straight line with "anchor points" marked near the top and bottom (comprising short descriptions of a very serious and relatively trivial problem[32]), and asking respondents to indicate where a problem sat on the line. The practice has since been adopted by other surveys, including the 2017 Sierra Leonean survey, and has been adapted into an equivalent numerical rating scale (NRS) in the case of, for example, the 2014 English and Welsh survey (conducted via telephone) and the World Justice Project's 2017 *General Population Poll* (conducted via various channels). Simple NRS based questions have also been used in other surveys, such as the 2016 Argentinian and Mongolian surveys.

The psychometric properties of such VRS and NRS approaches have not been tested, and they are unlikely to be as reliable as a fully developed multiple item scale.[33] However, a VAS can provide a simple, quick and adequate measure,[34] as can an NRS, which has the additional advantage of being capable of oral administration. Indeed, in other fields NRS approaches have demonstrated excellent test-retest reliability;[35] along with good sensitivity, without the practical difficulties of a VAS (Williamson and Hoggart (2005).[36]

Units of measurement

Contrasting with the "largely isolated" (Pleasence et al., 2016, p. 70) tradition of (largely sub-national) U.S. legal needs surveys that ask questions about household experience of justiciable problems, more than three-quarters of the national legal needs surveys detailed Table 1.1 asked about individual problem experience.[37]

Just five surveys ask about household experience. These include the access to justice module of the World Justice Project's 2016 *General Population Poll*; although the 2017 *General Population Poll* was then changed to ask about individual experience. In addition, a small number of surveys asked about the experience of respondents and their partners (the 2004, 2006 and 2008 Canadian surveys) or about respondents and their (non-adult) children (the 2005 Japanese survey, 1997 New Zealand survey and 2011 Taiwanese survey). And some individual experience-based surveys collected data from all adult members of households (such as the 2001, 2004 and 2006 to 2009 English and Welsh surveys), to enable household experience to be investigated alongside individual experience.[38]

It can be argued that "there are distinct benefits to the collection of household data, [such as that it] may more accurately reflect the experience of shared problems (i.e. those that are faced by families together), the linking (and counting) of which can be problematic in individual surveys" (Pleasence et al., 2013, p. 24). However, not all problems within households are shared. Some problems are between members of a household (raising obstacles to both the fact and nature of reporting), and individual respondents may be unaware or have a false impression of problems elsewhere within a household (especially when details are deliberately withheld). Moreover, households differ, and although individual data can in some cases be aggregated to household level (if information concerning whether problems are shared is collected), the reverse is generally not possible. Thus, surveys of individuals are generally preferable in the case of legal needs studies.

To properly reflect a population's experience of justiciable problems, individual respondents should be randomly selected. If a sample frame is composed of households (or similar), and if all members of a household are not interviewed, then individual respondents should be selected at random within households. For reasons similar to those just set out, proxy interviews should be avoided wherever possible. If proxy interviews are deemed necessary, then some questions (e.g. questions concerning domestic violence) become inappropriate.

In the case of surveys of individuals, even if problems can be included twice (e.g. within households) the standard unit of measurement for problem level analyses should be individually experienced problems.

Community problems

Just as household members may share problems, problems may also be shared by other groups of individuals, such as work colleagues and members of the wider community.

Although no legal needs surveys have been designed to measure the experience of justiciable problems by communities (as distinct from within communities), many surveys have nonetheless asked about problems commonly experienced across communities (such as those concerning expropriation, environmental damage, access to public services, etc.). The 2017-2018 Nepal survey went further than most, and also asked about a category of problems concerning "community resources".

As with problems shared within households, respondents can be asked whether their problems are shared more widely, and with whom. For example, the 2017 *General Population Poll* asked whether problems were shared with "other people, neighbours, or other members of your community" and whether people took the same position or collective action "to achieve a solution." Thus, it was possible to identify whether identified problems were instances of larger community problems *and* whether a community response was taken to such problems.

Questioning along these lines builds up a picture of the volume of shared problems. With additional questioning concerning the extent to which problems are shared, questioning could also shed light on the scale of community problems and (theoretically, at least, subject to sample structure) differences between communities.

Legal needs survey reference periods

A legal needs survey's reference period is "the time frame for which survey respondents are asked to report […] experiences of interest" (Lavrakas, 2008). Deciding on the appropriate reference period involves balancing two main factors: ensuring that a sufficient number of problems are reported to enable analysis and reporting as intended, and (particularly in the context of monitoring) the contemporaneity of survey data.[39] In deciding how many years to go back, it is important to recognise that recall becomes increasingly unreliable the further back in time it is extended. Moreover, different types of justiciable problems are associated with different "forgetting curves" (Tourangeau et al., 2000, p. 84) (i.e. patterns of recall error over time) (Pleasence et al., 2009). For example, consumer related problems tend to be forgotten more quickly than personal injuries, which, in turn, tend to be forgotten more quickly than divorce (Pleasence et al., 2009). The net effect of this is that the composition of problem samples varies with survey reference periods, and the proportionate increase in volume of problems reported diminishes as reference periods are extended. Experimental evidence indicates that increasing a legal needs survey's reference period from one to three years has only "a fairly modest" impact on problem reporting (Pleasence et al., 2016). Thus, the 2006 Hong Kong *Demand & Supply of Legal & Related Services* survey, which asked respondents to recall events from one year, five years and over the entire life course – within a single survey – recorded respective problem prevalence rates of 19%, 32% and 40%.

Looking at the surveys detailed in Table 1.1 and Table 1.2, slightly fewer than one-third have adopted a three-year reference period,[40] and four more a three-and-a-half-year reference period (where January 1st was used to anchor the reference period three calendar years prior to interview). The next most common reference periods were five years[41] and four years (the 10 HiiL *Justice Needs and Satisfaction* surveys), followed by one year.[42] Drawing on the review informing this Guide, the World Justice Project's *General Population Poll* access to justice module moved from a one-year to a two-year reference period between 2016 and 2017. In the context of the typical sample sizes of legal needs surveys, a one-year reference period is unlikely to yield sufficient problems to enable diverse or detailed analysis of respondents' problem resolving behaviour. A two-year reference period was also implemented by the 2017-2018 Nepalese survey and the 2017-2018 South African *Governance Public Safety and Justice Survey* Pilot.

While the vast majority of past legal needs surveys have been cross-sectional in their design, the English and Welsh *Civil and Social Justice Survey* switched to a panel design in 2010. This change of design gave rise to additional considerations regarding the survey's reference period and saw a switch from a three-year reference period to an 18-month reference period, to reflect the gap between surveys. Problems not concluded at the time of the 2010 survey were revisited in the 2012 survey.

Problem resolving behaviour

A central focus of legal needs surveys is problem resolving behaviour. This can extend to a broad range of activities, and past surveys have varied considerably in the types of activity and level of detail asked about.

Survey content is ultimately determined by the choice of questions, which reflect the interests and concerns of the survey's sponsors and stakeholders. However, in order to generate a comprehensive picture of respondents' problem resolving behaviour, three separate areas of activity *must* be addressed:

- Help seeking
- Use of processes
- Other activities that support problem resolution.

Process is discussed in the next section; being distinct in not requiring either initiation or engagement on the part of survey respondents. Help seeking and other activities that support problem resolution are discussed in this section.

Sources of help

All but one of the surveys detailed in Table 1.1 and Table 1.2, for which details are available,[43] explicitly asked whether or not help had been sought from a lawyer, professional or other source. In the majority of surveys, respondents were presented with a list of potential sources of help and invited to respond to each individually. In all but one of the remaining surveys, an open question was used. The anomaly was the 2011 Jordanian survey, which asked only a narrow question about whether an attorney was hired.

The 2007 Bulgarian survey was the only survey not to explicitly ask whether or not help had been sought from a lawyer, professional or other source. However, it did ask (through a broad open question) what respondents had done when faced with problems and, separately, whether they had sought "additional information". Thus, all of the surveys provided an opportunity for respondents to report help seeking.

As noted previously, more detailed questions can lower the risk of misinterpretation and/or neglect of relevant memories. However, when there are many potential answers, only limited specification may be possible, and care needs to be taken to avoid too narrow a focus. Care also needs to be taken to ensure that details are effectively communicated. Experimental evidence indicates that asking distinct and separate questions about sources of help can significantly increase reporting rates, compared to using a simple list format (Pleasence et al., 2016). In the context of online and other self-completion surveys – from which this evidence was drawn – this makes clear the importance of sustaining concentration across all question elements. In the context of other surveys, such as face-to-face surveys, it points to the value of presenting list items to respondents clearly and separately whenever possible.

The terminology used to describe sources of advice, in generic terms, has varied between surveys. Terms used to date have included "another person", "someone", "people", "professionals" and "organisations".[44] The most common phrasing has been "people or organisations", which was used in more than one-third of the surveys.

Past surveys have referenced numerous sources of help as examples or as the basis for lists: including lawyers, civil society organisations, the police, unions, community leaders and organisations, employers, politicians, government departments (central, regional and local), religious leaders, the media, health professionals, financial services, school staff, family and friends. It would be impossible to reference them all in any single survey, and inappropriate, as many are specific to particular places. Furthermore, terminology describing legal professionals and services varies from place to place. Consequently, more than 40 different terms have been used to do so in past surveys, including "lawyer", "attorney", "solicitor", "barrister", "notary", "paralegal", "legal executive", "legal consultant", "legal aid lawyer", "government lawyer", "insurance company legal service", "legal clinic", "legal advice office", "legal aid", "NGO with free legal advice", as well as various named services.

Previous legal needs surveys suggest that respondents often struggle to recall the exact name or (professional) nature of a source of help. This is not just a memory, but a comprehension, issue. It is therefore often unreasonable to expect a respondent to understand and recall the precise name or nature of an organisation or other source of help. The question should be asked, but issues regarding validity and reliability need to be understood.

Table 2.2 sets out a suggested taxonomy of sources of help to inform the drafting of legal needs survey questions and coding of responses. As with types of justiciable problems, a consistent approach would greatly increase the scope for comparison of findings.

A typology of sources of help might focus on various source characteristics, such as sector (i.e. government, commercial, civil society, community, etc.), degree of specialisation, extent of assistance, cost to clients (e.g. free or paid for), regulatory framework,[45] or manner of service delivery. However, mirroring the primary concern of the surveys detailed in Table 1.1 and Table 1.2– to establish respondents' recourse to independent and expert help – Table 2.2 first distinguishes between help obtained from (i) non-expert friends, family and acquaintances, (ii) legal and professional advice services, and (iii) other sources. Importantly, advice services included in the legal and professional advice services category must provide *some* information, advice or representation of a legal nature. Table 2.2 then distinguishes further between sectors, and then on other bases.

The categories included in Table 2.2 reflect those most often referred to in the reports of the surveys detailed in Table 1.1 and Table 1.2.[46] Some categories of sources are conceptually complex and difficult to communicate. Here, the experience of past survey authors can be particularly helpful. For example, HiiL's use of the phrase "designated formal authority", in its *Justice Needs and Satisfaction Surveys* captures the idea of a range of organisations that includes regulators, Ombudsman schemes and civil enforcement authorities.

Table 2.2. Illustrative standard sources of help categories for legal needs surveys

Help category	Primary sub-categories	Secondary sub-categories	Tertiary sub-categories	Quaternary sub-categories
Family, friends and acquaintances	With relevant expertise (code below)			
	Without relevant expertise			
Legal and advice sector	Government provided legal/advice services	Legal aid	Legal aid staff service	Attorney/solicitor/barrister
				Paralegal
			Provision through private practice	
		Other government legal services	Government legal/advice services	Public facing legal/advice service
				Offender release legal/advice service
				Other targeted legal/advice service
			Government legal department	
	Dispute resolution authorities (formal)	Police and prosecution authorities		
		Courts and tribunals	Judiciary	
			Staff	
			Enforcement	
		Designated formal authority/agency		
		Other formal dispute	Mediation, conciliation,	

		resolution authorities	arbitration
			Other
	Independent legal services provided through membership or association	Employment related	Through employer
			Through union / professional association
		Insurance legal/advice service	
		Other	
	Law centres, clinics and legal/advice	Law Centres	
	agencies (excl. government)	Independent legal/advice agencies	NGO/Charity
			University legal clinics
			Other
	Private sector lawyers	Universal	Attorney/solicitor
			Specialist advocate/barrister
			Notary
			Other
		Issue specific	
	Other independent advice services		
Other professionals	Health and welfare	Health professionals	
		Social workers	
	Financial		
	Other		
Other government	Administrative department	National, regional, local, etc.	
	Politician		
	Other		
Other civil society/charity	National, regional, local, etc.		
Other community	Community leader		
	Community organisation	Political	
		Non-political	
Religious			
Other	Employment related	Employer	
		Trade union / Professional body	
	Media		
	Other		

Information, advice and representation

The context and form of past legal needs surveys suggest that, when asking about sources of help, surveys have been principally concerned with help that is given personally (and sometimes only personalised forms of such help). This is particularly evident in relation to the (at least) 30 surveys, including all five iterations of the *English and Welsh Civil and Social Justice Survey* and 10 iterations of the *Justice Needs and Satisfaction Survey*, which separately asked about information obtained from, for example, websites, books, leaflets, self-help guides and other media (i.e. mass communication) sources.

With the development of sophisticated and intelligent web and app-based services, distinctions between plain information, help given personally and personalised help is likely to become increasingly blurred, requiring questions to adapt and capture more data about help obtained from online resources.

As regards levels of services, while distinctions between information, advice and representation are in general well understood by legal professionals – the first is generic, the second tailored to individual clients' circumstances, and the third involves action taken on behalf of clients – it is doubtful whether survey respondents easily recognise these sometimes subtle distinctions. Thus, if questions asking about help are intended to be restricted to particular levels of help, they must specify these levels clearly or inquire further into the matter through follow-up questions.

As with sources of help, the terminology used to describe help varies between surveys. Commonly used words have been "advice", "help", "information" and "assistance" (in order of prevalence), while the most used phrase has been "information or advice". The phrase "information, advice or help" has also been used. Although not the most commonly used term, "help" has been the term most often used on its own.

One problem with use of the term "help" is that it is too broad. So, for example, a respondent could report having obtained help from a court to resolve a problem, meaning that a court *process* helped to resolve the problem.

When drafting questions on sources of help, key considerations are which terms best reflect behaviour of interest, which will be best understood, and which will best assist recall.

Seeking, contacting and receiving

Past surveys have also varied in whether they have included a question or a combination of questions about help having been sought, contact having been made with sources of help, and help having been obtained. Initial questions concerning help have been phrased in terms of (in decreasing order of prevalence) "seeking", "getting", "contacting", "obtaining", "trying to obtain", "receiving", "consulting", "hiring" and "trying to contact".

With a significant minority of people who seek help failing to obtain it, asking only about whether help was sought, whether a source of (potential) help was contacted, or whether an attempt was made to obtain help, will leave unanswered the question of how many people managed to actually obtain help in resolving justiciable problems. Thus, most surveys which have asked about help seeking have also asked about whether help was obtained. However, some have not, such as the 2008 Australian and 2011 Moldovan surveys. This should be avoided.

Help from family, friends and the other party

Help from family and friends is generally very different in character to help received elsewhere. It is usually non-expert, not independent and informal. It is therefore important not to conflate such informal help with help sought from an independent source.

Some surveys, such as the 2016 Argentinian survey, have identified help from family and friends separately from help from other sources, while others have asked about all sources of help through the same question. In the case of surveys that have presented lists of potential sources of help to respondents, such as the World Justice Project's *General Population Poll*, family and friends has generally been expressly included as a list item.

Occasionally, help from family or friends will be expert, and if so, it is useful to identify this. However, to date, only relatively detailed surveys, such as the *English and Welsh Civil and Social Justice Survey,* have asked about the expertise and nature of advice obtained from family and friends, as well as from elsewhere.

Also distinct from independent help is help received from the other party to a dispute. This cannot be regarded as independent, whether expert or not. Thus, it should be explicitly excluded, or delineated within core questions designed to identify sources of help. If help provided by the other party is of particular interest, it should be asked about elsewhere.

Reference to "legal" help

As discussed in the context of survey framing and identification of justiciable problems, reference to 'legal' help should be avoided. Again, it is likely to narrow respondents' conceptions of the types of help being asked about and assumes they have an understanding of what constitutes 'legal'. Knowing a source of help will provide good indication of the character of help provided, and it is also possible to use follow-up questions to explore this in greater detail. This does not mean there should be no references to help from 'lawyers' or other 'legal' or named sources; although, again, the range of sources of interest should ideally be indicated in lay terms.

Help obtained on behalf of respondents

Reflecting the general tendency to inquire into individual (rather than household, etc.) problem experience, the great majority of surveys have asked only whether respondents *personally* sought/obtained help. An exception was the 2008 Australian survey, which asked whether "you or a relative or friend on your behalf" had sought/obtained help. Widening the scope of the question can have advantages. Importantly, it recognises that some people may not be able to, or choose not to, access help themselves.

A complete picture of problem resolving behaviour

While some surveys display an interest in only certain aspects of problem resolving behaviour, others are designed to be comprehensive. If a comprehensive picture is sought, then questions should address activities that go beyond obtaining information or advice, or utilising processes. These include evidence gathering and consideration of options.

If residual problem resolving behaviour is not investigated, then it is not possible to identify those respondents who took no action to resolve problems: a group often of interest to stakeholders. Despite this limitation, many survey reports have discussed inaction without a basis for its identification.

Process

As detailed above, there is a distinction between respondents' problem resolving behaviour and processes that form part of problem resolution. The latter can occur with or without initiation or engagement by the respondent. Thus, to maintain conceptual clarity, questions about processes should ideally be separate from those about other aspects of problem resolution.

To develop an accurate description of problem resolution, it is necessary to establish whether and what processes form part of problem resolving, who initiates them and whether different parties engage with them. This does not require detailed questioning about processes, only about whether process did or did not play a role in problem resolution. In fact, while some older surveys, most notably the *Paths to Justice* surveys, devoted significant questionnaire space to enquiring about respondents' experiences and navigation of formal processes, the rarity of formal processes and lay people's limited technical understanding and familiarity with them have resulted in more recent surveys shifting focus to early stage problem resolution decision-making.

The great majority of surveys listed in Table 1.1 and Table 1.2 have investigated processes used as part of problem resolution. The few exceptions, such as the 2006 New Zealand survey,[47] have focused narrowly on respondents' abilities to access help when needed.

Types of process

Surveys have asked about different types of processes. Surveys routinely include some focus on state courts and tribunals, as well as typically exploring "mediation" and "negotiation".[48] Some surveys have also explored other forms of resolution process.

Particular challenges face efforts both to draw up appropriate typologies of process in individual surveys and to compare the findings of different surveys. A great many different dispute resolution processes exist around the world, involving different forms of authority, different types of participant, different rules on standing, different approaches to resolution, and different rules of operation. Similar processes may be referred to using different names and dissimilar processes may be referred to using the same name. For example, although "mediation" may be technically defined as involvement of an independent third party to help different sides come to agreement, without taking sides, offering advice or imposing or requiring agreement, the term is commonly applied to many forms of intermediation, conciliation, arbitration and adjudication.

Table 2.3 sets out an illustrative taxonomy of process. Following the primary interest of past surveys in determining the identity of third parties involved in problem resolution, processes are initially split into five categories reflecting different identities ("state", "community", "religion", "other" and "none"), but then further divided according to different approaches to resolution (e.g. intervention, investigation, adjudication, mediation, etc.).

It is notable that past legal needs survey questions have often conflated different aspects of process, such as the identity of the individual or organisation responsible for the process and the nature of the process itself. In many cases, the result has been an inability to disaggregate these different aspects.

In contrast to Table 2.1, which lays out illustrative problem categories, Table 2.3 places substantial responsibility on survey authors to appropriately map different forms of locally available process into this taxonomy.

Table 2.3. Illustrative standard process categories for legal needs surveys

Process category	Primary sub-categories	Secondary sub-categories	Tertiary sub-categories	Quaternary sub-categories
No third party	Direct negotiation (personal)			
	Indirect negotiation (through representatives)			
State	Court/tribunal	Court	Hearing, paper based, online, etc. Investigation, adjudication, mediation, etc.	
		Tribunal		
		Enforcement service		
	Designated formal authority / agency (civil)	Regulator		
		Ombudsman	Investigation, adjudication, mediation, etc.	
		Other civil enforcement authority		
	Prosecution authority	Police	Investigation	
			Arrest / prosecution	
			Other	
		Other	Investigation	
			Arrest / prosecution	
			Other	
	Other government	Central	Investigation, adjudication, mediation, etc.	
		Regional		
		Local		
		Individual		
Community	Community leader or organisation (informal)	Investigation, adjudication, mediation, etc.		
	Indigenous/customary practice	Investigation, adjudication, mediation, etc.		
Religion	Court (*Shariah tribunals*, *Beth Din*, etc.)	Investigation, adjudication, mediation, etc.		
	Other			
Other	Family/friends			
	Independent third party (not connected to problem)	Mediation or conciliation	Mediation	
			Conciliation	
		Investigation, adjudication, etc.		

	Organisation connected to problem	Other party is the organisation / Other party is part of the organisation	Not Internet related	Investigation, adjudication, mediation, etc.
			Internet related (e.g. *Ebay Resolution Centre*)	
		Other party not the organisation	Not Internet related	Industry standards body
				Other
	Organised crime	Investigation, adjudication, mediation, etc.		

Contact with process bodies, process initiation and participation

The ways in which parties trigger a process for resolution varies considerably, as does the level of potential engagement on the part of the parties. Perhaps because of this, the terminology used in past surveys to ask about respondents' and others' involvement in processes has also varied considerably. Indeed, the terminology used in these questions has differed far more than in relation to other core legal needs survey questions.

As the terminology used in questions seeking to identify processes can have a significant bearing on the nature of what is identified, great care must be taken in the selection of terms, and the appropriateness of terms will vary along with processes.

For example, "contact" with a process body does not equate to either initiation, the existence of or participation in a process. Contact may relate to information or advice seeking; and even in this case does not denote success in achieving what is sought. Despite this, contact has been the most common term used to identify the involvement of courts and tribunals in dispute resolution. Towards the other end of the scale, asking about "participation" in a process will not necessarily identify all instances of process being used.

In addition to these terms, other terms that have been used in relation to courts and tribunals have included (in descending order of prevalence) "appear at", "go to", "filed a case/lawsuit", "turn to", "appeal to", "take to", "make a claim or make use of" and "initiate".

A narrower range of terms has been used to identify mediation and other processes in dispute resolution. For example, more than one-third of questions seeking to identify use of mediation have asked about "attendance" at mediation sessions, and another third about mediation being "arranged".

If surveys are to ascertain which party, including third parties, initiated a process, this can most efficiently be asked about as an immediate follow-on question (in respect of each process identified). Similarly, ascertaining the extent of respondents' involvement in processes is most efficiently addressed through follow-on questions.

Detail and specificity

As noted above, more detailed questions can lower the risk of misinterpretation and/or neglect of relevant memories. Also, as noted above, when questions centre upon lists, such as lists of processes, it is important to present each list item separately to respondents. Distinct and separate questions about processes have been found to substantially increase reporting rates, compared to the use of lists (unless items are individually presented) (Pleasence et al., 2016). Mediation, for example, was reported around four times as frequently when asked about separately, rather than as part of a list in an online survey.

Over half of the surveys in Table 1.1 and Table 1.2 used lists, which were usually read out to respondents, to ask about different processes. Most of the remaining surveys posed separate questions. A small number used open questions.[49]

Use of technical language and use of examples

Questions concerning resolution processes should also be constructed using lay language whenever possible. If specifically named processes are asked about or if technical language cannot be avoided, additional description should be provided, unless universal recognition can be assumed. If process categories are unclear, examples should be provided to clarify meaning using a range of examples broad enough to indicate a process's scope.

Reflecting the broad range of lay interpretations of the terms "mediation" and "conciliation", the *Paths to Justice Scotland Survey* provided 10 examples: Advisory, Conciliation and Arbitration Service (ACAS), Comprehensive Accredited Lawyer Mediators (CALM), Centre for Dispute Resolution (CEDR), Mediation Bureau, Academy of Experts, Chartered Institute of Arbitrators, National Family Mediation (NFM), Family Mediation Scotland (FMS), ACCORD and the SFLA. Evidently, fewer examples will generally suffice.

Whether and how justiciable problems have concluded

Whether or not problems have concluded

The majority of past surveys have asked whether identified problems have been concluded, with most using binary coding (concluded/ongoing) to record responses. The use of binary coding is inappropriate. There may be periods of time in which it is unclear whether problems have been concluded, or whether attempts to resolve them have been abandoned. Thus, a response option reflecting uncertainty is beneficial.

Moreover, there are aspects of problem conclusion that simplistic questioning may obfuscate. For example, disagreements or efforts to resolve problems may be concluded while problems persist, or the substance of problems may be concluded although disagreements persist. Moreover, respondents have sometimes reported that problems have been concluded, only to report them later in a survey as persisting but being "put up with" on a permanent basis.

To fully establish whether problems have been concluded, it is therefore necessary to inquire into whether problems are completely resolved (meaning they no longer exist, and there is no persisting active disagreement), otherwise settled (meaning that all parties have given up all actions to resolve them further), ongoing, or whether it is too early to tell.

The majority of past surveys with questions concerning conclusion have asked whether problems are "over" or "resolved". An explicit definition of such terms is rare, despite their evident ambiguity.

The small number of surveys that have not enquired about whether problems were concluded have focussed on problem resolving behaviour and process. However, it is important to determine whether problems have been concluded, as problem resolving behaviour and process related data can only be complete in respect of concluded problems.. Reporting ongoing problems as if they were concluded will lead to under-estimation of help seeking and process use.

Manner of problem conclusion

In all, more than thirty different category descriptions have been used in the surveys in Table 1.1 and Table 1.2 to ask about conclusion, although these can be reduced to eight principal categories, which are sometimes sub-divided and sometimes merged. These are:

- decision by a third party (often split between courts/tribunals and other third parties);
- mediation, conciliation and arbitration (often defined as being "formal" or "independent");
- action by a third party;
- agreement between the parties (often split between agreements reached "directly"/ "personally" and agreements through lawyers or other representatives);
- unilateral action by the other party;
- unilateral action by the respondent (often split between action to resolve the problem and action to avoid the problem (e.g. move home));
- the problem sorted itself out; and,
- the problem is being put up with.

Perceptions of process and outcome

To understand access to justice and legal need, one needs to know more than just the processes utilised and manner of conclusion. One must understand the quality of resolution process and outcome. Legal needs surveys can help to capture participants' experiences of different justice processes as well as assessment of outcomes.

The fact that a legal problem has been resolved by an institution does not mean that justice has been done. Around half of the surveys in Table 1.1 and Table 1.2 for which details are available[50] included questions exploring respondents' perceptions of "quality of process",[51] and a great majority included questions exploring perceptions of "quality of outcome".[52] The greater focus on outcomes suggests greater interest in perceptions of outcome among survey authors. However, "people's perceptions of procedural fairness are […] very important" (Van den Bos et al., 2001, p. 49) in shaping overall judgments of fairness.[53]

While the seminal surveys of the 1990s included questions concerning respondents' perceptions of process and outcome (including eight process related questions in the *Paths to Justice* surveys), the most influential surveys in this topic area have been HiiL's *Justice Needs and Satisfaction Surveys*. Historically, most past legal needs surveys have accommodated only a few questions in this area, but the ten *Justice Needs and Satisfaction Surveys* – informed by HiiL's *Measuring Access to Justice in a Globalising World* project[54] – have each devoted 19 questions to quality of process, and a further 23 to quality of outcome. Recognising the multidimensionality of process and outcome quality and drawing on a theoretical framework derived from extensive reviews of the literature (Klaming and Giesen, 2008); Verdonschot et al., 2008), the core questions investigating and seeking to measure perceptions of process address "procedural", "interpersonal" and "informational" justice (14 questions). The core questions investigating and seeking to measure perceptions of outcome address "distributive" and "restorative" justice, along with outcome "functionality" and "transparency" (20 questions).

Procedural justice refers to various properties that a procedure should possess "in order to be perceived as fair by its user" (Klaming and Giesen, 2008, p. 3) including "voice, neutrality, trustworthiness, consistency, and accuracy" (Gramatikov et al., 2011, p. 361). Interpersonal justice "reflects the degree to which people are treated with politeness, dignity, and respect by authorities and third parties involved in executing procedures or determining outcomes" (Colquitt et al., 2001, p. 427). Informational justice is concerned with "explanations provided to people that convey information about why procedures were used in a certain way or why outcomes were distributed in a certain fashion" (Colquitt et al., 2001, p. 427). Distributive justice concerns the fair distribution of benefits and burdens (that in this context constitute a justiciable problem's outcome),[55] while restorative justice "is the dimension of the outcome which rectifies the damage or loss suffered … [as a result of the] problem" (Gramatikov et al., 2011, p. 363). Functionality of outcome "is the extent to which the outcome solves the problem" (Gramatikov et al., 2011, p. 363), and transparency of outcome concerns explanations for outcomes and the ability to compare the outcomes of similar problems.

Seen through this lens, the *Paths to Justice* surveys' eight questions on perceptions of process concerned procedural and informational justice; while the United States *Comprehensive Legal Needs Study* focused on procedural and interpersonal justice. Among more recent surveys that have explored perceptions of process, the 2012 Colombian survey employed 21 questions[56] to address multiple aspects of procedural, interpersonal and informational justice including "voice", "neutrality" and "trustworthiness".[57] At the other end of the scale, the 2012 Georgian survey posed individual questions about procedural, interpersonal and informational justice respectively, while the 2016 Argentinian survey included single questions about interpersonal and informational justice. The 2011 Moldovan survey and World Justice Project's 2016 and 2017 *General Population Poll* included single questions on overall process fairness.

Few surveys, other than the *Justice Needs and Satisfaction Surveys*, have addressed the multiple dimensions of outcome quality, and while the *Justice Needs and Satisfaction Surveys* have devoted around two-dozen questions to exploring the dimensions of outcome quality described above, the 2017 Sierra Leonean survey – notable in also addressing all four dimensions – asked just one question in respect to each. When surveys addressed respondents' perceptions of outcomes, they usually asked only one or two questions using more or less the same format.

Among the 37 surveys known to have included supplementary questions on perceptions of outcomes, 36 asked about the extent to which outcomes were perceived to be "fair", "satisfactory" or both (24, 21 and 11 surveys, respectively). A significant minority of surveys also sought to identify the extent to which outcomes were favourable to respondents (a task most appropriate to zero-sum disputes) and/or the extent to which they were seen to meet respondents' objectives in acting (16 surveys, in both cases).

Defining the subject matter of process questions

With regard to the subject matter of inquiries into respondents' perceptions of process and outcome, questions may deal with either (i) specified processes (such as specific court or mediation processes), of which a number may be involved in resolving a particular problem; or (ii) the problem resolution process as a whole.

In the first case, in order to address all identified processes, a greater number of questions must be asked. However, inquiring into specific processes allows for comparisons to be drawn between processes. Although inquiring into the problem resolution process as a whole also allows for comparisons, the relatively ill-defined subject matter of questioning (owing to the inability to isolate individual processes for those who use more than one) is problematic.

The cost of resolving justiciable problems

Cost is commonly considered "a central barrier to obtaining legal assistance" (Pleasence and Macourt, 2013, p. 1) and, hence, a significant barrier to accessing justice and a factor in unmet legal need. Questions about the costs of legal assistance are often of central importance to national policymakers. Almost all of the surveys detailed in Table 1.1 and Table 1.2 inquired directly or indirectly into the cost of resolving justiciable problems.[58]

Almost all the surveys obtained information about cost concerns; most often indirectly, in the context of problem resolution strategy decision-making.[59] The great majority also asked direct questions about the financial costs incurred in seeking to resolve problems,[60] with levels of expenditure,[61] the nature of fee arrangements and subsidies commonly investigated. Very specific questions of interest to particular survey stakeholders have also sometimes been asked, such as whether costs were researched or negotiated.[62] However, the number of questions devoted to inquiring into the cost of problem resolution varied considerably, from 31 in the *Paths to Justice* surveys to just one in the 2016 Mongolian survey. Across all the surveys, the median number of questions asked was seven.

Those surveys that included only a small number of dedicated cost-related questions usually sought to determine whether respondents had to pay for legal services and how much they paid (e.g. the 2005 Japanese survey),[63] or how expensive services were considered to be (e.g. the 2015 Polish and 2016 Mongolian surveys). Some also asked about help or financial support obtained from legal aid or similar sources. This has been standard practice in surveys undertaken in jurisdictions with established legal aid schemes and in surveys intended to inform the institution or development legal aid.

Types of cost

HiiL's *Measuring Access to Justice in a Globalising World* project made evident that "the costs a claimant encounters on a path to justice can be very diverse" (Barendrecht et al., 2006, p. 13). Moreover, they can be measured "not only in terms of money, but also in terms of time[64] and emotional costs (e.g. stress)" (Barendrecht et al., 2006, p. 5). Just under half of the surveys reviewed sought to ascertain the total financial cost of resolving problems;[65] two-fifths sought to ascertain the cost in time;[66] and a similar number sought to establish the emotional cost.[67] However, only the *Justice Needs and Satisfaction Surveys* have sought to quantify all three of these costs types. They have also sought to quantify constituent costs of each type: first asking about respondents' expenditure on various aspects of problem resolution, then about the time spent engaging in various activities, and finally about the emotional impact of problem resolution processes and their impact on "important relationships".[68] Twenty-three questions, including sub-questions, were required to do this: nine on financial costs, nine on temporal costs, and five on emotional costs.

In quantifying the financial cost of resolving problems, specific cost items mentioned in past surveys have included: lawyer and other advisor fees, court and other process fees, travel costs, communication related costs, evidence and information collection costs (including the cost of professional witnesses), bribes/"kick-backs", reimbursement of witnesses' incidental costs, domestic costs (e.g. babysitter, house cleaner), and loss of salary/business (to enable problem resolution).

Sometimes, as with the two most recent Canadian surveys, respondents were given a list of cost items and asked to provide only their aggregate financial cost. This is likely to yield less accurate estimates than asking for the cost of the items separately, as was done in the *Justice Needs and Satisfaction Surveys*, and the 2010 Ukrainian and 2011 Moldovan surveys. In any event, to arrive at an aggregate figure, respondents need to address each constituent item. Asking about them individually both prompts and provides time for appropriate recollection. In the case of the last two surveys mentioned, cost questions also extended to the broader economic impact of problems themselves. This form of questioning about financial costs can therefore be functionally similar to the more detailed forms of questioning about problem impact discussed above.

In quantifying the time cost of resolving problems, the *Justice Needs and Satisfaction Survey* asked the most detailed questions; seeking separate estimates for the time spent on activities such as searching for a legal advisor, communication with advisors (and others), document preparation, attending hearings and "hanging around" (e.g. in lines, for hearings, etc.).

In quantifying the emotional cost of resolving problems, the *Justice Needs and Satisfaction Survey* asked how stressful processes had been, to what extent they made respondents feel frustrated, to what extent they made respondents angry, and to what extent processes were humiliating.[69]

"Free" services and financial support

The great majority of past surveys have sought to identify whether respondents had to personally pay for any legal services obtained, and half have sought to establish whether fees have been met, or contributed to, from elsewhere.[70]

The question of personal payment is not as straightforward as it seems. There is ambiguity in the case of services funded from pooled resources, such as legal expenses insurance or membership subscriptions (e.g. union subscriptions). Here, there are both direct and indirect payments, and questions should specify which payments are relevant.

In the case of subsidies, if subsidies must be applied for, then their existence is within the purview of individual respondents. However, respondents will not always understand or recall applications for financial support or the identity of subsidising bodies. For example, respondents may confuse an application for financial support with other documents they or an intermediary prepared. When subsidies are provided on other bases, their existence is unlikely to be within the purview of individual respondents. The origins of the funding of 'free' services can be both opaque and multifarious. For instance, free services may be provided as part of a marketing strategy, on a voluntary basis, through charitable support or from state subsidy. Respondents cannot ordinarily be expected to have insight into this matter.

Nor can respondents be expected to have insight into the amount of any subsidy if the subsidy is hidden from them. Indeed, even when financial support is provided from a source known to a respondent, and in relation to an individual case – whether through legal aid, by an employer or another source – details of the amount of support may never be known or, if known, may be forgotten more readily than for personal expenditure. Thus, in the context of a legal needs survey, extensive investigation into the nature and amount of financial support provided to respondents – along the lines of the 31 cost-related questions asked in the *Paths to Justice* surveys – is unlikely to deliver accurate results. It is noteworthy that the successor surveys to the *Paths to Justice* survey in England and Wales – the *English and Welsh Civil and Social Justice Survey* – included just 16 cost-related questions in 2001, 11 in 2004, 10 in 2006 and five in 2010.

While it is entirely appropriate to ask respondents whether they applied for/received support from legal aid, a union, legal expenses insurance, etc., further questioning can only reliably focus on costs personally met by respondents.

Legal capability and legal empowerment

The ability of individuals to respond effectively to justiciable problems – and, linked to this, the support that may be required to meet legal needs – varies with legal capability.[71] The concept of legal capability centres on the "range of capabilities" (Pleasence et al., 2014, p. 136) necessary to make and carry through informed decisions to resolve justiciable problems.[72] There is no consensus on the precise constituents of legal capability, but there is much agreement among recent accounts of the concept. All reference, to some extent, the following constituents: the ability to recognise legal issues;[73] awareness of law, services and processes; the ability to research law, services and processes; and the ability to deal with law related problems (involving, for example, confidence, communication skills and resilience).[74]

The great majority of surveys detailed in Table 1.1 and Table 1.2[75] included questions concerning one or more of these four constituents of legal capability. Most asked respondents about their awareness or familiarity (through prior use) of legal services.[76] The majority of questions concerned legal capability in general,[77] rather than referencing reported problems.[78] However, while a person's general legal capability is increasingly understood to play a role in legal problem resolution behaviour, specific capability in handling individual legal problems is important to understand in the context of legal need (being relevant to, for example, whether people obtain appropriate support).

Although questions about awareness of (and, sometimes, also prior use of) services is routine, only a handful of surveys have asked about respondents' professed knowledge of their legal position,[79] and always in relation to reported problems.[80] A few surveys (though not the same surveys[81]) have also posed questions about respondents' awareness of dispute resolution processes. This relative lack of questioning about legal understanding suggests a greater concern with people's ability to obtain information and support when required, than with their ability to independently progress legal cases.[82] This focus of concern may also partly explain the slightly greater number of surveys that have asked respondents whether they regarded justiciable problems as having a "legal" dimension, a matter now recognised as having a substantial bearing on whether help is sought from "legal" services.[83]

As regards the ability of individuals to deal with law related problems, a significant number of surveys[84] have investigated respondents' confidence in resolving justiciable problems (although just two of these surveys have done this in relation to reported problems: the 2005 Japanese[85] and 2012 Tajik survey). The majority of these surveys have adopted variants of the "subjective legal empowerment"[86] (SLE) questions used in HiiL's *Justice Needs and Satisfaction Surveys.* These have involved asking respondents how likely they think it would be that they would get a fair solution (or, separately, a solution and a solution that is fair[87]) to a justiciable problem. The questions focus on problems involving six types of opposing party: a debtor, an employer, a family member, a neighbour, a government authority and a retailer.

Questions such as these are simple to implement and give some insight into legal confidence. They can also provide a foundation for supplementary questions concerning knowledge of law and awareness of legal services. However, questions seeking to measure underlying traits (such as legal confidence) rather than observable phenomena, involve significant conceptual and technical challenges and require substantial testing. In the case of questions such as those used so far to investigate SLE, exploratory analysis[88] of data from two recent surveys – both undertaken for the specific purpose of developing standardised measures of legal confidence and attitudes to law – identified issues with their psychometric properties (Pleasence and Balmer, forthcoming),[89] indicating that additional developmental work is needed in order for them to function appropriately as an effective SLE scale. Alternative approaches to measuring legal confidence that were tested through these surveys – one based on independent questions, and one based on unfolding scenarios – yielded three working standardised legal confidence scales: a 6-item (scenario escalation based) "General Legal Confidence" (GLC) scale, a 6-item legal self-efficacy (LEF) scale, and a 4-item legal anxiety (LAX) scale (Pleasence and Balmer, forthcoming).

Generic aspects of legal capability

In addition to the unique aspects of legal capability, some generic aspects are also commonly asked about in legal needs surveys through demographic questions. For example, past demographic questions have addressed level of education, income, technological resources, social capital and disability. Thus, in drafting demographic questions for use in legal needs surveys, consideration should be given to their appropriateness as potential capability proxies.

Measuring legal need and unmet legal need

Despite their name, few legal needs surveys have sought to operationalise the concepts of legal need and unmet legal need for the purposes of measurement. This reflects the fact that measures of legal need are inevitably both crude and contentious, since the concept "cannot be measured directly" (Ignite Research, 2006, p. 10), is complex, contested and to a large extent political. Rather than seek to define and measure legal need, recent surveys have therefore tended simply to investigate *aspects* of need, such as the relative seriousness of problems,[90] legal capability, resolution strategy choices, and obstacles and regrets. This can provide a broad picture of the nature of the justiciable problems that people face, and people's capability, behaviour, success or failure in resolving them. It also provides a basis for survey stakeholders to apply their own concepts of legal need and unmet legal need, within the constraints of the data collected. This may often be a sensible approach. Although there are empirical aspects of legal need, evidently "there are normative aspects here as well" (Sandefur, 2016, p. 451).

Nevertheless, attempts continue to be made to develop and refine proxy measures of legal need and unmet legal need, with evident increasing complexity and sophistication (it being argued that "a more comprehensive approach … provides a better basis" for measurement[91]). Although competing definitions of legal need continue to be offered, the assumptions on which they are based are now far better appreciated and understood. While it may once have been assumed that the experience of "legal" problems without recourse to lawyers is equivalent to a "factual need" for legal services,[92] it is now well-recognised there can be many appropriate responses to problems with a legal dimension, some of which may involve neither input from legal services nor any reference to law. Commentators have pointed out the relevance of context, highlighting the relevance of advantages and disadvantages (including cost) of different potential responses to "legal" problems in determining legal need.[93] More recently, emphasis has also been placed on capability, options and choice.[94]

Thus, as described in Chapter 1. , it is now broadly agreed that legal need arises whenever a deficit of legal capability necessitates legal support to enable a justiciable issue to be appropriately dealt with. A legal need is therefore unmet if a justiciable issue is inappropriately dealt with as a consequence of the unavailability of (suitable) legal support to make good a deficit of legal capability. But the question remains as to what constitutes appropriateness, what forms of support might be necessary, who should act as arbiter and what comprises legal capability.

Explicit operationalisations of the concepts of legal need and unmet legal need have been undertaken in the context of the 2006 New Zealand,[95] 2012 Colombia[96] and 2016 Argentinian[97] surveys. In 2017, Colombia's Department of National Planning also developed an index of effective access to justice that relied heavily on legal needs measures.[98]

Recognising the limits of the proxy measures used, the New Zealand approach involved a three-way segmentation of need as "definitely having been met", "definitely not having been met" and possibly either met or unmet. A further distinction was made in cases in which need was deemed to have been met into cases that involved difficulties in securing help and cases that did not. In simple terms, legal need was deemed to have been met if there was agreement between the parties, a problem concluded through mediation, or a problem concluded with the help of someone other than a mediator or family and friends, and the if help was described as useful. Unmet legal need was taken to include cases where no action was taken because it was not known what to do, problem resolution was abandoned, and no help was sought because of specified barriers (including language, cost and fear). In addition, trivial problems and problems that resolved themselves were excluded from all calculations.

Also recognising the limits of the proxy measures used, the Colombian approach involved setting out various definitions of unmet legal need. In its widest interpretation, unmet legal need was taken to encompass all cases other than those in which parties were reported to have complied with a judgement. In its narrowest, it was taken to encompass only cases that either involved a judgement or settlement that was not complied with, involved no action being taken or action being abandoned and dissatisfaction with that decision, or were either concluded on still ongoing after a defined period of time. The authors commented, "even complex cases should have some kind of substantive decision after two years." (La Rota et al., 2012, pp. 99-100).

Figure 2.1. Logic tree for proxy measurement of legal need and unmet legal need

<table>
<tr><th>Duration</th><th>Seriousness</th><th>Legal awareness / understanding</th><th>Legal confidence</th><th>Process fairness</th><th>Expert help</th><th>Adequacy of support</th></tr>
<tr><td>Long</td><td>High/ Moderate/ Low</td><td>Yes/No</td><td>Yes/No</td><td>Yes/No</td><td>Yes/No</td><td>Yes/No</td></tr>
<tr><td rowspan="28">Short/Moderate</td><td rowspan="6">High</td><td rowspan="6">Yes/No</td><td rowspan="6">Yes/No</td><td rowspan="3">Yes</td><td rowspan="2">Yes</td><td>Yes</td></tr>
<tr><td>No</td></tr>
<tr><td>No</td><td>N/A</td></tr>
<tr><td rowspan="3">No</td><td rowspan="2">Yes</td><td>Yes</td></tr>
<tr><td>No</td></tr>
<tr><td>No</td><td>N/A</td></tr>
<tr><td rowspan="21">Moderate</td><td rowspan="13">Yes</td><td rowspan="5">Yes</td><td>Yes</td><td>Yes/No</td><td>N/A</td></tr>
<tr><td rowspan="4">No</td><td rowspan="2">Yes</td><td>N/A</td></tr>
<tr><td>N/A</td></tr>
<tr><td rowspan="2">No</td><td>N/A</td></tr>
<tr><td>N/A</td></tr>
<tr><td rowspan="8">No</td><td rowspan="4">Yes</td><td rowspan="2">Yes</td><td>Yes</td></tr>
<tr><td>No</td></tr>
<tr><td rowspan="2">No</td><td>N/A</td></tr>
<tr><td>N/A</td></tr>
<tr><td rowspan="4">No</td><td rowspan="2">Yes</td><td>Yes</td></tr>
<tr><td>No</td></tr>
<tr><td rowspan="2">No</td><td>N/A</td></tr>
<tr><td>N/A</td></tr>
<tr><td rowspan="8">No</td><td rowspan="8">Yes/No</td><td rowspan="4">Yes</td><td rowspan="2">Yes</td><td>Yes</td></tr>
<tr><td>No</td></tr>
<tr><td rowspan="2">No</td><td>N/A</td></tr>
<tr><td>N/A</td></tr>
<tr><td rowspan="4">No</td><td rowspan="2">Yes</td><td>Yes</td></tr>
<tr><td>No</td></tr>
<tr><td rowspan="2">No</td><td>N/A</td></tr>
<tr><td>N/A</td></tr>
<tr><td>Low</td><td>Yes/No</td><td>Yes/No</td><td>Yes/No</td><td>Yes/No</td><td>N/A</td></tr>
</table>

No legal need | Legal need | Met legal need | Unmet legal need

Like the New Zealand approach, the Argentinian operationalisation encompassed all four elements of the definitions of legal need and unmet legal need set out above: appropriateness, necessity, legal support and legal capability. The questions it drew upon asked about respondents' legal capabilities and satisfaction with assistance and outcomes, to enable unmet need to be measured as the proportion of respondents "who did not consider themselves capable of solving justiciable problems through their own knowledge and ability ... [and] were not satisfied with assistance received or with the outcome in cases in which they obtained no assistance" (Subsecretaría de Acceso a la Justicia (Ministerio de Justicia y Derechos Humanos), 2016, p. 23).

Figure 2.1 sets out a framework, in the form of a logic tree, for measuring legal need that draws upon the New Zealand, Colombian and Argentinian measures of legal need and unmet legal need. However, it references process fairness rather than outcomes – as process fairness can be addressed through policy, and fair outcomes are broadly reliant on fair processes – and introduces legal awareness/understanding.

Building on the New Zealand triviality filter, the framework not only excludes trivial problems from need calculations, but also assumes all of the most serious problems involve unmet need if expert help is not obtained. As has been argued in the case of advice in the police station (Pleasence et al., 2011c), some problems are so serious that a person will need legal support irrespective of their professed legal capability (at least in the "normative" or "comparative" senses set out in Bradshaw's taxonomy of social need) (Bradshaw, 1972). For example, anybody arrested on suspicion of a serious offence, such as rape or murder, needs legal support.

As an initial step, the framework includes a definition of legal need, which is either "met" or "unmet". No legal need arises in the case of trivial problems or in the case of moderately serious problems if respondents have legal knowledge, legal confidence and consider the resolution process fair.

Questions that can be used to populate the framework are detailed in Chapter 3. Chapter 4. also explores, more generally, how access to justice indicators can be constructed from legal needs surveys.

Consistency of approach and the comparability of legal needs survey findings

A broad range of factors affects the comparability of data from different legal needs surveys. The impact of methodological differences has been discussed extensively elsewhere (Pleasence et al., 2013a, 2016).[99] However there has been relatively little discussion of how data might be specified to promote comparability.

Data comparability requires that data at different levels of detail are investigated within a consistent conceptual and taxonomical framework, and that more detailed data can be made equivalent to less detailed data. This is possible only if more detailed data encompasses all, but no more than, the elements of less detailed data. Figure 2.2 illustrates the necessary relationship between data at different levels of detail in order for it to be comparable. As can be seen, all 16 items (and only these 16) feature in all five category sets. Thus, any category set can be aggregated to any lower detail category set. The category sets need not be constructed symmetrically, as in Figure 2.2. But each new level of detail must involve sub-dividing lesser detail categories in order to maintain compatibility. If there is re-allocation of items between sub-categories, the sets may become incompatible.

In the case of justiciable problem types, if an investigation of more narrowly defined problems involves asking about all constituent problem types of a broader (i.e. less detailed) category (as defined in a Table 2.1 type taxonomy), and problems are asked about in a way that allows them to be aggregated to the broader category without the inclusion of any additional problems, then there is full comparability between the more and less detailed problem category data.

Asking survey questions at different levels of detail will impact on responses. As has been noted above, the provision of additional detail in relation to, say, justiciable problems, increases accuracy of reporting and reported incidence (Pleasence et al., 2016). The more detail provided, the less respondents are left to interpret the scope of questions, and the lower the risk of misinterpretation and/or that relevant memories will be neglected.

Figure 2.2. Compatible category data at different levels of detail

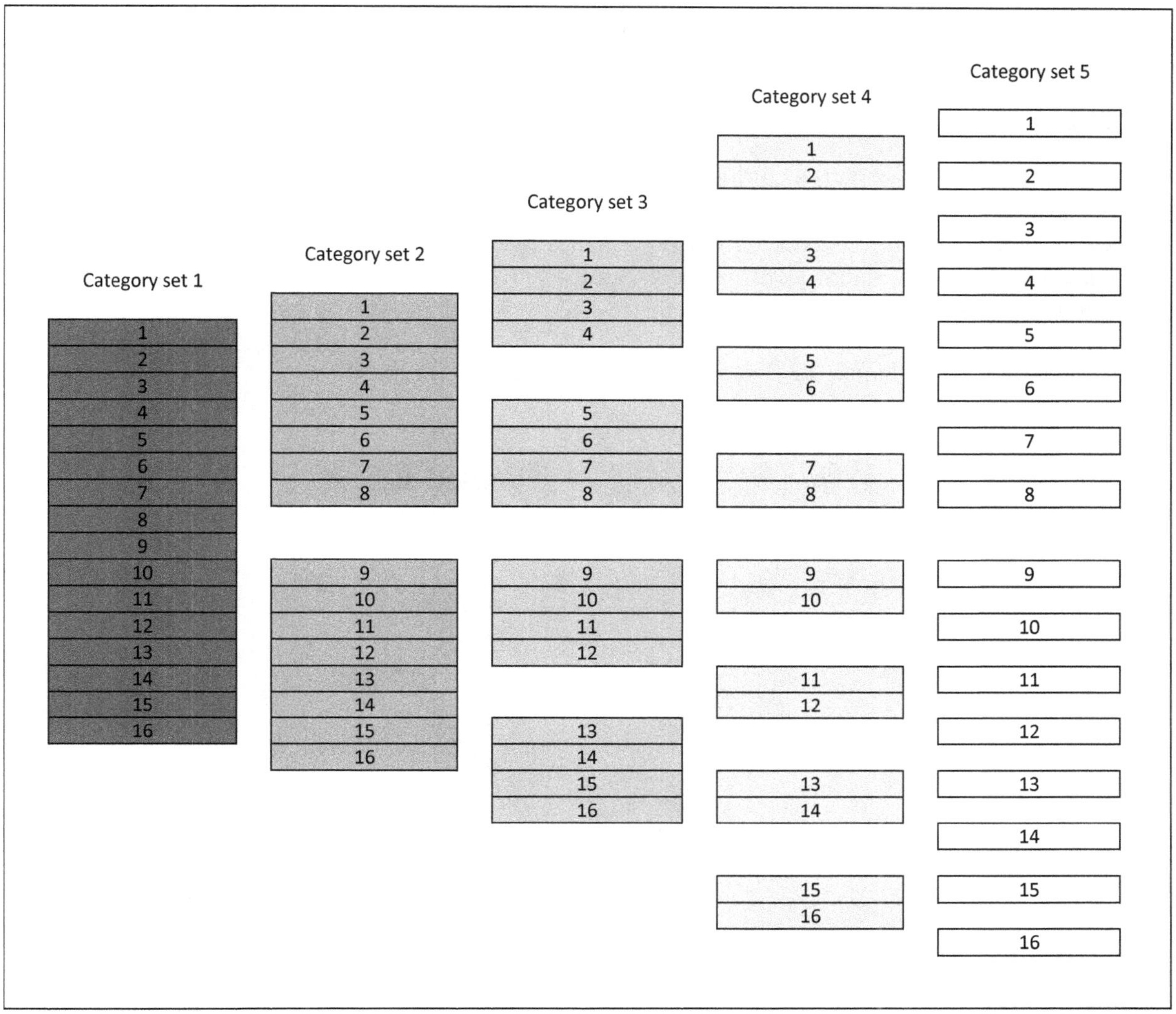

A framework for asking questions: survey structure

Legal needs surveys investigate people's experience of justiciable problems and, in particular, the strategies, the type of help sought and the processes used in their resolution. This subject matter involves the collection of multiple levels of data. Justiciable problems are unevenly distributed among organisations, households and individuals; some experience few or none, while others experience many. In turn, strategies, help seeking, and processes are unevenly distributed across problems. For example, some problems may involve one source of help, while others involve none or multiple sources. So, data can relate to, say, households and, within them, people and, within them, problems and, within them, sources of help, etc.

This has two important implications. The first is that, if unique data is required for multiple individual problems, strategies, sources of help or processes, then surveys must include "loops" and "sub-loops" of questions to systematically address each of these. The second is that it is impracticable to ask follow-up questions about each and every problem; nor, in the case of problems that are followed-up, detailed questions about each and every strategy, source of help or process. Numerical limits must be applied to avoid excessive length. The potential for follow-up is a function of the amount of detail sought and the duration of interviews.

A modular survey approach

Figure 2.3 illustrates the typical hierarchical structure of legal needs survey data. Sources of help and processes are nested within problems, which are nested within people, who are nested within households. Often legal needs survey data is compiled into separate person level and problem level datasets. Sources of help and process level datasets are also often possible.

Figure 2.3. Example legal needs survey data structure

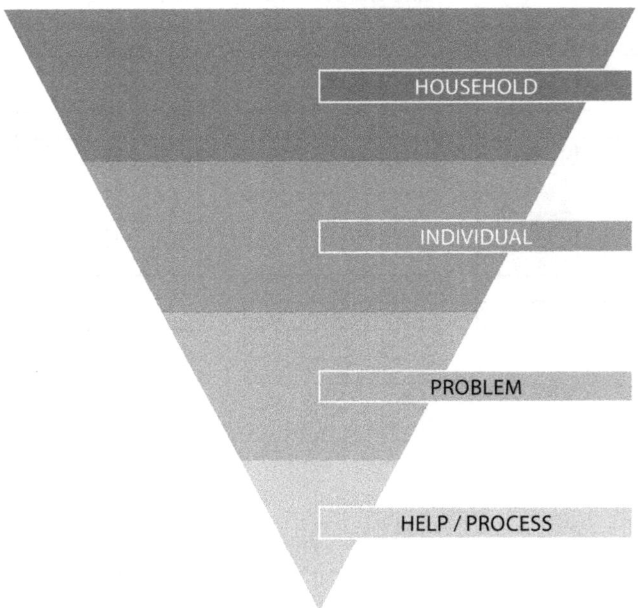

Hierarchical data of the type typically collected through legal needs surveys is most naturally reflected in a modular questionnaire design. Within a modular design, the various data strata become distinct subjects of enquiry, and questions concerning them constitute distinct "modules". Modules can be repeated within interviews, as necessary, in order to address, for example, multiple instances of problems. Within these modules, questions dealing with the same sub-topic can also be viewed as modules. These topic-based modules do not relate to distinct data levels, but this approach helps to give clarity to survey data, and facilitates survey design and analysis. Designing legal needs survey questionnaires as a combination of specific structural and topic-based modules – linking to data structure and the various topics of study – helps tie questionnaires to their defining research questions, clarify which topics are central and which peripheral, and make apparent the scale of sub-sampling required in order to keep interviews to a defined duration. If surveys are repeated, or questionnaires shared between surveys, a modular design makes the process of refinement relatively easy to manage, as modules can be worked on independently and substituted. Figure 2.4 illustrates a model legal needs survey questionnaire structure.

Figure 2.4. Model legal needs survey questionnaire structure

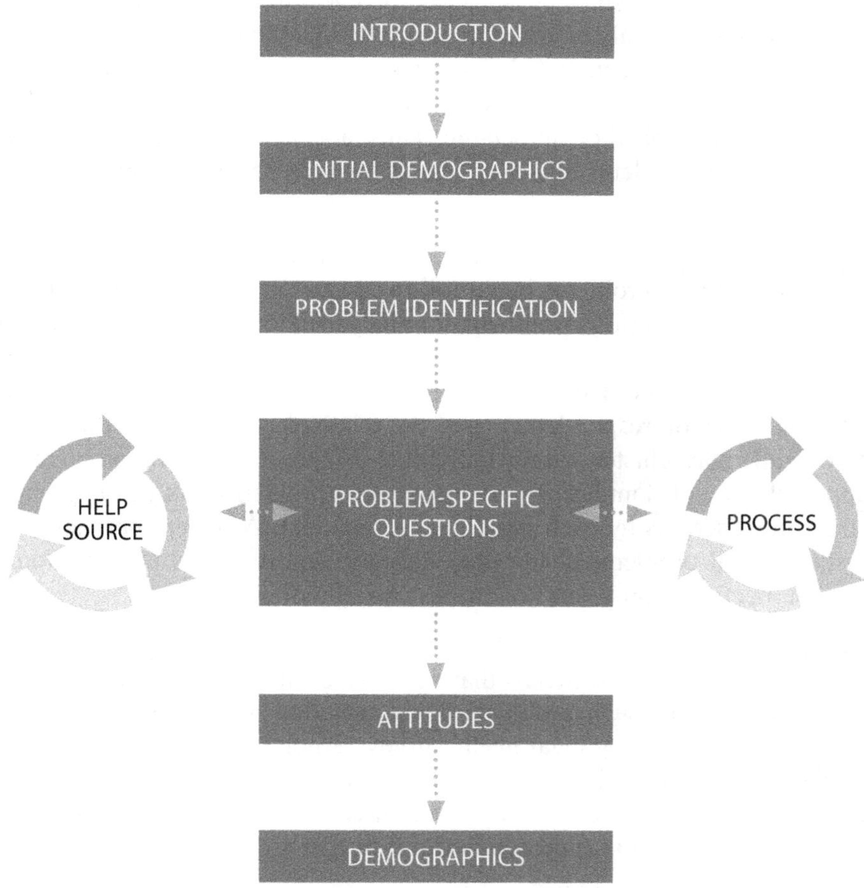

Sub-samples

Because some respondents report multiple problems – and, within problems, multiple sources of help or processes – and there is limited time available to ask follow-up questions, it is necessary to employ sub-sampling. This poses various methodological challenges. One example concerns how problems are reported. Respondents who report only one problem may provide data about "all" their problems, while those reporting many problems may provide data about only one or some. The resulting sample is far from representative of problems as a whole; and weighting down problems reported by those who report only one problem greatly reduces the effective sample size. Related to this is the challenge of determining an appropriate method of sub-sampling. No method is perfect (in practice, at least), but some methods are more problematic than others.

For the *Paths to Justice* surveys, single problems within problem categories were selected for follow-up,[100] and when more than one problem was reported in a category, the second most recent was selected for follow-up. The reason for selecting the second most recent problem (in preference to the most recent) was the increased likelihood that sufficient time would have elapsed for resolution to have been achieved. Given that a significant proportion of justiciable problems reported by respondents are not concluded by the time of the interview, this is a reasonable approach. It delivers data for a reasonably diverse set of problems, although older problems may not always play out in the same way as newer problems. Selection from only concluded problems is problematic, as many problems are ongoing at the time of interview. For example, the 2012 Macedonian survey – which adopted the *Paths to Justice* surveys' approach of selecting second most recent problems for follow-up – found that only a "disappointing" (Srbijanko et al., 2013, p. 60) 38.6% of reported problems had been concluded. Thus, a sample of concluded problems is likely to be much smaller than a sample of all problems. Also, while most ongoing problems will be new, some will be atypical or intractable. Thus, a sample of concluded problems fails to shed light on these problems and may bias it towards easier to resolve or less severe issues.

Another problematic yet common form of problem sub-sampling involves only respondents' most serious problems being followed-up. This has the superficial attraction of yielding a set of more serious problems for analysis. However, the resulting sample is even more difficult to characterise than samples obtained using the methods described above. The most serious problems of those respondents who report only one problem (a significant proportion of respondents) may be relatively trivial, and the most serious problems (overall) may cluster within individuals. Thus, samples of problems obtained via this approach are not samples of the most serious problems, but of the problems seen as being their most serious by each individual respondent. A better approach is to assess the seriousness of all problems at the time they are reported, and then randomly select from those that meet an appropriate seriousness threshold.

Compounding the difficulty of achieving a representative sample of problems for follow-up, the rarity of some problems means that aggressive sampling (in particular) can result in an unviable number of such problems being included in a sample, making analysis more difficult. Again, as many legal needs survey respondents report only one problem, this is a difficult issue to address. One approach that has been taken is to weight the probability of problem selection in favour of rarer problems, and thus select more of them. The disadvantage of this approach is that it further reduces sample efficiency.

Turning to sources of help, similar challenges are apparent to those just discussed in relation to problems. Surveys have asked about, for example, the first, last, most useful and most impactful source of help. All are problematic. The initial source of help is more likely to be inappropriate or a "stepping stone", and samples of them will yield a picture reflecting this. Last sources are more likely to be legal, in part because a person may only consult a lawyer as a final step. And samples of the most useful or most impactful sources will paint too pretty a picture of every source. Sub-sampling of advisors should therefore be avoided, or, if necessary, carefully designed with a mind to the questions that will be asked of the data.

Finally, no previous surveys seem to have sub-sampled processes. This reflects the limited number of processes ordinarily associated with individual problems and the limited number of processes that are followed-up. In earlier surveys, processes were a key focus of investigation, but now only a limited number of questions are generally asked about individual processes.

Notes

[1] For general guidance see, for example, Groves et al. (2009) and Wolf et al. (2016). For guidance in the context of developing and transition countries see, for example, UN Department of Economic and Social Affairs (2005). For guidance in the context of justice see, for example, Himelein et al. (2010).

[2] See, for example, *Webster's New World College Dictionary*.

[3] See, for example, Pleasence and Balmer (2012b) and Pleasence et al. (2015, 2017).

[4] As Genn (1997, p. 159) states, "For many people the law *is* the criminal law." Similar ideas were apparent in the findings of focus groups run in connection with the 2010 *Legal Capacity of the Ukrainian Population* survey. One legal expert is reported to have said that "During the Soviet period people felt ashamed of going to courts. They believed that courts only deal with criminals" (Kobzin 2011, p. 73).

[5] 24 of 50 surveys for which details are available eschewed legal terminology in their introduction.

[6] The difficulties involved in translating technical terms were evident in the case of the 2012 Georgian survey, about which it was observed, "at the initial stage of the survey, there was a problem of finding a Georgian term corresponding to the English 'justiciable event' that would be appropriate in the Georgian judiciary environment and clear to the public at large. After intensive consultations with experts, it was decided to use the term 'სამართლებრივი პრობლემა'" (Institute of Social Studies and Analysis 2012, p. 53).

[7] 35 of 51 surveys for which information is available.

[8] For example, in the case of the *English and Welsh Civil and Social Justice Survey*, problem descriptions were reviewed by lawyers working in the relevant fields, as well as being subjected to cognitive testing. In the case of the earlier *Paths to Justice* surveys, additional qualitative research was also undertaken to explore "the terminology used by the public when referring to 'justiciable events'" (Genn 1999, p. 16).

[9] 51 surveys in total.

[10] 49 of 51 surveys for which details are available.

[11] Mirroring this, these problems have tended to be asked about only in jurisdictions with a relatively low gross domestic product (GDP) (at purchasing power parity) per capita, as detailed in the International Monetary Fund's World Economic Outlook Database, October 2016. In the case of land, there were notable exceptions in the cases of Japan, New Zealand and the United Arab Emirates.

[12] The 2012 Tajikistan also asked about justiciable problem experience without reference to any problem categories or examples.

[13] Or even in a booklet setting out a full list of problems, as in the case of the 2017 iteration of the World Justice Project's *General Population Poll.*

[14] See, for example, Groves et al. (2009) and Schaeffer and Presser (2003).

[15] This practice also limits multiple counting of single problems. To avoid double counting, surveys have often adopted the practice, when asking about a series of problem types, of requesting that only problems that have not already been mentioned should be reported. This approach can distort the relative reporting rates of different problems. If possible, a better approach is to specify problems carefully (as in Table 2.1) to avoid overlaps between categories. This also more clearly allows for different aspects of problem clusters to be reported.

[16] Satisficing is linked to respondent ability, motivation and difficulty. Increasing length through a very large amount of repetitive problem types may decrease motivation/increase burden. This can reduce response rates and the completion of questionnaires, as well as lead to faster/shorter answering as the interview progresses (Galesic and Bosnjak 2009). In the context of legal needs surveys, randomisation of problem order (for problem identification) is prudent to counter resulting (and more general) order effects. Commencing follow-up questions only after all problems have been identified is similarly prudent in order to avoid flagging the effect of responses on questionnaire length. This also allows greater flexibility in sub-sampling

[17] Although the questionnaire was later amended to include a more traditional list of problem types.

[18] 32 of 52 surveys for which information is available.

[19] In addition to introducing the "difficult to solve" filter, the *Paths to Justice* surveys also excluded from follow-up problems about which respondents said that they had taken no action whatsoever … because the problem had not been regarded as important enough to warrant any action" (Genn 1999, p. 14).

[20] See, for example, Pleasence and Balmer (2013b).

[21] See, for example, Pleasence and Balmer (2017).

[22] The OECD's Glossary of Statistical terms defines "own account" workers as "self-employed persons without paid employees".

[23] Gindling and Newhouse (2013, p. 15) report that 52 per cent of workers in low income countries, and just 9 per cent in high income countries, work on their own account. This is largely associated with work in agriculture, with less of a difference if agriculture is excluded (18 per cent versus 8 per cent). Across all countries, 33 per cent of workers work on their own account (16 per cent if agriculture is excluded). As Gindling and Newhouse went on to explain, "as per capita income increases, the structure of employment shifts rapidly, first out of agriculture into unsuccessful non-agricultural self-employment, and then mainly into non-agricultural wage employment".

[24] For example, an owned business, self-employment, professional practice or farming.

[25] Evidently, for less common problem types, it will be less likely that reasonable estimates of the total incidence of personal and business related problems are possible.

[26] See, for example, Pleasence and McDonald (2013) and Kemp et al. (2007).

[27] In England and Wales, the 2014 Legal Problem Resolution Survey used a sample frame that drew on the previous year's Crime Survey for England and Wales, thus enabling links between victimisation survey data and legal needs survey data (Franklyn et al. 2017).

[28] United Nations Office on Drugs and Crime and United Nations Economic Commission for Europe (2010).

[29] 42 of 49 surveys for which information is available.

[30] Visual analogue scales were introduced by Hayes and Patterson (1921) but took many years to gain popularity (Streiner et al. 2015).

[31] For example, in the measurement of anxiety (Davey et al. 2007) and particularly pain (e.g. Hjermstad et al. 2011).

[32] Selected following the conduct of an online survey designed to explore the perceived relative seriousness of a broad range of short problem descriptions through a version of the VAS.

[33] The reliability of a scale is related to the number of items included.

[34] For example, Davey et al. (2007) proposed that either a single 5-point Likert scale or VAS could provide a simple, quick and adequate measure of anxiety when compared to the 20-item State-Trait Anxiety Inventory.

[35] For example, the field of pain research (Hawker et al. 2011).

[36] There have also been some instances of NRSs being more responsive than VASs and Verbal Rating Scales (Ferreira-Valente et al. 2011).

[37] 43 of 54 surveys for which information is available.

[38] While this form of cluster sampling allows for additional analyses of intra-household aspects on justiciable problem experience and problem resolving behaviour, this form of cluster sampling must be accounted for when conducting inferential statistical analyses. Some earlier surveys to adopt this data structure – including the original *Paths to Justice* survey – did not do so, resulting in the likelihood of underestimation of standard errors associated with model coefficients (Goldstein 2011, Rasbash et al. 2012). The appropriate approach for accounting for clustered data is to utilise multilevel models (Goldstein 2011, Rasbash et al. 2012).

[39] In general, reference periods assume respondents can place events accurately in time, but dates are the hardest to remember with any precision (Wagenaar 1986). One common phenomenon is "telescoping" events into a reference period (i.e. they seem closer than they actually were), although backward telescoping out of a reference period is also common (Groves et al. 2009). As time passes (and as reference periods are longer) errors in both directions increase (Rubin and Baddeley 1989).

[40] 15 of 49 surveys for which information is available.

[41] 10 surveys.

[42] 5 surveys.

[43] 1 of 49 surveys for which information is available.

[44] The need for terminology has occasionally been avoided in the case of list-based questions, by reference to "the following".

[45] Some jurisdictions, such as England and Wales, have relatively complex regulatory frameworks, reflected in some forms of segmentation. See, for example, Oxera Consulting Ltd. (2011).

[46] Additional distinctions could be incorporated into Table 2.2 but have not been in this instance.

[47] Although the 2006 New Zealand survey did ask about process in the context of outcomes, process would not necessarily have been identified in this manner.

[48] Around three-quarters of surveys in each case.

[49] Of the 45 surveys with relevant questions and for which details were available, 17 employed separate questions, 25 employed lists and 3 employed open questions.

[50] 26 of 48 surveys for which details are available.

[51] To adopt the language of Barendrecht et al. (2006).

[52] 40 of 48 surveys for which details are available.

[53] See, for example, Lind and Tyler (1988).

[54] See, for example, Barendrecht et al. (2006, 2010). The project was directed to developing a methodology to measure the cost and quality of access to justice.

[55] Verdonschot et al. (2008, pp. 7-8) summarise the potential criteria of distributive justice as being based on equity (proportionate to contribution), equality (equal shares), need (proportionate to individual needs), accountability (proportionate to volitional contribution) and efficiency (to maximise the welfare of the parties).

[56] The survey included 21 questions focused on process, 9 relating to courts and 12 to conciliation.

[57] The 2009 Bangladesh survey also notably included seven questions on process quality, including three on informational justice. It also asked about whether the community regarded the outcome as fair, although this would be beyond the purview of the respondent.

[58] Just 1 survey for which details are available – the 2016 Moldovan survey – did not ask about costs in any way.

[59] 45 of 47 surveys for which details are available.

[60] 44 of 47 surveys for which details are available.

[61] For reasons of sample efficiency, specificity and reliability, legal needs surveys are not well suited to establishing the typical or range of costs of different types of legal services. Thus, the Legal Services Board in England and Wales, the regulation authority for legal services, conducts supply side, in preference to demand side, research to establish these (Legal Services Board 2017).

[62] Such questions were asked in, respectively, the 2015 *Survey of Individuals' Handling of Legal Issues Survey* and 2012 *Legal Services Benchmarking Survey*, both commissioned by the Legal Services Board in England and Wales.

[63] Overall, 24 of 45 surveys for which details are available asked how much was paid for legal services. In total, 30 surveys asked how much was paid for legal services <u>or</u> how much was paid/incurred <u>in total</u> to resolve problems.

[64] And opportunity costs.

[65] 22 of 45 surveys.

[66] 12 surveys, comprising the 10 *Justice Needs and Satisfaction Survey* and the 2010 and 2012 *English and Welsh Civil and Social Justice Surveys.*

[67] 13 surveys, comprising the *Paths to Justice Surveys*, the 2001 *English and Welsh Civil and Social Justice Survey* and the 10 *Justice Needs and Satisfaction Surveys*.

[68] Important relationships were defined as "the respondent's relations with family, friends, colleagues, employer/s etc."

[69] A 5-point Likert scale was used for responses throughout. Other surveys, such as the earlier *Paths to Justice* surveys used blunter dichotomous questions.

[70] This is slightly different from asking about whether help or financial support was obtained from legal aid, which was marginally more common.

[71] Pleasence et al. (2014) for a definition and discussion of the concept of legal capability.

[72] See, above, n. 28.

[73] Which could be termed the "prefigurative" dimension of legal consciousness (McCann 2006).

[74] See, for example, Parle (2009), Collard et al. (2011), Coumarelos et al. (2012), Canadian National Action Committee on Access to Justice in Civil and Family Matters (2013), Pleasence et al. (2014), Pleasence and Balmer (forthcoming).

[75] 45 of 47 surveys.

[76] 22 and 14, respectively, of 47 surveys.

[77] 36 of 47 surveys.

[78] 18 of 47 surveys. Some general questions were asked about defined problem scenarios.

[79] 4 of 47 surveys, along with one further survey that asked respondents whether they had adequate knowledge for decision-making. The 2016 Argentinian survey asked about knowledge in this way, although there was no reference to law or rights within the question. In all, three surveys have asked whether respondents felt they had sufficient knowledge to act.

[80] The 2010 and 2012 *English and Welsh Civil and Social Justice Surveys* also quizzed respondents about their knowledge of law relating to four hypothetical scenarios and their own problems.

[81] Again 4 surveys. Only the 2016 Moldovan survey asked about knowledge of law and processes.

[82] It may also reflect the difficulty of assessing understanding of law, particularly in relation to identified problems. Levels of self-assessed legal understanding differ markedly from actual levels of understanding (Pleasence et al. 2015), and it is infeasible to test people on their understanding of a broad range of legal issues.

[83] 8 of 47 surveys. Pleasence et al. (2011); Pleasence and Balmer (2014).

[84] 19 surveys.

[85] Although the Japanese question was not framed in terms of confidence, it asked "Do you think you could obtain the desired outcome if you informed the other party of your claim?" See Murayama (2007).

[86] Defined by Gramatikov and Porter (2011, p. 169) as "the subjective self-belief that a person possesses [... in their] ability to mobilise the necessary resources, competencies, and energies to solve particular problems of a legal nature." Thus, subjective legal empowerment is a domain specific form of self-efficacy. It was most notably defined by Bandura (1997, p. 3) as referring to "beliefs in one's capabilities to organise and execute the courses of action required to produce given attainments".

[87] As in the *Justice Needs and Satisfaction Surveys*; thus involving 12 rather than 6 questions (in general).

[88] Based principally on Rasch analysis, which is used to ascertain whether questions in a group form the basis of an effective measure of a unidimensional domain (such as subjective legal empowerment) and, if so, to specify a scale. See, for example, Bond and Fox (2015).

[89] For example, in relation to person separation and differential item functioning. Person separation refers to the extent to which a scale discriminates between high and low scoring individuals. Differential item functioning refers to the extent to which a question may address different abilities for different sub-groups.

[90] Of particular relevance in the context of limited resources and access to justice policy centred on relative need.

[91] Subsecretaría de Acceso a la Justicia (Ministerio de Justicia y Derechos Humanos) (2016, p. 7).

[92] As Pleasence et al. (2001, p. 11) described the "background assumption" of much legal needs research in the 1960s and early 1970s.

[93] Such as Lewis (1973), Marks (1976) and Griffiths (1980).

[94] For example, the 1980 Hughes Commission (1980, paras. 2.09 and 2.10) influentially argued that legal need involves two distinct, staged, needs: the need for information about law and legal services to enable properly informed choices and the need for such support from legal services as is necessary if a legal solution is chosen: "In assessing the need for legal services, we must therefore think in terms of two stages - firstly enabling the client to identify and, if he judges it appropriate, to choose a legal solution; and secondly, enabling the client to pursue a chosen legal solution ..... When we speak of 'unmet need' we are concerned about instances where a citizen is unaware that he has a legal right, or where he would prefer to assert or defend a right but fails to do so for want of legal services of adequate quality or supply."

The Hughes Commission's definition of legal need centres on determining appropriate solutions by citizens in need. This reflects the Commission's preference for "felt need" (defined by those in need) over "expressed need" (felt need that is acted upon), "normative need" (defined by experts) and "comparative need" (assessed by comparison of service use by those with similar characteristics), to use Bradshaw's (1972) dominant taxonomy of social need. Aside from such a definition of legal need, there remain issues concerning the nature and extent of state responsibility to intervene to prevent individual needs going unmet, as described in the report of the 2005 Northern Irish survey (Dignan 2006, p. 4). Furthermore, given limited public resources, these issues must be considered alongside the effectiveness of services, citizens' resources and prioritisation of needs. Attention must be given to a further dimension of need - relative need - and draw on the theories of the hierarchy of needs (as done, most famously, by Maslow (1943)). In practice, the prioritisation of legal needs may depend upon whether the responsibility to meet them is considered a constitutional matter (i.e. grounded in the rule of law) or a welfare matter (i.e. grounded in general welfare service provision).

[95] See Legal Services Agency (2006), Ignite Research (2006).

[96] See La Rota et al. (2012).

[97] See Subsecretaría de Acceso a la Justicia (Ministerio de Justicia y Derechos Humanos) (2016).

[98] See Colombia's Department of National Planning: http://dnpsig.maps.arcgis.com/apps/Cascade/index.html?appid=b92a7ab2fe6f4a06a6aec88581d6873e

[99] A stark illustration of the impact of methodological change on findings is provided at n. 183.

[100] Subject to an overall cap on problems followed-up that was rarely exceeded.

References

Bandura, A. (1977), *Self-Efficacy: Toward a Unifying Theory of Behavioral Change*, Englewood Cliffs, Prentice-Hall, NJ.

Barendrecht, M., M. Gramatikov, I. Giesen, M. Laxminarayan, P. Kamminga, L. Klaming, J.H. Verdonschot and C. van Zeeland (2010), *Measuring Access to Justice in a Globalising World,* HiiL, The Hague.

Barendrecht, M., Y.P. Kamminga and J.H. Verdonschot (2008), "Priorities for the justice system: Responding to the most urgent legal problems of individuals", TILEC Discussion Paper No. 2008/011, TISCO Working Paper No. 001/2008), Tilburg University Faculty of Law, Tilburg.

Barendrecht, M., J. Mulder and I. Giesen (2006), *How to Measure the Price and Quality of Access to Justice?,* Tilburg University, Tilburg.

Bond, T. and C.M. Fox (2015), *Applying the Rasch Model: Fundamental Measurement in the Human Sciences*, 3d edition, Routledge, New York.

Bradshaw, J. (1972), "Taxonomy of social need", in G. McLachlan (ed.), *Problems and Progress in Medical Care: Essays on Current Research,* 7th series, Oxford University Press, London.

Canadian National Action Committee on Access to Justice in Civil and Family Matters (2013), *Responding Early, Responding Well: Access to Justice Through the Early Resolution Services Sector,* National Action Committee on Access to Justice in Civil and Family Matters, Ottawa.

Chen, K.-P., K.-C. Huang, Y.-L. Huang, H.-P. Lai and C.-C. Lin (2012), "Exploring advice seeking behavior: Findings from the 2011 Taiwan Survey of Justiciable Problems", Paper presented at the Law and Society Association Conference, Honolulu, 7 June 2012.

Collard, S., C. Deeming, L. Wintersteiger, M. Jones and J. Seargeant (2011), *Public Legal Education Evaluation Framework,* University of Bristol Personal Finance Research Centre, Bristol.

Colquitt, J.A., D.E. Conlon, M.J. Wesson, C.O.L.H. Porter and K.Y. Ng (2001), "Justice at the millennium: A Meta-analytic review of 25 years of organizational justice research", *Journal of Applied Psychology,* Vol. 86, pp. 425-445.

Coumarelos, C., D. Macourt, J. People, H.M. McDonald, Z. Wei, R. Iriana and S. Ramsey (2012), *Legal Australia-Wide Survey: Legal Need in Australia,* Law and Justice Foundation of New South Wales, Sydney.

Davey, H.M., A.L. Barratt, P.N. Butow and J.J. Deeks (2007), "A one-item question with a Likert or visual analog scale adequately measured current anxiety", in *Journal of Clinical Epidemiology,* pp. 356-360.

Dignan, T. (2006), *Northern Ireland Legal Needs Survey,* Northern Ireland Legal Services Commission, Belfast.

Farrow, T.C.W., A. Currie, N. Aylwin, L. Jacobs, D. Northrup and L. Moore (2016), *Everyday Legal Problems and the Cost of Justice in Canada,* Canadian Forum on Civil Justice, Toronto.

Ferreira-Valente, M.A., J.L. Pais-Ribeiro and M.P. Jensen (2011), "Validity of four pain intensity rating scales", in *Pain,* Vol. 152(10), pp. 239-404.

Franklyn, R., T. Budd, R. Verrill and M. Willoughby (2017), *Findings from the Legal Problem Resolution Survey*, Ministry of Justice, London.

Galesic, M. and M. Bosnjak (2009), "Effects of questionnaire length on participation and indicators of response quality in a web survey", in *Public Opinion Quarterly,* Vol. 73(2), pp. 349-360.

Genn, H. (1999), *Paths to Justice: What People Do and Think About Going to Law,* Oxford.

Genn, H. (1997), "Understanding civil justice," in *Current Legal Problems*, Vol. 50(1), pp.155–187.

Goldstein, H. (2011), *Multilevel Statistical Models*, 4th edition, Wiley Chichester.

Gramatikov, M.A. and R.B. Porter (2011), "Yes i can: Subjective legal empowerment", *Georgetown Journal on Poverty Law and Policy,* Vol. 18(2), pp. 169-199.

Gramatikov, M.A., M. Barendrecht and J.H. Verdonschot (2011), "Measuring the costs and quality of paths to justice", in *Hague Journal of the Rule of Law,* Vol. 3, pp. 349-379.

Gindling, T.H. and D. Newhouse (2013), *Self-Employment in the Developing World: Background Paper for the World Development Report 2013,* World Bank, Washington, DC.

Griffiths, J. (1980), "A comment on research into legal needs", in E. Blankenburg (ed.), *Innovations in the Legal Services*, Oelgeschlager, Gunn and Hain, Cambridge, Mass.

Groves, R.M., F.J. Fowler, M.P. Couper, J.M. Leprowski, E. Singer and R. Tourangeau (2009), *Survey Methodology,* 2nd edition, John Wiley and Sons, Hoboken, New Jersey.

Hawker, G.A., S. Mian, T. Kendzerska and M. French (2011), "Measures of adult pain: Visual Analog Scale for Pain (VAS Pain), Numeric Rating Scale for Pain (NRS Pain), McGill Pain Questionnaire (MPQ), Short-Form McGill Pain Questionnaire (SF-MPQ), Chronic Pain Grade Scale (CPGS), Short-Form 36 Bodily Pain Scale (SF-36 BPS), and Measure of Intermittent and Constant Osteoarthritis Pain (ICOAP)" in *Artrhritis Care and Research,* Vol. 63(S11), pp. S240-S252.

Hayes, M.H.S. and D.G. Patterson (1921), "Experimental development of the graphical rating method", in *Psychological Bulletin,* Vol. 18, pp. 98-99.

Himelein, K., N. Menzies and M. Woolcock (2010), "Surveying justice: A practical guide to household surveys", *Justice and Development Working Paper Series*, Vol. 11/2010, World Bank Justice Reform Practice Group, Washington, DC.

Hjermstad, M.J., P.M. Fayers, D.F. Haugen, A. Caraceni, G.W. Hanks, J.H. Loge, R. Fainsinger, N. Aass, S. Kaasa and EPCRC (2011), "Studies comparing numerical rating scales, verbal rating scales, and visual analogue scales for assessment of pain intensity in adults: A systematic literature review", in *Journal of Pain and Symptom Management,* Vol. 42, pp. 1073-1093.

Ignite Research (2006), *Report on the 2006 National Survey of Unmet Legal Needs and Access to Services*, Legal Services Agency, Wellington.

Institute of Social Studies and Analysis (2012), *KAP Survey Concerning Justiciable Events in Georgia,* Open Society – Georgia Foundation, Tblisi.

Kemp, V., P. Pleasence and N.J. Balmer (2007), *The Problems of Everyday Life: Crime and the Civil and Social Justice Survey,* Centre for Crime and Justice Studies, London.

Klaming, L. and I. Giesen (2008), "Access to justice: The quality of the procedure", *TISCO Working Paper Series on Civil Law and Conflict Resolution Systems*, Vol. 002/2008, University of Utrecht, Utrecht.

Kobzin, D., A. Chernousov, R. Sheiko, M. Budnik, M. Kolokolova and S. Scherban (2011), *The Level of Legal Capacity of the Ukrainian Population: Accessibility and Effectiveness of Legal Services,* International Renaissance Foundation and Kharkov Institute of Social Research, Kharkov.

La Rota, M.E., S. Lalinde and R. Uprimmy (2013), *Encuesta Nacional de Necesidades Jurídicas Análisis General y Comparativo Para Tres Poblaciones*, Dejusticia - Centro de Estudios de Derecho, Justicia y Sociedad, Bogota.

Lavrakas, P.J. (2008), *Encyclopaedia of Survey Research Methods,* Sage, Thousand Oaks, California.

Legal Services Agency (2006), *Technical Paper: Defining Legal Need and Unmet Legal Need,* Legal Services Agency, Wellington.

Legal Services Board (2017), *Prices of Individual Consumer Legal Services 2017: An Analysis of a Survey of Prices Quoted for Commonly Used Legal Services,* Legal Services Board, London.

Lewis, P. (1973), "*Unmet legal needs*", in P. Morris, R. White and P. Lewis (eds.), *Social Needs and Legal Action,* Martin Robertson, Oxford.

Lind, E.A. and T.R. Tyler (1988), *The Social Psychology of Procedural Justice*, Plenum, New York.

Marks, F.R. (1976), "Some research perspectives for looking at legal need and legal services delivery systems" in *Law and Society Review*, Vol. 11, pp. 191-205.

Maslow, A.H. (1943), "A theory of human motivation," in *Psychological Review*, Vol. 50, pp.370-396.

McCann, M. (2006), "On legal rights consciousness: A challenging analytical tradition", in B. Fleury-Steiner and L.B. Nielsen (eds.), *The New Civil Rights Research,* Ashgate, Aldershot.

Murayama, M. (2007), "Experiences of problems and disputing behaviour in Japan", in Meiji Law Journal, Vol. 14, pp. 1-59.

OXERA (2011), *A Framework to Monitor the Legal Services Sector*, Oxera (for the Legal Services Board), Oxford.

Parle, L.J. (2009), *Measuring Young People's Legal Capability*, Independent Academic Research Studies and PLEnet, London.

Pleasence, P. (2006), *Causes of Action: Civil Law and Social Justice*, 2nd edition, The Stationery Office, Norwich.

Pleasence, P. and N.J. Balmer (forthcoming), "Development of a general legal confidence scale: A first implementation of the Rasch measurement model in empirical legal studies," *Journal of Empirical Legal Studies.*

Pleasence, P. and N.J. Balmer (2017), "It's personal: Business ownership and the experience of legal problems", *Justice Issues*, Vol. 24, Law and Justice Foundation of New South Wales, Sydney.

Pleasence, P. and N.J. Balmer (2014), *How People Resolve 'Legal' Problems,* PPSR (for the Legal Services Board), Cambridge.

Pleasence, P. and N.J. Balmer (2013), *In Need of Advice: Findings of a Small Business Legal Needs Benchmarking Survey,* PPSR (for the Legal Services Board), Cambridge.

Pleasence, P. and D. Macourt (2013), *What Price Justice? Income and the Use of Lawyers,* Law and Justice Foundation of New South Wales, Sydney.

Pleasence, P. and H. McDonald (2013), *Crime in Context: Criminal Victimisation, Offending, Multiple Disadvantage and the Experience of Civil Law problems,* Law and Justice Foundation of New South Wales, Sydney.

Pleasence, P., N.J. Balmer and C. Denvir (2015), *How People Understand and Interact with the Law*, Legal Education Foundation, London.

Pleasence, P., N.J. Balmer and C. Denvir (2014), *Reshaping Legal Services: Building on the Evidence Base,* Law and Justice Foundation of New South Wales, Sydney.

Pleasence, P., N.J. Balmer and S. Reimers (2011b), "What really drives advice seeking behaviour? Looking beyond the subject of legal disputes", *Oñati Socio-Legal Series,* Vol. 1(6).

Pleasence, P., N.J. Balmer and R.L. Sandefur (2016), "Apples and oranges: An international comparison of the public's experience of justiciable problems and the methodological issues affecting comparative study", *Journal of Empirical Legal Studies,* Vol. 13(1), pp. 50-93.

Pleasence, P., N.J. Balmer and R.L. Sandefur (2013a), *Paths to Justice: A Past, Present and Future Roadmap,* Nuffield Foundation, London.

Pleasence, P., N.J. Balmer and T. Tam (2009), "Failure to recall," in R.L. Sandefur (ed.), *Access to Justice,* Emerald, Bingley.

Pleasence, P., Z. Wei and C. Coumarelos (2013b), "Law and disorders: Illness/disability and the response to everyday problems involving the law", *Updating Justice*, Vol. 30, Law and Justice Foundation of New South Wales, Sydney.

Pleasence, P., N.J. Balmer, A. Patel, A. Cleary, T. Huskinson and T. Cotton (2011a), *Civil Justice in England and Wales: Report of Wave 1 of the English and Welsh Civil and Social Justice Survey,* Legal Services Commission, London.

Pleasence, P., A. Buck, T. Goriely, J. Taylor, H. Perkins and H. Quirk (2001), Local Legal Need, London Legal Services Commission.

Pleasence, P., V. Kemp and N.J. Balmer (2011c), "The justice lottery? Police station advice 25 years on from PACE," *Criminal Law Review,* Vol. 11, pp. 3-18.

Rasbash, J., F. Steele, W.J. Browne and H. Goldstein (2009), *A User's Guide to MLwiN, v2.26*, Centre for Multilevel Modelling, University of Bristol, Bristol.

Rubin, D.C. and A.D. Baddeley (1989), "Telescoping is not time compression: A model," *Memory and Cognition,* Vol. 17(6), pp. 653-661.

Sandefur, R.L. (2016), "What we know and need to know about the legal needs of the public", *Carolina Law Review,* Vol. 67, pp. 443-459.

Schaeffer, N.C. and S. Presser (2003), "The science of asking questions", in *Annual Review of Sociology,* Vol. 29, pp. 65-88.

Srbijanko, J.K., N. Korunovska and T. Maleska (2013), *Legal Need Survey in the Republic of Macedonia: The Legal Problems People face and the Long Path to Justice,* Open Society Foundation – Macedonia, Skopje.

Streiner, D.L., G.R. Norman and J. Cairney (2015), *Health Measurement Scales,* 5th edition, Oxford University Press, Oxford.

Subsecretaría de Acceso a la Justicia Ministerio de Justicia y Derechos Humanos (2017), *Diagnosticode Necesidades Jurídicas Insatisfechas y Niveles de Acceso a la Justicia,* Subsecretaría de Acceso a la Justicia Ministerio de Justicia y Derechos Humanos, Buenos Aires.

Torangeau, R., L.J. Rips and K. Rasinski (2000), *The Psychology of Survey Response*, Cambridge University Press, Cambridge.

United Nations Department of Economic and Social Affairs (2005), *Household Sample Surveys in Developing and Transition Countries,* United Nations, New York.

United Nations Office on Drugs and Crime and United Nations Economic Commission for Europe (2010), *Manual on Victimization Surveys,* United Nations, Geneva.

van den Bos, K., E.A. Lind and H.A.M. Wilke (2001), "The psychology of procedural and distributive justice viewed from the perspective of fairness heuristic theory", in R. Cropanzano (ed.), *Justice in the Workplace: From*

Verdonschot, J.H., M. Barendrecht, L. Klaming and P. Kamminga (2008), "Measuring access to justice: The quality of outcomes", *TISCO Working Paper Series on Civil Law and Conflict Resolution Systems*, Vol. 007/2008, Tilburg University, Tilburg.

Wagenaar, W.A. (1986), "My memory: A study of autobiographical memory over six years", *Cognitive Psychology*, Vol. 18(2), pp. 225-252.

Williamson, A. and B. Hoggart (2005), "Pain: A review of three commonly used pain rating scales", *Journal of Clinical Nursing,* Vol. 14(7), pp. 798-804.

Wolf, C., D. Joye, T.W. Smith and Y.-C. Fu (2016), *The Sage Handbook of Survey Methodology,* Sage Publications, London.

Chapter 3. Model Questions, Model Structure and Short-Form Illustrative Questionnaire

This Chapter sets out a series of model core legal needs survey questions, along with explanations of their form. It also describes the range of topics that have been addressed through past legal needs surveys, and then situates the model questions within an illustrative short-form questionnaire.

Model core legal needs survey questions

The following paragraphs introduce and explain model questions for: identifying justiciable problems, gauging problem seriousness, determining problem impact, identifying sources of help, categorising problem resolving behaviour, establishing the nature of processes used, ascertaining if and how problems have been concluded, investigating (if relevant) reasons for not obtaining independent advice, exploring people's perceptions of dispute resolution processes and outcomes, estimating the cost of problem resolution, examining legal capability, and finding out problem start and end dates. The model questions are informed by the full range of legal needs surveys undertaken to date. Explanations link to the broader methodological discussion in Chapter 2.

The questions are primarily designed for use in short-form questionnaires but are also nested in the illustrative long-form questionnaire set out in Annex B. Indication is provided as to how questions can be adapted to collect more or less granular data if necessary.

The diversity of justice institutions, services, practices and norms around the world entails that questions may sometimes need to be adapted to reflect the understanding, experience and options available for specific sample populations. While the questions have been designed to be broadly applicable, appropriate scrutiny and testing should always be undertaken ahead of implementation.

Problem identification (Annex A; Figure A.1)

A model question for identifying justiciable problems is:

> *I am going to read you a list of problems and disputes that people commonly experience in everyday life. In each case, can you tell me whether you have personally experienced such a problem in the past two years; by which I mean a problem that started since [DATE] or started before then, but continued afterwards?*
>
> *Please only include problems that you have had yourself, not problems experienced by a business you run, in the course of self-employment or by an employer, and not situations where you represented or helped somebody else with their problem. And please only mention problems once.*

This question is appropriate for both long- and short-form questionnaires. For longer questionnaires, all problems of interest should be presented to respondents individually. Show cards, or even comprehensive problem type booklets, have commonly been used to facilitate this process.[1] For shorter questionnaires, problem categories, along with brief descriptions and examples, can be presented instead. Care should be taken to ensure that descriptions and examples are sufficiently clear to indicate the full range of problems in a particular category, while minimising the likelihood that non-justiciable problems will be reported.[2]

The model question for problem identification uses the phrase "problems and disputes" to indicate the character of the issues under study. These terms have been adopted as a pair in more than half of the national legal needs surveys detailed in Table 1.1 and Table 1.2.[3]

To avoid any reference to law, the question refers to problems and disputes commonly experienced "in everyday life". To promote reliability, respondents are presented with a simple (dichotomous) question asking whether they have experienced problems, rather than how many problems they have experienced. If, as is generally the case, the total number of problems experienced is of interest, this can be ascertained through an immediate follow-up question (e.g. "How many such problems have you experienced in the past two years?")

The reference period is two years. Although uncommon in the past,[4] a two-year period is increasingly considered a good timeframe for achieving a balance between maximising problem reporting, data accuracy and contemporaneity.[5] Reflecting this, the World Justice Project's *General Population Poll* moved to a two-year reference period in 2017, and the same was adopted for the 2017-2018 Nepalese survey and 2017-2018 South African *Governance Public Safety and Justice Survey* Pilot.

Allied to the reference period, the model question makes clear that problems should be reported if they existed within the reference period, irrespective of when they started. Many of the surveys detailed in Table 1.1 and Table 1.2 have followed this *Paths to Justice* survey inspired rule of inclusion, but others have been silent on the matter. Here, a rule is made explicit to ensure clarity, and the choice of rule reflects the fact that the main focus of interest in legal needs surveys tends to be on problem resolving behaviour and experience, which manifests across the full lifetime of a problem. The rule increases the number of problems that will be reported. Importantly, it also increases the number of problems that have been concluded and problems of a more serious nature about which data is captured in a manner that does not undermine the coherence of the sample.[6]

The question is directed to identifying problems experienced by respondents personally, rather than within households, etc., to promote data accuracy, best reflect the general nature of experience and provide flexibility for data disaggregation and aggregation, as discussed in the previous chapter.

The question clearly excludes problems experienced by a respondent in running a business, an employer, or anyone respondents may have represented or helped to resolve a problem. It also emphasises that problems should only be reported once, as there is a significant risk of double-counting when potentially overlapping problem types or categories are presented to respondents. This is often the case when problems are defined in broad terms but can also occur with multi-dimensional problems.

An example set of 12 core problem categories, descriptions and examples – for use in short-form questionnaires – is set out in Table 3.1.[7] The examples used to illustrate the categories have been drawn from previous surveys, with phrasing modified for greater relevance across all jurisdictions. If individual problem types need to be identified, this can be done through follow-up.[8]

Randomisation should be employed when presenting problem types or categories to respondents in order to mitigate issues stemming from fatigue and satisficing behaviour.

Table 3.1. Example categories with forms of presentation and illustrative examples

Category	Form of presentation	Illustrative examples
Consumer	Problems or disputes to do with defective or undelivered goods or services	Such as difficulties obtaining a refund, billing errors, or disputes with utility providers (such as water, electricity, gas, telephone or Internet), or professionals (such as accountants, lawyers, mechanics, plumbers, etc.).
Community resources	Problems or disputes to do with community resources	Such as denial of or unfair access to the benefits of community land/forest/water groups, disputes over community resource governance, and disputes over fees and revenues.
Land	Problems or disputes to do with land or buying and selling property	Such as disputes over title or boundaries, problems to do with land grabbing, expropriation, mining, or environmental damage, or problems to do with land transfers or building permits
Housing	Problems or disputes to do with housing	Such as problems or disputes with a landlord or tenant, concerning, for example: poor maintenance, the terms of a lease, eviction or becoming homeless; also problems concerning an owners' corporation, problems with neighbours (for example, excessive noise or threatening behaviour).
Family	Problems or disputes to do with family and relationship break ups	Such as divorce, access to or custody of children, child support, disputes over property division, children being taken into care, [violence or harassment]*, guardianship or adoption, or inheritance.
Injury / illness	An injury caused by someone else, or injury or illness caused by an accident at work, working conditions, or negligent or wrong medical treatment (including dental and other healthcare treatment).	
Employment / labour	Problems or disputes to do with employment or labour	Such as dismissal, unpaid wages, poor working conditions, denial of rights, discrimination, harassment, unfair disciplinary procedures, changes to contract terms.
Social protection	Problems or disputes to do with government payments	Such as disputes concerning your entitlement to, or the amount of, suspension of, or registration for government payments; for example, social safety net assistance, state pension and education grants or loans.
Abuse by state officials	Problems or disputes to do with abuse by state officials	Such as threatening, discriminatory or corrupt treatment by the police, [military]*, [a customary authority]*, or other government official.
Public services/ administration	Other problems or disputes to do with government and public services	Such as problems to do with citizenship or residency status, obtaining a passport, [identity document,]* or other public documentation; obtaining access to or being excluded from public services, such as healthcare and education; fairness of examinations; tax disputes or disputes with other government bodies.
Debt	Problems to do with debt	Such as being behind and unable to pay money you owe, action by a creditor for non-payment (including harassment), or the prospect of bankruptcy.
Money	Other problems or disputes to do with money and with financial services	Such as insurance claims being denied, repeated unfair bank charges, credit rating inaccuracy, problems collecting money owed to you, or being misled about insurance, a pension, or other financial product you acquired.

However, when a problem might reasonably fall within a number of categories or types, questions should be designed to ensure reliability. To do this, some categories or types may need to be presented in a particular order. If this is the case, randomisation should apply to the groups so constituted, rather than to individual categories.

Table 3.2 sets out additional categories that are often incorporated into legal needs surveys, but which are distinct in character from the categories set out in Figure 2.1. These additional categories are concerned with business and crime. As well as being distinct, the three categories in Figure 2.1 should be asked about separately, unless measures have been taken to prevent conceptual conflation as discussed in Chapter 2. . Reflecting this, the model question expressly excludes business related problems from its scope.

Table 3.2. Problems concerning business and crime

Problem category	Model question	
Business	Problems or disputes to do with a business that you own	Such as disputes concerning sales, purchases, or business premises; or problems concerning permits, regulations, tax assessment, insolvency, employees, corruption, demands for "protection", intellectual property or the use, acquisition or expropriation of land or property.
Crime: Victimisation	Being a victim of any crime	Such as theft, attempted theft, fraud, threats, violence or sexual violence or abuse.
Crime: Arrest	Have you been arrested, charged or prosecuted for any alleged offence (other than a motoring offence that cannot lead to disqualification)?	

The problem descriptions in Table 3.1 and Table 3.2 are drafted in lay terms to promote recognition and avoid overly narrow interpretations that might stem from public misconceptions of law. As far as is possible, they are drafted to make a legal dimension inevitable.

As the law varies between jurisdictions, some problem descriptions will not be appropriate universally and others may require further explanation. However, care has been taken to select examples that have broad applicability. Nevertheless, when using the descriptions in Table 3.1 and Table 3.2, they should always be reviewed by legal and community experts ahead of use.

As sociocultural norms vary among jurisdictions, errors introduced into surveys by inaccurate responses (respondent error) will also vary. For example, social desirability bias is likely to vary considerably among jurisdictions in relation to domestic violence. It is known that "in countries with strong cultural pressure to keep violence behind closed doors or simply to accept is as natural, non-fatal violence is likely to be underreported" (Fraga, 2016, p. 78).

While the majority of past legal needs surveys have included domestic violence – domestic violence has been found to be catalytic in relation to wider population experience (Pleasence et al., 2003) – it is to be noted that the United Nations Department of Economic and Social Affairs *Guidelines for Producing Statistics on Violence Against Women – Statistical Surveys* argue that "surveys designed to address a broad array of crime- or health-related or other issues cannot accommodate the broad range of questions needed to study violence against women in all its complexity" (United Nations Department of Economic and Social Affairs, 2014, p. 8). They continue:

"Certain drawbacks are evident when a module on violence against women is inserted into an already lengthy questionnaire on other topics. For example, the question wording and ordering may not facilitate disclosures of violence, especially if introductory statements or questions that cue respondents to think about violence occurring in private settings or incidents involving intimate partners have not been introduced. Compared to dedicated surveys, the breadth of questions that can be included in surveys on other topics is also limited, thereby reducing the opportunities for disclosure of experiences of violence. Finally, less attention is usually paid to the sensitisation of interviewers to violence-related issues during their training, the need for interviewers to develop a rapport with respondents, privacy and confidentiality issues surrounding the interview and other ethical and safety issues, all of which can have a significant negative impact on the willingness of respondents to report violence." (United Nations Department of Economic and Social Affairs (2014, p. 8-9)

Importantly, if domestic violence (or other forms of violence or harassment in, say, a neighbourhood or employment context) is included in legal needs surveys, then – as the guidelines further add – "ethical considerations are of upmost importance … [and] care must be taken … to consider how each aspect of the survey design and implementation will affect the safety and well-being of the respondents and, indeed, of the interviewers." (United Nations Department of Economic and Social Affairs (2014, p. 7).

To obtain a clearer picture of the nature of problems reported through the model problem identification question, the simplest method is to follow it up, for example, with questions asking what problems were about and/or whether and with whom the problems were shared.

Problem seriousness (Annex A; Figure A.2)

A model question for gauging problem seriousness is:

Thinking about the problem as a whole, consider a scale of 1 to 10, where 1 represents the least serious type of problem you could face and 10 represents the most serious.

To provide some examples, a score of 8 might be [ANCHOR 1] and a score of 2 might be [ANCHOR 2].

What number best represents the seriousness of your problem?

Again, this question is appropriate for both long- and short-form questionnaires. It provides a basis for both substantive analysis and the filtering out of trivial problems from follow-up (i.e. by omitting from follow-up any problem not perceived to be as serious as the lower anchor problem description). It is based on the seriousness question developed for the 2010 *English and Welsh Civil and Social Justice Panel Survey*. While the psychometric properties of the scale have not been tested, and the question is likely to be less reliable than a multiple item scale (no examples of which have yet been developed),[9] it has proved to be simple to implement.

The form of the question is textual, rather than graphical, so that it can be used across surveys delivery via different means without the need for adaptation.

No anchor problem descriptions are included in the model question text, as suitable problem descriptions are likely to vary between populations. [10] It is important to have a high degree of accord as to the seriousness of selected problem descriptions. Moreover, the wording of anchors must be considered carefully, as it can make a significant difference to measurement.[11]

Problem impact (Annex A; Figure A.3)

A model question for determining problem impact is:

Did you experience any of the following as part of or as a result of this problem?

a) ill-health or injury

b) high levels of stress

c) damage to a family relationship

d) being harassed, threatened or assaulted

e) damage to your property

f) loss of employment

g) having to move home

h) financial loss

i) fear or loss of confidence

This question is fairly concise, but can be lengthened or shortened if required. Some surveys have investigated a greater range of impact areas – including stigma, alcohol/drug problems, denial of public services, problems concerning education and problems concerning documentation – but those in the model question represent the most common (and commonly asked about).

There may also be interest in particular aspects of model question impact areas, such as unemployment (as an aspect of loss of employment) and homelessness (as an aspect of moving home).

The model question extends to elements of justiciable problems, as well as impacts that follow from justiciable problems. Both are relevant to the cost of justiciable problems, as well as to the potential benefits of interventions that might prevent justiciable problems from arising. If interest is only in impacts following from justiciable problems, the words "as part of" can be removed. However, if this is done, it should be emphasised that harms experienced "as part of" problems should not be reported.

Identifying sources of help (Annex A; Figure A.4; Figure A.5; Figure A.6)

Two model questions which together can be used to identify sources of help are:

1. *Did you, or somebody acting on your behalf, obtain information from any of the following sources, to help you better understand, resolve or prepare to resolve [the problem]?*

   a) A website or "app"

   b) A leaflet, book or self-help guide

   c) Newspapers or magazines

   d) Television, video or radio

2. *(Apart from anything you have told me about already) Did you, or someone acting on your behalf, obtain information, advice or representation from any of the following people or organisations to help you better understand or resolve [the problem]?*

Please exclude any help provided by the other party.

The first question asks about information obtained via the media (i.e. all modes of mass communication); the second about information, advice and representation otherwise obtained from people or organisations.

Both questions ask about help obtained personally or through someone acting on the respondent's behalf. This is to more fully capture the totality of help seeking. The questions also require help to have been "obtained" so as to exclude instances of unsuccessful help seeking. In the absence of additional questions in this area, this formulation provides greatest insight into unmet legal needs. In a longer questionnaire, a more comprehensive account of problem resolving behaviour can be acquired by asking about both successful and unsuccessful attempts to obtain help. Unsuccessful attempts to obtain help may also be investigated through the model residual activity question presented in the next chapter, although details will be limited.

Both questions refer to help obtained "to help better understand or resolve" problems rather than "to try to resolve" problems to clearly incorporate help obtained prior to, or separate from, decisions to take action.

The second question asks about "information, advice or representation" to clarify the types of help of interest and prevent reporting of people or organisations responsible for dispute resolution processes. The term "help" has been avoided, as it is broader in scope than information, advice and representation.

The second question also uses the phrase "people or organisations". Although not a critical design issue in the case of closed questions, the phrase is the most appropriate for open ones. It indicates that all sources of help should be included. However, the question explicitly states that help obtained from the other party should be excluded. The question will also naturally exclude information obtained via mass media, which was asked about in the first question. To emphasise the distinction, the second question starts by excluding anything respondents have already reported.

As always, questions concerning sources of help should be constructed using lay language whenever possible. If the identity of a particular, say, legal service needs to be known, then it is preferable to use generic terminology in the first instance and follow-up with more specific questions about identity.

Finally, the second question centres upon a list of categories of sources of help, an example of which is set out in Figure A.6. Figure A.6 list will prompt respondents to recall help sought from the full range of sources in Figure 2.3 and thus enable data to be recorded in a manner that is consistent with that table's structure.

For shorter-form questionnaires, an open version of the second question could be used instead. If an open question is adopted, additional sources of help should be probed for. An open form of the second question is:

(Apart from anything you have told me about already) did you, or someone acting on your behalf, obtain information, advice or representation from any person or organisation to help you better understand or resolve [the problem]? For

example, from family or friends; from a lawyer, professional advisor or advice service; a court, government body, or the police; a trade union or employer; a religious or community leader or organisation; an [NGO/civil society organisation/charity][12]*, a trusted person or organisation or anybody else?*

Please exclude any help provided by the other party.

Process (Annex A; Box A.1)

A model question and follow-ups for establishing the nature, and initiator, of processes are:

1. *(Apart from anything you have told me about already) Did any of the following things happen as part of [the problem] or sorting it out? When I say "you" here, I mean you or somebody acting on your behalf.*
    - *a) You communicated with the other party*
    - *b) You or the other party made a claim to, or made use of, a court (or tribunal)*
    - *c) [If applicable] You or the other party made a claim to, or made use of, an [Indigenous/ customary] dispute resolution process (e.g. [examples])*
    - *d) [The problem] was reported to the police (or other prosecution authority)*
    - *e) You or the other party turned to, or action was taken by, a formal designated authority or agency, such as [examples, e.g. Ombudsman, regulator (e.g. [example]) or enforcement authority (e.g. consumer protection authority)]*
    - *f) You or the other party turned to, or action was taken by, another state authority (e.g. [examples])*
    - *g) You or the other party turned to, or action was taken by, a religious authority*
    - *h) You or the other party turned to, or action was taken by, a community leader or organisation (e.g. [example])*
    - *i) You participated in formal mediation, conciliation or arbitration (e.g. [examples])*
    - *j) You or the other party made use of a formal appeals process operated by the other party or independently*
    - *k) You, the other party or somebody else turned to, or action was taken by, another third party for adjudication, mediation or intervention*
    - *l) There was no negotiation or third party involvement*
2. *[For each positive response (a to k), respondents to then be asked]*

   Who initiated this action? [PROMPT ONLY IF NECESSARY]
    - *a) You*
    - *b) The other party*
    - *c) The third party responsible for the process*
    - *d) Another third party.*

3. *[If the respondent did not initiate processes b to h or j and k]*

   Did you respond to this action?

The model process question begins by excluding anything that respondents have already reported. This emphasises that the question concerns processes and not information, advice or representation, already addressed in earlier questions.

The question then asks whether any of 11 distinct processes "happen[ed] as part of [the problem] or sorting it out". These processes follow the typology set out in Table 2.3 and are defined with reference to the body responsible for the process rather than with the process (which is often but not always implicit). The 11 process categories in the question include four state provided processes, two community processes, one religious authority process, negotiation between the parties and three "other" categories of process. In five of the 11 categories, the question requires examples or detail to be included, so as to make clear the types of authority/ process. For example, category (c) refers to traditional dispute resolution processes, which are still common in many jurisdictions.

Reflecting the need for appropriate terms and phrases, the model process question uses seven different phrases to identify the 11 process. The most common phrase, "turn to", appears five times, "made use of" three times and "made a claim to" twice. The term "contact" is too general. Phrases such as "appear at" and "participate in" are also inappropriate in all cases other than mediation (which requires engagement), as they suggest a need for engagement on the part of the respondent. The phrase "appeal to" may be inappropriate if it suggests prior process when there need be none.

Some of the response categories for the model process question refer only to respondents' activities, some to the activities of respondents and the other party, and some to any activity. The distinctions mirror the nature of the processes concerned. Thus, only the respondent and other party in a dispute are relevant to the advancement of civil court process; the same is not true of, for example, criminal investigation.

For each process identified, the first follow-up question asks who initiated the process. The appropriate options will vary depending upon the nature of the process.

If a respondent did not initiate an identified process, the second follow-up question asks whether the respondent responded to any action.

For shorter-form questionnaires an open process question may be necessary. A model open process question and follow-up are:

1. *Did you, somebody acting on your behalf, the other party or anybody else, make a claim to a court (or tribunal), or turn to any other third-party individual or organisation – such as [institutional examples] or a community or religious leader [or respected family member] – to adjudicate, mediate or intervene to help resolve [the problem]?*
2. *[For each process specified]*

   Did you, or somebody acting on your behalf, initiate or respond to this action?

   a) *Initiated action*

   b) *Responded to action*

   c) *Neither initiated, nor responded to, action*

If necessary, a further follow-up question could be used to identify who initiated processes, if not respondents.

The reference to a respected family member should be included if a family member might potentially act to adjudicate, mediate or intervene to resolve a problem (other than by representing the respondent in negotiation or another dispute resolution process; which should be coded accordingly). As the report of the 2015 Uganda survey commented, "The family is a central institution for dispute resolution in Uganda, along with the broader informal network consisting of friends and neighbours. This is not surprising given the traditional value of the family in dispute resolution as well as the lack of access to the formal justice system, which incentivises a heterogeneity of responses to justice problems, particularly for women and especially for those who are poor" (Piest et al., 2016, p. 80).

Given the complexity of the model process question, and sometimes substantial variation in the nature of dispute processes between jurisdictions, it is particularly important to review process questions through cognitive testing and piloting.

Residual problem resolving behaviour (Annex A; Figure A.7)

In order to appropriately categorise problem resolving behaviour, it is necessary to capture data concerning any form of problem resolving behaviour on the part of the respondent that is not captured by the model sources of help questions or the model process question.

A model question for identifying residual problem resolving behaviour is:

> *(Apart from anything you have told me about already) Did you, or somebody acting on your behalf, do anything else to help you better understand or resolve [the problem], such as obtain or organise evidence or make an insurance claim?*

The question is presented so as not to limit responses to pre-determined behaviours. A similar question was used in the *Paths to Justice* surveys, to ask about the residual activity of those who did not contact sources of help. The examples provided (namely, "obtaining or organising evidence" and "making an insurance claim") represent a potentially significant component of problem resolving behaviour. Consideration of options, and communication with the other side that falls short of "trying to resolve the problem" (asked about in the model process question), might also fall within residual activity.

Importantly, the residual problem resolving behaviour question should be asked *after* the model process question. If the short form of model process question is used, then the residual problem resolving behaviour question should also include the example of "communicate with the other party".

Fact and manner of conclusion (Annex A; Figure A.8 and Figure A.9)

A model question for identifying the fact of problem conclusion is:

> *Is [the problem] ongoing or done with? By "done with" I mean that the problem is either resolved or that it persists, but you and everybody else have permanently given up all efforts to resolve it further. [PROBE FULLY]*
>
> *a) Ongoing*
>
> *b) Too early to say*

c) *Done with - problem persists, but all have given up trying to resolve it further*

d) *Done with - problem resolved*

This question is appropriate for both long- and short-form questionnaires. It seeks to ascertain whether or not problems are ongoing or "done with", in the sense that there is no prospect of any future attempts being made to resolve them. The question requires careful coding and – if relevant – careful follow-up, as it allows for problems to be treated as if they have been concluded, even though they may persist. This accurately reflects the reality of lived problems, which are often simply "put up with".

The phrase "done with" is preferred to other previously used wording (notably "over" or "resolved"), as it suggests no change in the future rather than the non-existence of a problem. However, as the intended meaning is relatively complex, the question goes on to provide a definition. The definition of "done with" is central to the question, so it should not be shortened or removed to save time. It is important that it refers to the intentions of both the respondent and the other party and that the intentions be "permanent" in nature.

A model question for identifying the manner of problem conclusion is:

Which of the following statements best reflects how the problem outcome was ultimately brought about?

The problem outcome was ultimately brought about by:

a) *a court (or tribunal) judgment*

b) *a decision or intervention by another formal authority*

c) *mediation, conciliation or arbitration*

d) *action by another third party*

e) *agreement between you and the other party*

f) *the other party independently doing what you wanted*

g) *you independently doing what the other party wanted*

h) *your moving away from the problem (e.g. moving home, changing job)*

i) *the problem sorting itself out*

j) *you and/or all other parties giving up trying to resolve the problem*

Again, the question is appropriate for both long- and short-form questionnaires. It is presented in a closed form, as the data sought is particular and an open question is less conducive to a succinct and relevant response.

The question is designed to be comprehensive. The model covers all 30 categories referenced in past surveys.

There is some scope for more succinct delivery of the question. For example, process questions can be used to restrict the categories read/shown to respondents. For instance, if there has been no court process, then the corresponding (first) outcome category is redundant. However, such efficiencies place additional burden on earlier questions and must be carefully considered.[13]

Reasons for advice not being obtained[14] (Annex A; Figure A.10)

A model question for investigating, if relevant, reasons for independent advice having not been obtained is:

> *Why didn't you obtain independent advice to help resolve the problem?*

The question can be either open or closed. In the above instance, the range of potential responses is well understood (with model categories set out in Figure A.10). The main considerations concerning the form of the question will be the length of the question and data quality. A speedily delivered open question is likely to be quicker, while a closed question is likely to generate a broader range of responses from individual respondents.

The question is designed to allow multiple responses. If there is interest in the relative significance of response items in individual cases, then respondents could be asked to identify the main reason, rank responses or indicate the degree of importance of each reason. Although each of these requires more time, they yield a greater level of insight.

Perceptions of the quality of process and outcome (Annex A); Model questions for exploring perceptions of the dispute resolution process and problem outcome are:

> *Do you feel the outcome of this problem was basically fair to everybody concerned?*

> *Regardless of the outcome of this problem, do you feel the process through which the outcome was reached was basically fair to everybody concerned?*

The model questions are most suited to short-form questionnaires. In their suggested form, they are best suited to capturing binary data. If the aim is to investigate multiple dimensions of perceptions of process and outcome, longer-form questionnaires are preferable because of their greater scope. They can also be used in addition to a shorter questionnaire.

The model questions explore the dispute resolution process and problem outcome as a whole rather than individual processes (e.g. specific court processes, mediation, etc.) and individual process outcomes. Past legal needs surveys have tended to adopt this approach, as it requires fewer questions and reflects the relative rarity of most processes (thus limiting options for analysis and reporting). If, as in the *Paths to Justice* surveys, there is interest in the quality of individual processes and process outcomes, then the model questions should be prefaced by explicit reference to those processes. For example, they could be prefaced in a manner such as, "Thinking about the claim made to a court as part of this problem …"

Both model questions ask about fairness; the most fundamental dimension of process and outcome quality. They ask about "basic" fairness, to indicate that minor deficiencies of fairness should be disregarded. They also ask about fairness "to everybody concerned", to shift the focus away from respondents' personal satisfaction.

The process question is clearly differentiated from the outcome question by an explicit instruction to disregard outcome.

To provide a degree of measurement, the model questions can be reformulated to use, say, a 4-point Likert scale (e.g. "very fair", "somewhat fair", "somewhat unfair" and "not fair at all"[15]):

> *How fair do you feel the outcome of this problem was to everybody concerned?*

Regardless of the outcome, how fair do you feel the process through which the outcome was reached was to everybody concerned?

Again using a Likert scale (e.g. "strongly agree", "agree", "disagree", "strongly disagree"), the model questions can also be incorporated into a question matrix:

To what extent do you agree or disagree with the following statements about the problem?

- *The outcome of this problem was fair to everybody concerned.*
- *Regardless of the outcome, the process through which the outcome was reached was fair to everybody concerned.*

If there is interest in investigating the different dimensions of process quality and outcome, then additional questions are required. The *Justice Needs and Satisfaction Surveys* have included a substantial question-set to permit relatively complex measurement of process and outcome quality. Other surveys have sought only a basic indication of one or more quality dimensions. This requires fewer questions, but care must be taken to align questions with the concepts of interest.

If single questions are used to reflect the dimensions of process and outcome quality detailed in Chapter 2 (procedural, interpersonal, informational, distributive and restorative justice, along with outcome functionality and transparency), the starting point for question design should be definitions of these dimensions. This was the approach taken for the 2017 Sierra Leonean survey, in which the questions concerning outcome quality were closely tied to the "criteria for evaluating outcomes of paths to justice" (Verdonschot et al., 2008, p. 12). set out in the course of the *Measuring Access to Justice in a Globalising World* project.

Example questions covering the seven dimensions, again using a Likert scale for responses, are:

To what extent do you agree or disagree with the following statements?

a) The process was fair, and I had opportunity to explain my position.

b) I was treated with respect.

c) Processes and decisions made were clearly explained.

d) The outcome involved a fair distribution of benefits and burdens.

e) Any loss or harm arising from the problem (e.g. financial or concerning relationships) has been made good.

f) The problem was solved in a timely matter and is unlikely to recur.

g) The outcome was much the same as for other people in similar situations.

The cost of justiciable problem resolution (Annex A; Figure A.12)

A model question for estimating the cost of justiciable problem resolution is:

***Excluding** indirect payments – such as insurance premiums or membership subscriptions – but **including** payments made by family members and friends*

Did you, personally, have to pay for any of the following in order to resolve the problem?

a) Lawyer and other advisor fees

b) Court, mediation or other administrative fees

c) Telephone calls and correspondence

d) Collecting information or obtaining evidence (incl. reimbursement of witnesses' costs)

e) Travel (e.g. bus fares or petrol to visit an advisor)

f) Lost business or salary, from taking time off work (e.g. to obtain advice)

g) Bribes / kick-backs (Remember, your answer is confidential)

h) Incidental domestic costs (e.g. childcare)

The model cost question provides a platform for investigating both the affordability and proportionality of the cost of problem resolution. The question is designed to establish whether respondents have personally incurred any financial costs in acting to resolve a specific justiciable problem. The form of the question was inspired by the approach taken by HiiL's *Justice Needs and Satisfaction Surveys* and the 2014 *Everyday Legal Problems and the Cost of Justice in Canada Survey*. The wording of the question also draws on the 2010 Ukrainian, 2014 English and Welsh and 2017 Indian surveys.

The scope of the question is defined and clarified in the preamble, which states that it relates to payments made "in order to resolve" a specified problem, rather than costs incurred simply as a result of encountering a problem. The preamble also excludes indirect payments by respondents, such as insurance premiums or membership (e.g. union) subscriptions, but it includes payments made by family members and friends. In both cases, if the scope of the question is not explicitly stated, there is a risk that respondents will interpret the question inconsistently.

The question centres on a list of cost items. The item list serves both to define the scope of the question and to assist respondents in recalling expenditures they may have incurred. The question permits data to be captured for each list item, although global data could also be captured. If interest only extends to legal costs, the list can be shortened or the question adapted to reference legal costs without a list being used.

In asking about bribes and kick-backs, the question includes a confidentiality reminder to allay concerns respondents may have.

To establish the level of costs incurred by respondents, one of three approaches can be adopted. The first is subjective. Respondents are asked how expensive, or difficult to meet, the costs were (similar to in the 2015 Polish survey and 2016 Argentinian survey). This gives insight into the extent to which costs present an obstacle to accessing justice. If this approach is adopted, the follow-up question might be: "How difficult was it to find the money to pay for this/these things?"

The second approach is more objective. The respondent is asked a single question in order to establish the aggregate costs incurred. For example, the 2014 Canadian survey simply asked, "Approximately how much in total did it cost to deal with this problem?"

This question may be harder for respondents who have incurred costs of multiple types and so may be less reliable than the third approach.

The third approach is to ask about the amount of each type of cost separately, as was done in the *Justice Needs and Satisfaction Surveys*, and calculate the total from the figures supplied: "Approximately how much did you have to pay for [cost item]?"

The last two approaches are attractive in that they provide a basis for cost-benefit type calculations. However, they do not naturally indicate the extent to which costs were a burden to respondents.

Beyond affordability and proportionality – the latter of which can be investigated either through a subjective value-for-money type question, such as employed in the 2012 Colombian survey,[16] or through enquiring as to respondents' objectives and/or seeking to quantify outcomes – if there is interest in particular forms of financial support for legal services or processes, these can be asked about in a number of ways. One way is to ask:

> *Apart from family or friends, did anybody, or any organisation, pay or part-pay for [the help you received from [advisor]/[process] fees[17]]?*

Then an open question can be used to ask who provided the financial support. Alternatively, specific forms of support can be enquired about through single questions, such as:

> *Did you receive financial assistance from legal aid?*

Or, a list-based question can be used:

> *Did any of the following pay or part-pay for [the help you received from [advisor]/[process] fees[18]]?*

Legal capability (Annex A; Figure A.13)

A first model question for examining legal capability in relation to an identified problem is:

> *To what extent do you agree or disagree with the following statements about the problem?*
>
> a) *I understood or came to understand my legal rights and responsibilities.*
>
> b) *I knew where to get good information and advice about resolving the problems.*
>
> c) *I was able to get all the expert help I needed.*
>
> d) *I was confident I could achieve a fair outcome.*

This question is appropriate for both long- and short-form questionnaires. It addresses a respondent's awareness of legal rights and responsibilities, awareness of services and legal confidence in relation to an identified problem. It is optimised for identifying unmet legal need. For speed and efficiency, the question employs a common stem to ask respondents about the extent to which they agree with statements relating to these three aspects of legal capability, along with a further statement that concerns whether respondents obtained all the help they felt they needed. The first statement contains elements of questions used in past surveys to investigate knowledge of rights and responsibilities at the time the problem arose, modified to incorporate knowledge acquired subsequently. This is because, if seeking to identify unmet legal need, it is important to recognise knowledge acquired during the problem resolution process. The second statement investigates knowledge of legal services. It adopts phrasing from the

2014 Canadian survey.[19] The third statement concerns legal confidence and uses phrasing similar to that used in the 2016 Tajik survey.

A second, complementary, model question for examining legal capability in relation to an identified problem is:

> *Which of the following describe the problem? You can choose more than one option, or none.*
>
> *a) Bad luck / part of life*
>
> *b) Bureaucratic*
>
> *c) A family or private matter*
>
> *d) Legal*
>
> *e) Political*
>
> *f) A social or community matter*
>
> *g) Economic*
>
> *h) None of these*

This question concerns the ability of respondents to recognise legal issues. It is appropriate for both long- and short-form questionnaires, but its length means its inclusion in shorter questionnaires may be problematic.

The question is based on one introduced in the 2010 *English and Welsh Civil and Social Justice Panel Survey,* a version of which was also included in the 2016 Argentinian survey. It gives insight into both awareness of law and the way in which problems are characterised. This links to perceptions of appropriate fora for problem resolution. By mixing the "legal" response category with other potential descriptions, the question avoids being leading.[20] The other potential descriptions included in the question constitute common characterisations of justiciable problems. Other descriptions, such as "criminal", have also been included in the past. If there is particular interest in characterisation, then a response of "none of these" could be followed up with a question such as, "How would you characterise the problem?"

An issue with the question as formulated is that it is set in the present, meaning it reveals characterisation in hindsight rather than when the problem began. However, the question is simpler to administer in this form and is likely to benefit from greater accuracy than one seeking to situate respondents at the time when a problem began. Moreover, characterisation is of significant interest at all stages of problem experience.

Together, the two model legal capability questions address the four broad aspects of legal capability discussed in Chapter 2. The questions do this in relation to particular problems, but legal capability can also be asked about in general.

Questions concerning general recognition of legal issues have never been asked, and only the *English and Welsh Civil and Social Justice Survey* has asked about general legal understanding. This was done through a series of lengthy vignettes in which legal knowledge questions were embedded.[21] Past general capability questions have tended to relate to only awareness of services and legal confidence.

In the case of awareness of services, a mixture of open and closed questions have been used. The former have asked respondents where they might get help to deal with specific problems (e.g. the 2016 Moldovan survey), the latter whether they have heard of (or "know something about"[22]) services presented to them in a list or whether they know where they could get help, if needed (e.g. the 2012 Tajik survey). There are advantages and disadvantages to using both open and closed questions. For example, "the strength of the open questions is that there are virtually no false positives," while "the disadvantage of the open form of the question is that it may provide a low estimate of active knowledge, because some people who could recognise the correct answer, or retrieve it given more time, will fail to retrieve it in a survey situation" (Fowler, 1995, p. 69).

As regards the form of open questions, the 2016 Argentinian survey asked about sources of "legal advice", the 2016 Mongolian survey asked about help for problems such as those detailed in earlier problem identification questions, and the 2014 English and Welsh survey asked about help for hypothetical problems. All three approaches are legitimate, but because of people's generally narrow interpretation of things "legal", there are concerns about using the first approach in jurisdictions in which legal advice is frequently provided outside traditional legal services. A model form of question, which can be easily adopted to each approach, is:

Where can people get independent expert advice about X?"

Turning to closed questions, past surveys have sometimes presented respondents with a list of sources of help to determine their knowledge about them. A model form of such a question is:

Which of the following do you know something about?[23]

It is also possible to ask respondents how much they known about where help can be obtained, although this again requires clarifying the nature of the help and/or the problems it relates to. A model form of such a question is:

How well do you know where people can get independent expert advice about [problem description]?

In relation to legal confidence, both the HiiL SLE questions (which are presented in blocks) and the recently developed standardised measures of legal confidence (such as the GLC scale) provide excellent models.[24] An example of the SLE form of question is:

Imagine you had a conflict with your employer, for example, a conflict over your dismissal. How likely is it that you would get a fair solution to the problem?

The GLC scale, the most robust of three standardised legal confidence scales – at least, for use in the United Kingdom – is constructed as follows (with a 4-point Likert scale response-set: "very confident", "quite confident", "not very confident", "not confident at all"):

If you found yourself facing a significant legal dispute – such as being unreasonably sacked by your employer, injured as a result of someone else's negligence, involved in a dispute over money as part of a divorce, or facing eviction from your home – how confident are you that you could achieve an outcome that is fair and you would be happy with in the following situations?

a) *Disagreement is substantial and tensions are running high.*

b) *The other side says they "will not rest until justice is done".*

c) *The other side refuses to speak to you except through their solicitor.*

d) *A notice from court says you must complete certain forms, including setting out your case.*

e) *The problem goes to court, a barrister represents the other side, and you are on your own.*

f) *The court makes a judgement against you, which you see as unfair. You are told you have a right to appeal."*

Finding out problem start and end dates

Model questions for finding out the start and end dates of identified problems are:

1. *Can you tell me roughly what month and year the problem started?*
2. *[If the problem is done with, but persists]*

   And when did you and everybody else give up all actions to resolve the problem?
3. *[If the problem is done with and fully resolved]*

   And when did it conclude?

Beyond core questions

The model questions presented above are intended to serve as a core set of questions relevant for national and global statisticians and policymakers. They are not intended to inhibit the collection of more in-depth data, nor are they intended to limit the scope of future legal needs surveys. Rather, they are intended to provide a form and phraseology for key questions that heeds the lessons of past surveys. They are also intended to provide a sufficient basis for meaningful indicators of access to justice, including basic measurement of levels of legal need and unmet legal need. This is discussed further in Chapter 4.

Legal needs surveys: additional topics of investigation

Past legal needs surveys have investigated a broad array of topics. Many of these topics have been explored in this and the previous chapter. However, there are many others that legal needs surveys have and can legitimately explore. Annex C sets out a complete list of topics addressed in past surveys. The following paragraphs provide a summary.

In relation to problem experience, aside from topics already discussed in this chapter, topics have included:

- The substance of problem (e.g. money, property, changing behaviour, apology, etc.)
- Who is considered to be responsible for the problem
- Links to other identified justiciable problems (including "problem clustering")
- The nature of other party/parties (including their demographics and relative power)
- Relationships with other party/parties
- Whether problems involve discrimination
- The existence and extent of disagreement
- Whether problems are shared with other people (households and communities)

In relation to obtaining help, aside from topics already discussed in this chapter, topics have included:

- How respondents find out about/chose sources of information and help
- Factors in choice (e.g. distance, cost, reputation, ethnicity, etc.)
- The extent to which options are researched
- Nature of Internet use
- Obstacles/barriers to access (e.g. opening hours, distance, cost, language, etc.)
- Distance and mode of travel to sources of help
- When help is obtained
- The timeliness of assistance
- The sequence of sources of information/help
- Links between the use of different sources (e.g. signposting, referral, etc.)
- The nature of information/help sought
- The nature of information/help obtained
- Whether any information/advice suggests objectives would not be met
- The form of communication with sources of help
- Whether help is obtained through an intermediary
- Satisfaction with/utility of information/help obtained
- Reasons for satisfaction/dissatisfaction
- Responses to being dissatisfied (complaint, advice, etc.)
- The impact of obtaining help on social, health, and economic circumstances
- Details of unsuccessful attempts to obtain information/help
- Whether there was consideration of (any/further) information/help

In relation to dispute resolution processes, aside from topics already discussed in this chapter, topics have included:

- Whether and how many hearings/sessions
- Whether respondent attends hearings/sessions
- Tasks undertaken by respondent in hearings/sessions
- Whether the respondent (and other party) is represented, and by who
- Whether the respondent is pressed to give particular testimony
- Bribery/threats as part of processes
- Reasons for choice of process
- The duration of process
- The sequence of processes

- The language used in processes and availability of translation
- Whether processes are discriminatory
- The utility of processes

And in relation to problem resolution in general, aside from topics already discussed in this chapter, topics have included:

- Whether respondents thought problems would be resolve without action
- The delay until first action was taken
- Whether previous experience influenced strategy
- Whether respondents regret how they handled problems
- What they wish they had done/had known
- Whether and what help would have improved outcome

By and large, legal needs surveys routinely ask a bank of general attitudinal questions concerning the justice system. Some mirror the questions discussed in relation to perspectives on process or outcome; others are concerned with trust in the justice system, equality of justice and accessibility of justice.[25]

And, apart from justiciable problem related data, all surveys collect (sometimes extensively[26]) demographic data, which is used to explore the social patterning of problem experience and behaviour. Demographic data has also been incorporated into analyses of the impact of justiciable problems, the general clustering of problems (both justiciable and other), and links between justiciable problems and wider social, economic and health problems.

Given the strong association between justiciable problem experience and morbidity/disability, there is good reason to consider health/disability status a core aspect of demographic data. Similarly, broader associations between justiciable problem experience, disadvantage and poverty make a similar case for data relating to employment, family status, housing type, income, language, migration, social safety net assistance, etc.

As with other data, for demographic data to be comparable between surveys, it must be collected in comparable form. Thus, unless there is good reason to do otherwise, standard/common forms of demographic questions should be adopted whenever possible; and if international norms exist, they should be adopted. Not only does this promote comparability, it also promotes data quality – as significant focus is placed on refining demographic questions by national and supranational statistical agencies.

From questions to questionnaire

As discussed in relation to the model legal needs survey structure in Figure 2.4, longer legal needs survey questionnaires are best constructed as a combination of specific structural and topic-based modules, which link to data structure and the various topics of study discussed in the preceding text. This helps to appropriately represent data structure within questionnaires and tie questionnaires to their defining research questions; clarifying which topics are central and which are peripheral.

This section situates the model questions discussed above in an illustrative short-form questionnaire, which is introduced with an explanation of the content and ordering of the questionnaire. Summary explanatory notes are also provided alongside the questionnaire components in Table 3.3. The questionnaire set out in Table 3.3 collects only the smallest amount of data required to build a basic picture of the experience of justiciable problems. This is done in a conceptually coherent manner, and it permits a rudimentary measurement of legal and unmet legal needs using the framework set out in Figure 2.1. Such measurement would involve data from questions 3, 6, 14, 17, 18, 21, 22 and 23. It is not suggested that these questions represent the ideal measurement tool - far from it. Professed knowledge of rights is a poor substitute for an objective test of legal knowledge. Thus, the latter is preferable. However, an objective test – even a short quiz – is unlikely to be practicable in any but the most comprehensive (or narrow) surveys. In fact, professed knowledge can be "disastrously wrong" (Sandefur, 2016, p. 453). Similarly, legal confidence would best be assessed with a standardised measure, such as those recently developed in England and Wales (Pleasence and Balmer, forthcoming), and process fairness would be best addressed through detailed measures rather than single questions.

Measurement of legal needs and access to justice is discussed further in Chapters 2 and 4.

The questionnaire set out in Table 3.3 is too short to fully reflect the model legal needs survey structure in Figure 2.4, but it is built on the same conceptual foundations. Moreover, indication is provided of the points at which supplementary questions and looping question modules might be added.

While care has been taken to draft questions suitable to a variety of modes of delivery, the illustrative short-form questionnaire is most suited to face-to-face delivery, with show-cards to assist delivery. Adaptation to other modes of delivery should be relatively straightforward.

An illustrative expanded version of the questionnaire is set out in Annex B.

As noted in relation to the model questions, the diversity of justice institutions, services, practices and norms around the world means that questions may need to be adapted to specific populations. As with all questionnaires, questions should be carefully scrutinised and tested. The complexity of the subject matter also increases the importance of training for those collecting and/or coding data.

Illustrative short-form legal needs survey questionnaire

The illustrative short-form legal needs survey questionnaire set out in Table 3.3 commences with an introduction that sets the scene for the survey. It introduces the interviewer and the nature of the survey,[27] and provides information necessary to ensure that the ethical requirements for personal interviews and collection of personal data are met. These requirements vary from jurisdiction to jurisdiction, and care should always be taken to use appropriate text when introducing a survey.

Following the introduction, initial demographics are obtained. If there is an interest in general legal capability, questions addressing that should be included at this point, as long as they are formulated to avoid drawing attention to the "legal" focus of the questionnaire. Placing such questions here will help to engage respondents, particularly those who go on to report no justiciable problems. It also means that respondents will not have been exposed to questions providing names of sources of help, processes, etc.

Then comes the foundation question upon which the remainder of the questionnaire is built, namely the problem identification question (Q1). This question determines the scope of the survey. If the question is poorly worded, then out-of-scope problems will be followed-up and/or in-scope problems will be missed. The greater and more accurate the detail of problem descriptions, the more effective the question. Q1 references the problem descriptions set out in Table 3.1.

For each category in which problems are reported, Q2 ascertains the number of problems that have been experienced. This then leads to Q3, which asks about the seriousness of problems. Q3 is asked at this early point in the questionnaire as the data it generates will be used to identify the pool of problems sufficiently serious for follow-up. Data generated by this question is also of broader interest. It can contribute to measuring unmet legal need using the framework set out in Figure 2.1, enable the relative seriousness of problems to be investigated, and explored as a predictor of strategy choices, etc. For efficiency, Q2 and Q3 should be asked immediately after respondents report problems in any problem category.

If there is interest in asking about problems experienced in a business capacity, an appropriate identification question should be asked at this point.

Q4 asks about the nature of those problems selected for follow-up. These are randomly selected from the pool of identified problems with seriousness scores over a defined threshold. The number of problems followed-up will depend upon the time available for interviews. Although Q4 is not one of the core model questions discussed above, it validates Q3 data and provides examples for reporting.

If there is interest in identifying problems that are shared (e.g. within households, communities, etc.), this should be asked about at this point, when the focus is on the nature of problems.

Q5 and Q6 ask about information, advice and representation. As discussed above, these two questions are used to distinguish between help obtained via mass communication channels and help received personally. For respondents who received no help, Q20 later asks for reasons, provided that problems have concluded. Although it is possible to ask a variant of Q20 immediately after Q6, it is not known at this point whether the problems have been concluded, so further response categories would need to be added to reflect that respondents may intend to obtain advice in the future. When interest is primarily in legal advice, then the routing for this section can be amended to ask about only that. Q6 also contributes to measuring unmet legal need using the Figure 2.1 framework.

Q7 then asks about process. As discussed above, questions about process should be asked separately to questions about help and other problem-solving behaviour. This is important because people do not necessarily choose or even engage with process. When processes are identified in Q7, the following question establishes who initiated them. For the sake of efficiency, Q8 should be asked of each process type as soon as it is reported. Likewise, Q9 – which asks whether respondents responded to formal process brought against them – should immediately follow all instances of Q8 in the manner of a loop.

Q10 is the problem and resolving behaviour "catch-all" question, without which it is impossible to be certain whether respondents took any action to understand or resolve their problems.

Q11 determines whether problems have been concluded. If they have, Q12 establishes the manner of conclusion. It is important not to conflate process (addressed in previous questions) with the manner in which problems are concluded. They are linked but distinct.

Q13 and Q14 concern quality of outcome and process. Q14 can also contribute to measuring unmet legal need using the Figure 2.1 framework.

Q15 and Q16 ask about the costs of problem resolution. First, respondents are presented with a series of cost items and asked if they incurred them. Then, they are asked to estimate associated costs. If interest is limited to legal service costs and process fees, then a shorter Q15 is appropriate, although it will not provide the same insight in benefit-cost analysis. Q15 can also be shortened by not asking about each cost item separately, but the breadth of items will result in the data being ambiguous.

Together, Q17 and Q18 address the four broad aspects of legal capability discussed in Chapter 2. The two questions also provide data that can be used as part of the process of measuring unmet legal need using the Figure 2.1 framework. Q18 comprises a question matrix, which can be expanded to explore further aspects of legal capability.

Q19 asks about problem impact. If there is a particular interest in benefit-cost analysis, Q19 items can be followed-up for the purposes of estimating costs. For example, use of health services can be investigated, or welfare claims.

Finally, in terms of problem data, Q21 to Q23 establish problem start and (if relevant) end dates. This provides reasonable estimates of problem duration that, as well as being of interest in their own right, provide greater flexibility in the forms of analysis that can be employed with legal needs survey data. Sampling both ongoing and concluded problems raises the issue of how to deal with ongoing problems in analysis and reporting. Including ongoing problems in estimates of, say, use of lawyers poses the problem that ongoing problems may involve lawyer use after the time of interview. Analysis needs to consider "censored'" observations to arrive at an accurate estimate. This can be achieved by using appropriate forms of analysis, such as event history analysis, which takes into account both concluded and on-going problems when modelling problem duration.[28]

If there is interest in asking about attitudes to the justice system, the appropriate place to do so is after the problem data has all been collected. This placement means that responses will benefit from respondents' reflections on their own experience of justiciable issues. Attitudinal questions usually concern levels of access to justice, equality of justice and trust in the justice system. They can be asked globally or of constituent elements of the justice system. Care should be taken to avoid technical language, for the reasons set out elsewhere in this Guide.

Finally, in terms of substantive data, core demographic data is obtained (other than that already obtained at the outset). If there is interest in the social patterning of problems and/or links between justiciable problems and wider social, economic and health problems, then core demographic data should cover age, gender, ethnicity, employment status, family status, health/disability status, housing type, income, language, migration status, social safety net assistance, etc.

The questionnaire ends with closing remarks and, if necessary, a request for permission to recontact the respondent.

Table 3.3. Illustrative short-form legal needs survey questionnaire

Content	Explanatory notes
Introduction	
Good morning/afternoon/evening. My name is … and I am with … who have been commissioned by … to conduct a survey to find out how people deal with a range of issues people can face in everyday life, such as with housing, work, or within families; and the types of help that are needed and used to do this. Your [address/telephone number] has been randomly selected for inclusion in the survey, as one of an intended sample of *x* [addresses/ telephone numbers across the country], as it is important that we collect information about the experience of a representative group of people. The questions should take about … minutes, and to achieve a fully random sample I would like to ask them of the person at this address who will be the next to have a birthday and is currently *y* years old or above. Would that be you, and if not, could I speak to that person? [Repeat if necessary] Any answers you give are confidential, and participation in the survey is entirely voluntary. If you agree to participate, you may choose to skip a question if you do not wish to answer it or to end the interview. No information that identifies you will be shared or used in any report of the survey's findings. [Additional text to meet ethical requirements, as required] Do you agree to participate?	An introduction serves to frame a survey and to ensure that ethical requirements for personal interviews and the collection of personal data are met. An introduction should also engage respondents, motivating them to complete the questionnaire. Thus, text should be added to explain the importance of the survey in a manner likely to resonate with potential respondents. As discussed in Chapter 2, reference to law and the use of technical language should be avoided in the introduction to a legal needs survey, and justiciable problems should be described in lay terms. If incentives are offered for participation in a survey, details should also be included in the introduction.
Initial demographics	
[Basic demographics and demographics for routing]	For efficiency, some legal needs survey questions can be filtered by demographics. For example, if business related problems are asked about following Q3, then an initial demographic question could be used to identify who is to be asked.
If general legal capability questions are included in a questionnaire, they should be placed either here or ahead of the additional demographics section (at the end of the questionnaire). A benefit of including general legal capability questions here is that they can help to engage respondents; particularly those who go on to report no justiciable problems. Placing questions here also means that respondents will not have been exposed to questions providing names of sources of help, processes, etc. However, if capability questions are placed here they must be formulated to avoid drawing attention to the 'legal' focus of the questionnaire.	
Problem identification	
1. I am going to read you a list of problems and disputes that people commonly experience in everyday life. In each case, tell me whether or not you have personally experienced any such problem in the past two years, by which I mean a problem that started since [DATE] or started before then, but continued afterwards. (Please only include problems that you have had yourself, in a private capacity, not problems experienced by a business you run, in the course of self-employment or by your employer, and not situations where you represented or helped somebody else with their problem.) Please only mention problems once. a) Since [DATE] have you had any problems or disputes to do with defective or undelivered goods or services – such as difficulties obtaining a refund, billing errors, or disputes with utility providers (such as water, electricity, gas, telephone or Internet), or professionals (such as accountants, lawyers, mechanics, plumbers, etc.)? b) Since [DATE] have you had any problems or disputes to do with community services – such as denial of or unfair access to the benefits of community land/forest/water groups, disputes over community resource governance, and disputes over fees and revenues?	This is the most important question in the questionnaire. It determines the scope of the survey. If the question is poorly worded, then out-of-scope problems will be followed-up and/or in-scope problems will be missed. The greater and more accurate the detail of problem descriptions, the more effective the question will be. The question is the first asked, as all other questions rely upon data obtained from it. If respondents have experienced problems in a category, then Q2 and Q3 should be asked immediately for the sake of efficiency. If Q2 > 1, then Q3 should be looped for up to x number of problems. The sub-questions mirror the Table 3.1 categories and examples. An alternative and common approach is to provide show cards setting out (say) the example problems included within Table 3.1, or a full set of problems of interest.

Content	Explanatory notes
c) Since [DATE] have you had any problems or disputes to do with land or buying and selling property – such as disputes over title or boundaries, problems to do with land grabbing, expropriation, mining, or environmental damage, or problems to do with land transfers or building permits? d) Since [DATE] have you had any problems or disputes to do with housing – such as problems or disputes with a landlord or tenant, concerning (for example), poor maintenance, the terms of a lease, eviction, becoming homeless; or problems concerning an owners' corporation; or with neighbours (over, for example, excessive noise or threatening behaviour)? e) Since [DATE] have you had any problems or disputes to do with family and relationship break ups – such as divorce, access to or custody of children, child support, disputes over property division, children being taken into care, guardianship or adoption, or inheritance? f) Since [DATE] have you had any problems or disputes to do with an injury caused by someone else, or an injury or illness caused by an accident at work, working conditions, or negligent or wrong medical treatment (including dental and other healthcare treatment)? g) Since [DATE] have you had any problems or disputes to do with employment or labour – such as dismissal, unpaid wages, poor working conditions, denial of rights, discrimination, harassment, unfair disciplinary procedures, and changes to contract terms? h) Since [DATE] have you had any problems or disputes to do with government payments – such as disputes concerning your entitlement to, the amount of, suspension of or registration for government payments having to do with, for example, social safety net assistance, state pension and education grants or loans? i) Since [DATE] have you had any problems or disputes to do with abuse by state officials – such as threatening, discriminatory or corrupt treatment by the police or another government official? j) Since [DATE] have you had any problems or disputes to do with government and public services – such as problems to do with citizenship or residency status; obtaining a passport or other public documentation; obtaining access to or being excluded from public services, such as healthcare and education; fairness of examinations; tax disputes or disputes with other government bodies? k) Since [DATE] have you had any problems or disputes to do with debt – such as being behind and unable to pay money you owe, action by a creditor for non-payment (including harassment), or the prospect of bankruptcy? l) Since [DATE] have you had any other problems or disputes to do with money and with financial services – such as insurance claims being denied, repeated unfair bank charges, credit rating inaccuracy, problems collecting money owed to you, or being misled about insurance, a pension, or other financial product you acquired?	Show cards can speed up the process of running through lists for some respondents. If there is interest in including business related problems, then one of the strategies outlined in Chapter 2 should be adopted. Either business problems can be asked about separately, following completion of initial problem identification, or the text that excludes business problems can be removed or modified, along the lines of the 2017-18 Nepalese survey, to include "problems experienced through a business that provides you with self-employment (but not an enterprise providing employment to others)". Respondents can then be asked whether problems were faced in a personal or business capacity during follow-up.
2. [For each Q1 problem category reported, ASK IMMEDIATELY (i.e. do not wait until all Q1 categories have been asked about)] How many such problems have you experienced in the past two years? Please count problems of the same type, where the other party remains the same, as one problem.	
3. [For each Q1 problem category reported, ASK IMMEDIATELY for all / up to x number of problems. If Q2 > 1 ask about problems in order of recency, starting with the most recent] Thinking about the problem as a whole, consider a scale of 1 to 10, where 1 represents the least serious type of problem you could face and 10 represents the most serious. To provide some examples, a score of 9 might be [ANCHOR 1] and a score of 2 might be [ANCHOR 2].	What number best represents the seriousness of your problem? This question is asked at this early point in the questionnaire as the data it generates will be used to identify the pool of problems sufficiently serious for follow-up. Data generated by this question is also of broader interest. It can contribute to measuring unmet legal need using the framework in Figure 2.1, enable the relative seriousness of problems to be investigated and explored as a predictor of strategy choices, etc.

Content	Explanatory notes
Core question loop	
[Randomly select y number of problems from the pool of identified problems with seriousness scores of 3 or more. For each selected problem, ask Q4 to Q23. If there are no such problems, go to the next section]	
I am now going to ask you some questions about [PROBLEM 1, etc.] 4a. What was the problem about? [Code to detailed Table 2.1 categories] 4b. Did you share this particular problem with other people, neighbours, or other members of your community (as in the case of some problems concerning, for example, the environment or communal land)? 4c. [If 4(b) = Yes] Who did you share it with? Household member(s) Other friend(s) or family member(s) Work colleague(s) Neighbour(s) Community Other	Questions 4(a), (b) and (c) are not core model questions. They are included here to verify Q3 data, provide examples and further define the nature of the problems reported. Questions 4(b) and 4(c) identify whether problems are shared. They indicate the extent to which justiciable problems are experienced across populations.
5. Did you obtain any information from the Internet, an app, a video, printed material or the media to help you better understand or resolve the problem? a) A website or "app" b) A leaflet, book or self-help guide c) Newspapers or magazines d) Television, video or radio	
6. (Apart from anything you have told me about already) Did you, or someone acting on your behalf, obtain information, advice or representation from any of the following people or organisations to help you better understand or resolve [PROBLEM 1, etc.]? Please exclude any help provided by the other party. [ASK EACH SEPARATELY] a) Family, friends or acquaintances (excluding people whose job is to advise on problems such as these; please mention these people in their professional capacity) b) A lawyer, professional advisor, advice service or advice helpline (such as [examples] (specify) c) A court [or tribunal] or other dispute resolution organisation (such as [examples]) or the police (specify) d) A national, regional or municipal government department, agency, council or a politician (specify) e) Your employer, a trade union, a professional or trade association (such as [examples]) (specify) f) A health, welfare, financial services or other professional (specify) g) A community or religious leader or organisation, an [NGO/charity], or trusted person or organisation (specify)	Further specification is included in the question to enable coding in the set of categories based on the Table 2.2 taxonomy. An open form of this question could also be used here: "Apart from anything you have already told me, did you or someone acting on your behalf obtain information, advice or representation from any person or organisation to help you better understand or resolve the problem? For example, from family or friends; a lawyer, professional advisor or advice service; a court, government body or the police; a health or welfare professional; a trade union or employer; a religious or community leader or organisation; an [NGO/charity], a trusted person or organisation or anybody else?" [PROBE] If Q6 (particularly in its open form) is asked ahead of Q5, there is a risk that information obtained via mass communication channels will be reported in Q6, preventing a clear distinction between this and help received personally.

Content	Explanatory notes
h) Any other person or organisation	Any additional questions concerning particular sources of help should loop following Q6.
7. (Apart from anything you have told me already) Did any of the following things happen as part of [PROBLEM 1, etc.] or sorting it out? When I say "you" here, I mean you or somebody acting on your behalf. [ASK EACH SEPARATELY] a) You communicated with the other party b) You or the other party made a claim to, or made use of, a court (or tribunal) c) [If applicable] You or the other party made a claim to, or made use of, an [Indigenous/ customary] dispute resolution process (e.g. [examples]) d) [PROBLEM 1, etc.] was reported to the police (or other prosecution authority) e) You or the other party turned to, or action was taken by, a formal designated authority or agency, such as [examples, e.g. Ombudsman, regulator (e.g. [example]) or enforcement authority (e.g. consumer protection authority)] f) You or the other party turned to, or action was taken by, another state authority (e.g. [examples]) g) You or the other party turned to, or action was taken by, a religious authority h) You or the other party turned to, or action was taken by, a community leader or organisation (e.g. [example]) i) You participated in formal mediation, conciliation or arbitration (e.g. [examples]) j) You or the other party made use of a formal appeals process operated by the other party or independently k) You, the other party or somebody else turned to, or action was taken by, another third party for adjudication, mediation or intervention l) There was no negotiation or third party involvement	As with Q6, an open form of this question could also be used here: Did you, somebody acting on your behalf, the other party or anybody else, make a claim to a court (or tribunal), or turn to any other third-party individual or organisation – such as [institutional examples] or a community or religious leader [or respected family member] – to adjudicate, mediate or intervene to help resolve [PROBLEM 1, etc.]? [PROBE] Questions about process are separate from those about help, as respondents do not necessarily choose or even engage with processes. Thus, it is distinct from help seeking and other problem solving behaviours.
8. [For each positive Q7 response for *a* to *k*] Who initiated this action? [READ OUT ONLY IF NECESSARY] a) The respondent b) The other party c) The third party responsible for the process d) Another third party.	For efficiency, Q8 should be asked of each process type the moment it is reported. Likewise, Q9 should immediately follow all instances of Q8.
9. [If the respondent did not initiate processes *b* to *h* or *j* and *k*] Did you respond to this action?	Any additional questions concerning particular processes should loop following the full completion of Q7, Q8 and Q9.
10. Did you, or somebody acting on your behalf, do anything else to help you better understand or resolve the problem, such as communicate with the other party, obtain or organise evidence, or make an insurance claim? [OPEN] a) Communicated with the other party b) Obtained or organised evidence c) Made an insurance claim d) Other (SPECIFY)	Without this "catch-all" question, it is impossible to be certain whether respondents took any action to understand or resolve reported problems.

Content	Explanatory notes
11. Is the problem ongoing or done with? By "done with" I mean that the problem either has been resolved or that it persists, but you and everybody else have given up all efforts to resolve it further. [PROBE] a) Ongoing b) Too early to say c) Done with - problem persists, but all have given up trying to resolve it further. d) Done with - problem resolved	This is an essential question for enabling coherent data analysis. Problems that are ongoing and problems that have been concluded are not equivalent. For example, unmet needs within ongoing problems may go on to be met. The wording used here is careful to suggest finality.
12. [If Q11 = *c* or *d*, otherwise go to Q17] Which of the following statements best reflects how the problem outcome was ultimately brought about? The problem outcome was ultimately brought about by … [ASK EACH SEPARATELY] a) a court (or tribunal) judgment b) a decision or intervention by another formal authority c) mediation, conciliation or arbitration d) action by another third party e) agreement between you and the other party f) the other party independently doing what you wanted g) you independently doing what the other party wanted h) the problem sorting itself out i) your moving away from the problem (e.g. moving home, changing job) j) [Only if Q10 = c] … you and/or all other parties giving up trying to resolve the problem	It is important not to conflate process (as asked about in previous questions) with the manner in which problems conclude. They are linked but distinct.
13. Do you feel the outcome of this problem was basically fair to everybody concerned? a) Fair to everybody concerned b) Not fair to everybody concerned	Q13 and Q14 concern quality of process and outcome. Q14 can also contribute to measurement of unmet legal need using the framework set out in Figure 2.1
14. Regardless of the outcome of this problem, do you feel the process through which the outcome was reached was basically fair or unfair to everybody concerned? a) Fair to everybody concerned b) Not fair to everybody concerned	Any additional questions about perceptions of process and outcome should accompany Q13 and Q14.
15. Excluding indirect payments – such as insurance premiums or membership subscriptions – but including payments made by family members and friends, [did you/have you], personally [have/had] to pay for any of the following in order to resolve the problem: [ASK EACH SEPARATELY] a) Lawyer and other advisor fees b) Court, mediation or other administrative fees c)Telephone calls and correspondence d) Collecting information or obtaining evidence (incl. reimbursement of witnesses' costs) e) Travel (e.g. bus fares or petrol to visit an advisor)	If interest is limited to legal service costs and process fees, then a shorter Q15 is appropriate; although it will not provide the same insight in benefit-cost analysis: "Excluding indirect payments – such as insurance premiums or membership subscriptions – but including payments made by family members and friends, [did you/have you], personally [have/had] to pay for [the help you received from [advisor]/[process] fees]?" If respondents report costs for a category, then Q16 should be asked immediately for the sake of efficiency.

Content	Explanatory notes
f) Lost business or salary, from taking time off work (e.g. to obtain advice) g) Bribes / kick-backs (Remember, your answer is confidential) h) Incidental domestic costs (e.g. childcare)	Q15 can be shortened by not asking about each cost item separately, but the breadth of items will result in the data being quite ambiguous.
16. "Approximately how much [did you have/have you had] to pay for [cost item]?"	If a shorter version of Q15 is used, then Q16 should be phrased as follows: "Approximately how much in total did it cost you to deal with this problem?" This phrasing is not appropriate if individual cost items have been identified, as respondents will in any event need to add the cost of the items. Another approach is to ask the following: "How difficult was it to find the money to pay for this/these things?" A more complete picture of costs can be obtained by also asking: "Apart from family or friends, did anybody, or any organisation, pay or part-pay for [the help you received from [advisor]/ [process] fees]" Any additional questions about the cost of problem resolution should integrate with Q15 and Q16.
17. Which of the following describe the problem? You can choose more than one option, or none. [ASK EACH SEPARATELY] a) Bad luck / part of life b) Bureaucratic c) A family or private matter d) Legal e) Political f) A social or community matter g) Economic h) None of these	Q17 and Q18 together address the four broad aspects of legal capability discussed in Chapter 2. The two questions also provide data that can be used as part of the process of measuring unmet legal need using the framework set out in Figure 2.1.
18. To what extent do you agree or disagree with the following statements about the problem? [strongly agree, mainly agree, mainly disagree, strongly disagree] a) I understood or [came/have come] to understand my legal rights and responsibilities b) I [knew/know] where to get good information and advice about resolving the problem c) I [was able/have been able] to get all the expert help I needed d) I [was/am] confident I [could/can] achieve a fair outcome	The question matrix in Q18 can be extended to explore further aspects of legal capability, or additional questions can be added after Q18.

Content	Explanatory notes
19. Did you experience any of the following as part of or as a result of this problem? [ASK EACH SEPARATELY] a) ill-health or injury b) stress c) damage to a family relationship d) being harassed, threatened or assaulted e) damage to your property f) loss of employment g) having to move home h) financial loss i) loss of confidence or fear j) problems to do with your education k) problems with alcohol or drugs	If there is particular interest in benefit-cost analysis, Q19 items can be followed-up for the purposes of estimating costs. For example, use of health services or welfare claims can be investigated.
20. [If 6 = NO to all items] Why didn't you obtain independent advice to help resolve [PROBLEM 1, etc.]? [PROBE] [DO NOT READ] [CODE ALL THAT APPLY] a) No dispute with anybody/thought other side was right b) Problem resolved without need to get advice c) Did not think needed advice d) Did not think problem important enough e) Concerned about the time it would take f) Concerned about the financial cost g) Advisors were too far away h) Thought it would be too stressful i) Thought it would damage relationship with other side j) Was scared to take action/get advice k) Didn't know where/how to get advice l) Didn't think it would make any difference to outcome m) Had tried seeking advice before and not found it useful n) Other (SPECIFY)	As well as providing valuable strategic information concerning obstacles to advice, this question also provides data that can be used as part of the process of measuring unmet legal need using the framework set out at in Figure 2.1 If the interest is primarily in legal advice, then the routing for this question can be amended to ask about only this.
21. Finally, can you tell me roughly what month and year the problem started?	Establishing problem start and end dates provides greater flexibility in using ongoing problems within analyses.
22. [If Q11=c] And when did you and everybody else given up all actions to resolve the problem?	
23 [If Q11=d] And when did it conclude?	
[End of core question loop]	

Content	Explanatory notes
If access to justice related attitude questions are included in a questionnaire, they should appear here; as they will then benefit from respondents' reflections on their own experience of justiciable issues.	
[Attitudinal questions commonly concern levels of access to justice, equality of justice and trust. They can be asked globally, or of constituent justice system elements. Technical language should be avoided.]	
Additional demographics	
[Sensitive and additional demographics]	e.g. health status, poverty proxies, etc.
Concluding remarks	
[If there is interest in recontacting respondents, consent should be obtained at this point.]	

Notes

[1] Examples of the content of show cards can be found in Ipsos MORI (2012). Beyond show cards, the World Justice Project's *General Population Poll* made use of booklets to present respondents with lists of the justiciable problems asked about.

[2] In drafting problem descriptions within justiciable problem identification questions, a central concern is to ensure they suggest *both* the full range of justiciable problems of interest *and* only justiciable problems. Evidently, as descriptions become broader, risks associated with the former tend to improve at the expense of risks to the latter. In the case of longer surveys, both risks can be addressed by increasing the number of problem descriptions included (at both the problem category and constituent problem type levels). This enables scope to be maintained alongside more rigorous problem specification. However, in the case of shorter surveys, compromise can sometimes be unavoidable.

[3] 28 of 47 surveys, for which information is available, including all 10 HiiL *Justice Needs and Satisfaction* surveys and all five instances of the *English and Welsh Civil and Social Justice Survey*, a survey that involved substantial developmental work over a period of more than a decade. The terms were also used together – along with the terms "abuses" and "crimes" – in the 2009 Bangladesh survey. The terms have also been used separately from each other in a majority (14) of the remaining surveys.

[4] Only the 2004 Slovakian survey, the 2017-2018 Nepalese survey and the 2017 iteration of the World Justice Project's *General Population Poll* adopted a two-year reference period.

[5] If surveys are repeated more regularly than every two years or the focus is a shorter time span, then a shorter reference period may be appropriate. For example, the panel form of the *English and Welsh Civil and Social Justice Survey* adopted an 18-month reference period to mirror the period between waves of the survey. Periods longer than two years offer diminishing returns (in terms of maximising problem reporting). However, it may sometimes be necessary to extend a reference period beyond two years to yield the sample size required for proposed forms of analysis. For example, after pre-testing, the 2018 *Nationwide Legal Needs and Access to Justice Survey* in South Korea moved from a two year to a four year reference period to increase the volume of problem data the survey would yield (Kim and Choi, 2018).

[6] In the absence of information on problem start dates, the adoption of this rule means that data conveys problem prevalence rather than incidence (as these concepts are understood in epidemiology). "Prevalence" relates to cases existing in a time period; "incidence" to cases occurring within a time period.

[7] The surveys detailed in Table 1.1 normally incorporated between 10 and 20 problem categories (with 14 to 16 the most common numbers). A small number of surveys incorporated more.

[8] The 2006 New Zealand survey – which initially asked about only five problem categories – followed-up by individually asking about 92 constituent problem types, when relevant. As most respondents reported no problems in most categories, this approach resulted in a substantial amount of time being saved. The approach was reprised for the 2017 New Zealand survey.

[9] The reliability of a scale is related to the number of items included.

[10] For reference, the English and Welsh Civil and Social Justice Survey anchors at the "serious" end alluded to regular physical abuse by a partner and at the "less serious" end to a faulty "moderately expensive electrical item". Elsewhere, the World Justice Project's *General Population Poll* incorporated anchors using the following text: "For example, a score of 2 might be a problem with a neighbor over a noisy party and a score of 8 might be being made homeless."

[11] See, for example, Seymour et al. (1985).

[12] Include the most appropriate term

[13] In addition, some responses to questions on outcomes are recorded under the first category. Again, this restricts the number of categories available to respondents. However, there are instances in which multiple processes are used within problem resolution, and relying on the ordering of the category list requires both that it be hierarchical (so that if two categories being potentially applicable, the first is always the appropriate choice) and that respondents understand that they should clarify say how the process *ultimately brought about* the problem outcome. While it may be argued that the categories *are* hierarchical and that the question clearly indicates that the selected process must have *ultimately brought about* the problem outcome, the safest route to accurate data is communication of the full category list.

[14] This question is included here, in preference to a question concerning reasons for inaction, as it more directly links to the example approach to measuring unmet legal discussed in Chapter 2.

[15] As in the case of the 2010 and 2012 *English and Welsh Civil and Social Justice Surveys.*

[16] The 2012 Colombian survey asked about respondents' satisfaction with processes on the basis of "the money you spent compared to the result you obtained."

[17] The appropriate text will reflect survey sponsor interest and responses to earlier sources of help and process questions.

[18] The appropriate text will reflect survey sponsor interest and responses to earlier sources of help and process questions.

[19] The 2014 Canadian survey also asked a series of questions relating to legal capability: recognition of legal issues, knowledge of where "to obtain good information and advice about resolving the problem," knowledge of the type of assistance needed, and knowledge necessary "to deal with the problem." However, the questions did not closely mirror the aspects of legal capability set out in Chapter 2, nor did they benefit from the greater efficiency of a "grid" style formulation.

[20] This is in contrast to the alternative approach of asking if respondents are "aware … the problem was related to the law" (as adopted in the 2005 Japanese survey).

[21] In the case of both recognition of legal issues and legal understanding, general inquiry is complicated by the need for substantial questionnaire space. A range of subject areas must be explored, and sufficient contextual detail must be provided to enable clarity and certainty. While it would be possible to ask a simple question about a respondent's legal knowledge (such as, "In general, to what extent do you know about legal rights and responsibilities in everyday situations, such as the workplace, accidents, the family, and housing?"), this would inevitably involve self-assessment, and self-assessed legal understanding may differ markedly from actual understanding (Pleasence and Balmer 2012, Pleasence et al. 2015, Pleasence et al. 2017).

[22] 2010 *English and Welsh Civil and Social Justice Panel Survey.*

[23] A more nuanced version of the same question would be, "How much do you know about what each of the following do?"

[24] In the latter case, see Pleasence and Balmer (forthcoming).

[25] In addition to the standardised measures of legal capability mentioned above, two standardised measures of attitudes to justice have also been developed, both demonstrating reasonable psychometric properties. One is

the nine-item *Perceived Inaccessibility of Justice* (IOJ) scale, the other the six-item *Perceived Inequality of Justice* (PIJ) scale (see Pleasence and Balmer (2018).

[26] For example, in addition to information collected about the identity and relationships between members of households surveyed, the 2010 *English and Welsh Civil and Social Justice Panel Survey* asked 73 separate demographic questions, including 24 questions concerning respondents' health.

[27] Engaging respondents and motivating them to complete questionnaires can be challenging if the subject matter of the survey is not of personal concern. Careful consideration should therefore be given to how surveys can best be introduced to respondents. Sometimes incentives, such as money or postage stamps, are used to boost response rates.

[28] Steele (2008) presents a common form of analysis; Pleasence and Balmer (2013) give an example in a legal needs survey context.

References

Fowler, F.J. Jr. (1995), *Improving Survey Questions: Design and Evaluation,* Sage, Thousand Oaks.

Fraga, S. (2016), "Methodological and ethical challenges in violence research", in *Porto Biomedical Journal,* Vol. 1(2), p. 77-80.

Ipsos MORI (2012), *The English and Welsh Civil and Social Justice Panel Survey: Wave Two Technical Report,* Ipsos MORI, London.

Kim, S. and S. Choi (2018), "Reflections and lessons from the 2018 Nationwide Legal Needs and Access to Justice Survey in South Korea", unpublished report prepared for the Judiciary of the Republic of Korea.

Piest, J., M. Gramatikov, S. Muller, K. Heijstek-Ziemann and J. Sallali (2016), *Justice Needs in Uganda: Legal Problems in Daily Life,* HiiL, The Hague.

Pleasence, P. and N.J. Balmer (forthcoming), "Development of a general legal confidence scale: A first implementation of the Rasch measurement model in empirical legal studies," *Journal of Empirical Legal Studies.*

Pleasence, P. and N.J. Balmer (2018), "Measuring the accessibility and equality of civil justice", *Hague Journal on the Rule of Law*, Vol. 10(2), pp. 255-294.

Pleasence, P. and N.J. Balmer (2013), *In Need of Advice: Findings of a Small Business Legal Needs Benchmarking Survey,* PPSR (for the Legal Services Board), Cambridge.

Pleasence, P. and N.J. Balmer (2012), "Ignorance in bliss: Modeling knowledge of rights in marriage and cohabitation", in *Law and Society Review,* Vol. 46(2), pp. 297-333.

Pleasence, P., N.J. Balmer, A. Buck, A. O'Grady, M. Maclean and H. Genn (2003), "Family problems: What happens and to whom?" in *Family Law,* Vol. 33, pp. 497-501.

Pleasence, P., N.J. Balmer and C. Denvir (2017), "Wrong about rights: Public knowledge of key areas of consumer, housing and employment law in England and Wales", *Modern Law Review*, Vol. 80(5), pp. 836-859.

Pleasence, P., N.J. Balmer and C. Denvir (2015), *How People Understand and Interact with the Law*, Legal Education Foundation, London.

Sandefur, R.L. (2016), "What we know and need to know about the legal needs of the public", *Carolina Law Review,* Vol. 67, pp. 443-459.

Seymour, R.A., J.M. Simpson, J.E. Charlton and M.E. Phillips (1985), "An evaluation of length and end-phrase of visual analog scales in dental pain", *Pain*, Vol. 21, pp. 177-185.

Steele, F. (2008), "Multilevel models for longitudinal data", *Journal of the Royal Statistical Society. Series A: Statistics in Society*, Vol. 171(1), pp. 5-19.

United Nations Department of Economic and Social Affairs (2014), *Guidelines for Producing Statistics on Violence Against Women,* United Nations, New York.

Verdonschot, J.H., M. Barendrecht, L. Klaming and P. Kamminga (2008), "Measuring access to justice: The quality of outcomes", *TISCO Working Paper Series on Civil Law and Conflict Resolution Systems*, Vol. 007/2008, Tilburg University, Tilburg.

Chapter 4. Legal Needs Surveys and Access to Justice Indicators

This Chapter explores how indicators derived from legal needs surveys can fit into broader measures of access to justice and inclusive development. It then describes how national and global indicators can be formulated to help drive meaningful progress.

Multidimensionality of access to justice

In 2008, the United Nations Commission on Legal Empowerment of the Poor estimated that more than half the world's population live outside the effective protection of law. This provides profound context to United Nations Sustainable Development Goal (SDG) 16.3, to "promote the rule of law at the national and international levels and ensure equal access to justice for all."[1] Failure to ensure effective access to civil justice results in substantial social costs and undermines inclusive development. Justiciable problems commonly concern matters of basic welfare, compound disadvantage, diminish opportunities and result in considerable public expenditure.

A better and nuanced understanding of access to civil justice is crucial for developing more effective policies, models and financing. National and global policy and measurement frameworks too often fail to meaningfully account for civil justice issues. Legal needs surveys are a tool to give visibility to legal problems, drive policy responses and understand progress towards access to justice for all.

Efforts to construct measures of access to justice must start from the understanding that access to justice is a multidimensional concept, the breadth of which "heavily depends on how society receives the meaning and scope of justice" (Yuthayotin, 2015, p. 66). Even narrowly construed to refer only to the administration of the law, the concept of justice extends to many aspects of everyday life and encompasses institutional, procedural and outcome related dimensions. However, the concept is increasingly recognised to extend beyond formal process to informal dispute resolution and ultimately to social justice and the distribution of welfare, resources and opportunity.

The working definition of access to justice offered in Chapter 1. centred on the ability of people to obtain just resolution of justiciable problems in compliance with human rights standards; if necessary, through impartial formal or informal institutions of justice and with appropriate legal support. The reference to conformity with human rights standards both extends the concept beyond local legal frameworks (which may conflict with accepted international norms) and indicates standards for independent adjudication.

This definition suggests at least seven distinct dimensions/sub-dimensions of access to justice:

- The substance of law
- The availability of formal or informal institutions of justice
- The quality of formal or informal institutions of justice
- The availability of legal assistance
- The quality of legal assistance
- The quality of outcomes
- Legal capability and empowerment

Moreover, the operationalisation of the constituent concepts of legal need and unmet legal need, which are detailed in Chapter 2. , suggests further dimensions/sub-dimensions of access to justice:

- Timeliness of outcomes

- Legal knowledge
- Awareness of dispute resolution options
- Quality of process
- Awareness of assistance services
- Adequacy of assistance services

In addition to these, further dimensions and sub-dimensions have been set out by others. For example, the final report of HiiL's *Measuring Access to Justice in a Globalising World* project set out three dimensions of the cost and quality of access to justice: costs of procedure, quality of procedure and quality of outcome. It also sets out nine sub-dimensions: monetary costs, opportunity costs, stress and emotions, procedural justice, interpersonal justice, informational justice, distributive justice, restorative justice, functionality and transparency (Barendrecht et al., 2010).

Certain dimensions also attach to specific types of justiciable problem. Yuthayotin's framework for access to justice in business to consumer e-commerce, for example, which extends to the "protection of all aspects of justice" (Yuthayotin, 2015, p. 67), incorporated dimensions relating to the information necessary to allow informed decisions, the nature of transactions, the functioning of the marketplace, and the recognition of consumer rights and their role in the market. Linked to this, levels of access to justice will inevitably vary between justiciable problem types, meaning that being able to disaggregate broad civil justice indicators by problem type can be valuable.

Similarly, access to justice may vary considerably between population groups and vulnerable population groups may face specific barriers to access. For this reason, it is important to design and disaggregate indicators that highlight and are responsive to key demographic characteristics. Thus, the US *Justice Index*, which assesses laws, rules, and practices across the United States and was published in 2014 and 2016, incorporated access to justice dimensions of language access and disability access. Such an approach exposes differences among population groups. This resonates with the UN General Assembly's broader call for SDG data to be "disaggregated by income, sex, age, race, ethnicity, migration status, disability and geographic location and other characteristics relevant in the national contexts."[2] The UN's Inter-Agency and Expert Group (IAEG) responsible for global SDG indicators has established a working group on disaggregation that is exploring strategies to operationalise and expand opportunities for disaggregation. In general, comprehensive and well-chosen social and demographic data helps facilitate disaggregation. In addition, as discussed in Chapter 1, a number of past legal needs surveys have used oversampling and additional samples to improve understanding of marginalised groups.

Finally, dimensions of access to justice can also be dimensions of other social goals, meaning that legal needs-based indicators can further increase understanding of how policies in other sectors can be strengthened to drive progress. The Global Fund to Fight AIDS, Tuberculosis and Malaria, for example, found that "factors such as stigma, discrimination and criminalization drive [particular] populations underground and away from the health services they need."[3] Such health problems require corresponding justice-oriented approaches. Although SDG indicators in Goal 3 track health outcomes, they fail to account for the many ways injustice and health interact. Legal needs surveys could provide a complement by identifying and clarifying the relationship between health priorities and access to justice priorities. Through the introduction of civil justice indicators, policymakers will be able to better understand common legal problems and sources of advice. This will identify sectoral links in particular contexts and enable a more granular understanding of sustainable development across the SDG framework.

Principles for defining access to justice indicators

Access to justice indicators should be directed towards aspects of access to justice for which meaningful change is both a priority and feasible. Priorities should be defined through collaborative processes inclusive of government, civil society and affected communities. It is also important that indicators are sufficiently sensitive to register such progress as is reasonable to expect. This section describes principles for developing legal needs-based civil justice indicators.

Objectives

Indicators ultimately seek to "answer the question of how much, or whether, progress is being made toward a certain objective."[4] Access to justice indicators can be developed through operationalising defined dimensions of access to justice where operationalisation is defined as "the process of converting concepts into their empirical measurements or of quantifying variables for the purpose of measuring their occurrence, strength and frequency" (Sarantakos, 1993, p. 46).

At different levels, civil justice indicators can respond to a multitude of priorities, such as articulating "access to justice as a societal goal, and establishing the relationship between access to justice and poverty reduction; creating incentives to … expand access to justice; producing data and findings that empower reformers to expand access to justice in public institutions and in areas of law and policy in which they possess expertise … and expanding sources of funding for civil legal aid … and courts" (Columbia Law School and the National Center for Access to Justice, 2016, p. 6). They are also tools to provide project level measurements of progress. They can also be used to track impacts, cutting across institutions, organisations and populations (Vera Institute, 2003, p. 3).

"Just outcome" is at the core of the working definition of access to justice described above. Other dimensions generally support this: just law, fairness of process and appropriate support for those facing problems are guarantors and proxies of just outcomes (as well as hallmarks of constitutional integrity and legitimacy, which are the subject of SDG goals beyond SDG 16). Thus, when defining broad indicators, important consideration should be given to establishing the total number of justiciable problems and the problems considered the most important.[5] The next step is to measure key proxies of just outcomes for these problems, including fairness of process and adequacy of different forms of support.

Form

Indicators can be simple or complex and use single or multiple sources of data. The form and nature of access to justice indicators is inevitably determined within a context of limited availability of data and resources. Such constraints were surely a dimension of the IAEG's 2015 decision to define access to justice and rule of law through just two criminal justice themes: pre-trial detention and crime reporting rates (Columbia Law School and the National Center for Access to Justice, 2016, p. 5). These constraints also exist at a national level, where resources and data availability regularly impede contextualised understanding of access to civil justice.

Simple single data source indicators are typically easier to comprehend, define and communicate. They can also offer strong links to specific policies. Two further benefits of using a single data source are transparency and logistical simplicity. However, if goals are complex, then simple indicators can only partially address them.

"Baskets" of indicators, which bring together simple single variable indicators to provide "a combination of supplementary and complementary indicators to reflect … priorities and planning" (Virtual Network for the Development of Indicators on Peaceful, Just and Inclusive Societies for Goal 16, 2015, p. 22), can offer a more holistic and balanced assessment of progress.[6] Multiple indicators can sometimes be combined in a complex single indicator (for example, through an index, such as the Colombian *Index of Effective Access to Justice,* described in the next section).

Multiple indicators can also be used to illuminate stages of a progression. For example, a simple pie-chart might illustrate the proportion of problems (overall, of a defined level of seriousness, of a particular type, etc.) in which people took no action for reasons that are a concern (capability, inaccessibility of support, etc.), took no action for other reasons, obtained inadequate support (overall, of a defined type, etc.) and obtained adequate support (overall, of a defined type, etc.).

As well as providing a fuller picture, the benefits of multiple or complex indicators include the reduced risk of creating "perverse incentives … [that] may be counterproductive to … broader goals" (Virtual Network for the Development of Indicators on Peaceful, Just and Inclusive Societies for Goal 16, 2015, p. 23).

However, the construction of complex indicators is often contested and involves increased logistical complexity, more complicated communication and the dilution of associations with particular policies. Consequently, a balance must be struck in determining the form of indicators.

All indicators must be defined in their scope. In the case of access to civil justice, scope must be defined with reference to, for example, problem type and population group. For example, indicators could relate to a single problem type or to a small or large set of problems, or to the general population or a smaller defined population. As noted above, indicators should reflect priorities and be directed towards aspects of access to justice for which meaningful change is feasible.

Careful consideration must also be given to the denominators used for indicators. For example, an indicator of the volume of appropriate advice that uses a denominator of population size may go down if problems decrease in number, while a similar indicator using problem number as a denominator might be expected to go up in the same circumstances. Evidently, the use of both indicators provides a balance.

Subject matter

Table 4.1 sets out the many dimensions of access to justice suggested in this and previous chapters. Each could be the subject matter of access to justice indicators. Legal needs surveys can provide indicators across a broad range of the dimensions listed. As Table 4.1 suggests, sometimes they can uniquely do so. In other areas their use is less suitable. Indicators from surveys have particular value in providing the perspective of individuals, communities, businesses, etc.; potentially doing so across the wide universe of justiciable problems. Simple indicators that legal needs surveys can provide include:

- the incidence of justiciable problems (of defined types),

- the level of awareness of defined support services,
- the proportion of people acting and failing to act to resolve problems (or failing to act for defined reasons),
- the proportion of people obtaining and failing to obtain defined support (or failing to obtain defined support for defined reasons),
- the proportion of people experiencing defined obstacles to defined support,
- the proportion of problems in respect of which defined support was obtained,
- the proportion of problems in which adequate support was obtained,
- the proportion of problems resolved in a manner (i.e. overall process) perceived as fair,
- the proportion of problem outcomes perceived as fair,
- the cost of problem resolution, and
- the level of perceived accessibility of justice.

Legal needs survey data is thus a valuable complement to administrative and other forms of data that can also provide access to justice indicators, particularly relating to legal support and dispute resolution processes. Where these other data sources are weak, legal needs surveys are often strong. Where legal needs surveys are weak, other data sources are often strong.

Table 4.1. Access to justice dimensions and relevant data sources

Access to justice dimension	Sub-dimension	Typical data sources
Substance of the law	Adherence to international norms	Expert review
	A2J related legislative provision	Expert review
Incidence of justiciable issues / problems	Volume of issues / problems	Legal needs survey data
	Seriousness of issues / problems	Administrative data, legal needs survey data
	Cost (impact) of issues / problems	Administrative data, legal needs survey data
Favourability of the environment (i.e. structural and institutional barriers beyond the justice system)	Remoteness	Geospatial data
	Broadband availability	Administrative data
	General (personal) capability	Administrative data / general survey data
Provision of public legal information	Law / dispute resolution / assistance	Administrative data
Legal capability / legal empowerment	Knowledge of the law	Survey data
	Awareness of sources of help	Survey data
	Awareness of dispute resolution options	Survey data
	Legal confidence / Subjective legal empowerment	Survey data

Legal assistance	Availability of legal assistance	Volume • Number of providers • Range of providers • Level of public funding • Form of public funding • Sustainability of public funding	• Administrative data / Institutional survey data • Administrative data / Institutional survey data / legal needs survey data • Administrative data / Institutional survey data • Administrative data / Institutional survey data • Administrative data / Institutional survey data
		Physical access • Geographical access • Disability access	• Geospatial data • Administrative data / observation data / user and institutional survey data
		Socio-economic access • Actual cost • Affordability • Language • Other	Administrative data / user and institutional survey data / legal needs survey data
		Actual use of legal assistance services • Absolute / caseload • Relative (per justiciable issue)	• Administrative data / user and institutional survey data / legal needs survey data • Legal needs survey data
	Quality / appropriateness of legal assistance	Regulation	Expert review / administrative data
		Quality	File review / administrative data / user survey data
		Satisfaction	Administrative data / user survey data
		Trust / perceptions	General survey data / survey data
		Adequacy / appropriateness • Specific service • Overall	• Administrative data / user survey data • Legal needs survey data
Process	Availability of formal / informal institutions of justice	Volume of provision • Number of courts, etc. • Rage of institutions • Level of public funding	• Administrative data / institutional survey data • Administrative data / institutional survey data / legal needs survey data • Administrative data / institutional survey data
		Physical access • Geographical access • Disability access	• Geospatial data • Administrative data / observation data / user and institutional survey data
		Socio-economic access • Actual cost • Affordability • Language • Other	• Administrative data / user and institutional survey data / legal needs survey data • Administrative data / user and institutional survey data / legal needs survey data • User survey data • Administrative data / user and institutional survey data
		Actual use of institutions • Absolute / caseload • Relative (per justiciable issue)	• Administrative data / user and institutional survey data / legal needs survey data • Legal needs survey data

	Quality of formal/informal institutions of justice	Quality of procedure • Procedural justice / fairness • Interpersonal justice • Informational justice	Expert review / file review / observation data / user survey data
		Quality of decisions • Distributive justice • Restorative justice • Functionality • Transparency	Expert review / file review / user survey data
		Satisfaction	User survey data
		Trust / perceptions	Survey data
		Adequacy / appropriateness • Specific service • Overall	 • User survey data • Survey data
	Overall process quality	Quality of procedure • Procedural justice / fairness • Interpersonal justice • Informational justice	Legal needs survey data
	Overall process cost (to individuals)	• Actual cost • Affordability	Legal needs survey data Legal needs survey data
Overall outcome quality		Timeliness	Legal needs survey data
		Compliance / enforcement • Specific service • Overall	 • Administrative data / user survey data • Legal needs survey data
		Other aspects of quality • Distributive justice • Restorative justice • Functionality	Case reviews / legal needs survey data
		Perceptions	Legal needs survey data
Cost of access to justice		Monetary cost • Actual cost • Affordability	Legal needs survey data
		Opportunity cost	Legal needs survey data
		Stress and emotions	Legal needs survey data
Inclusivity		Socio-economic disaggregation	Administrative data / legal needs survey data

Process

The process by which access to justice indicators are developed has a significant impact on their utility. Indicators are effective when they are developed through and support an inclusive and deliberative process.

Defining and contextualising people's legal problems and the possible means for resolving them is a challenge. Meaningful engagement with frontline service providers, community groups and wider stakeholders in the delivery of justice equips them with a deeper understanding of the measurement process, which, in turn, is likely to generate trust and encourage those organisations to act on findings.

Access to justice, in particular, implicates a wide range of government agencies and civil society organisations in measurement. Each agency or organisation can play a role in interpreting findings and driving programmatic and policy reform. Governments, civil society organisations and others have worked together to define indicators, generate data and debate progress. Developing access to justice indicators through legal needs surveys should build on these experiences.

Using legal needs-based access to justice indicators

Increasingly legal needs surveys are used to inform national priorities and track progress. In recent years, debates around the SDG framework have provided new opportunities for policymakers to link access to justice with broader developmental themes. This section will summarise how legal needs-based indicators can contribute to a more informed and ultimately more effective policy environment for access to justice.

National and thematic indicators

Legal needs surveys have historically been used as a tool to provide a strategic evidence base for access to justice policy decisions. Surveys are increasingly being used to provide indicators that complement and supplement those derived from administrative or other sources of data. Given the breadth of information gathered through legal needs surveys, national policymakers are able to develop contextually specific and operational indicators for policy reform.

In addition to the three surveys which operationalised the concepts of legal need and unmet legal need (detailed in Chapter 2), two additional surveys have been used to provide access to justice indicators for development and strategic planning purposes.

The *English and Welsh Civil and Social Justice Survey* was originally commissioned, in 2001, to provide indicators to monitor progress against two government departmental Public Service Agreement (PSA) targets concerning access to justice (within the context of the 2000 Spending Review) (HM Treasury, 2000; Legal Services Research Centre, 2003). The first target, to increase the number of people who receive suitable assistance in priority areas of law involving fundamental rights or social exclusion[7] was a simple legal need related target. The indicator was calculated by dividing the number of priority area justiciable problems that had been resolved and for which suitable assistance was received – defined as including problems that were in a priority area of law, that had concluded and about which assistance had been successfully obtained from a lawyer, solicitor, law centre, trade union, professional body, Citizen's Advice Bureau, another advice agency, local authority advice service and/or other public authority – by the total number of survey respondents. This target was later replaced by a proportional target, in which the denominator was replaced by the total number of resolved justiciable problems in priority areas. Further "explanatory" indicators also took account of "the degree of helpfulness or satisfaction with advice" (Legal Services Research Centre, 2003, p. 12).

The second target – to reduce the proportion of disputes which are resolved by resorting to the courts – was associated with a departmental objective to improve people's knowledge and understanding of their rights and responsibilities, including how to resolve disputes that affect them. Policymakers sought to understand how resolution could be conducted in a way and at a cost proportionate to the issue at stake. This indicator was associated with an objective to make civil and family law clearer and more easily enforceable, giving priority to key government objectives in tackling social and economic issues.

The legal needs module incorporated into the 2016 Colombian *Quality of Life Survey* contributed 9 of the 13 exclusively survey-based indicators making up the *Index of Effective Access to Justice*, along with the denominator for a tenth indicator. One of the nine indicators concerned legal capability (the proportion of respondents who did nothing to resolve justiciable problems because they did not know what to do or where to obtain assistance). One concerned access to legal assistance and was similar in form to the first English and Welsh indicator (proportion of problems about which respondents obtained assistance from a legal professional). Two concerned access to justice institutions (the proportion of respondents who did nothing to resolve justiciable problems because of cost, time or procedural complexity; the proportion of respondents using justice institutions who reported problems ending through a decision or agreement). Two concerned procedural fairness (the proportion of respondents with needs still pending because of poor-quality dispute resolution provision; the proportion of respondents using justice institutions that reported they would use them again). Three concerned compliance (the proportion of problems concluded by complying with a decision or agreement following the use of a justice institution; the proportion of problems taken to justice institutions that were "resolved"; the difference in the experience of men and women as regards the previous indicator).

While the *Index of Effective Access to Justice* demonstrates the breadth of access to justice indicators that legal needs surveys can contribute to, their potential is greater still. The short- and longer-form legal needs surveys set out in the previous Chapter and in Annex B include questions relevant to 37 of the 54 secondary dimensions of access to justice listed in Table 4.1.

Global indicators

The SDGs provide a new forum for access to justice advocates to define critical global dimensions of access to justice. The omission of civil justice in the two official SDG 16.3 indicators spurred new debate around how to understand and track progress towards access to justice at a global level. In 2017, members of IAEG and the United Nations Statistical Commission formally acknowledged that two criminal justice indicators were insufficient to measure the breadth of SDG 16.3, which relates to the rule of law and access to justice for all. To address this limitation, the IAEG recommended the addition of a global indicator focused on "access to civil justice" into the global SDG framework.[8] Over the course of 2019, the IAEG is expected to consult on a specific global indicator to measure "access to civil justice".

The push for inclusion of "access to civil justice" builds on the knowledge that the majority of justiciable problems are not dealt with by courts or tribunals. Administrative data relating to courts and other justice institutions says little about the extent to which needs are met and justice is achieved across problems as a whole. As people obtain assistance with problems from many places, administrative data relating to assistance is fragmented and can, at best, only talk to the minority of problems for which assistance is obtained.

For all of the reasons explored in this document, legal needs surveys represent an important tool for understanding global progress towards access to justice. They present a picture of progress impossible to obtain from other data sources, and can provide indicators that uniquely extend to people's full experience of justiciable problems. Thus, legal needs surveys can complement existing global indicators reliant on administrative and victimisation survey data, to help provide a more comprehensive global picture of access to justice.

In addition to advancing progress towards 16.3, a legal needs-based indicator focused on access to civil justice would also present a valuable complement to other SDGs. As described in Chapter 1, common legal needs across countries connect to SDG priority areas, including: land, property and housing (Goal 1: End Poverty, Goal 15: Life on Land), employment (Goal 8: Decent Work), health (Goal 3: Ensure healthy lives), family issues (Goal 5: Achieve gender equality, Goal 8: Decent Work), social protection (Goal 1: End Poverty) and economic and consumer issues (Goal 10: Reduce inequality). By including a legal needs-based indicator, policy makers will be able to better understand the ways in which justice systems interact with developmental priorities and, therefore, devise more multidimensional strategies.

The specific formulation of a *single*, *global* legal needs-based indicator will be challenging. For all the reasons discussed in this document, access to civil justice is most strategically understood and measured through multidimensional assessments. Nonetheless, in the years leading up to the adoption of the initial SDG indicator framework, a Virtual Network for the Development of Indicators on Peaceful, Just and Inclusive Societies for Goal 16 recommended a civil justice 16.3 indicator in the initial consultation process. This proposed indicator – "the proportion of those who have experienced a dispute in the past 12 months who have accessed a formal, informal, alternative or traditional dispute resolution mechanism and who feel it was just" – includes important elements for a headline global civil justice indicator. However, its reference to formal, informal, alternative or traditional dispute resolution mechanisms is unwieldy and restrictive (considering the very many paths to justice people take and the difficulties, detailed in Chapter 2, in defining dispute resolution processes in a way appropriate across all jurisdictions). Additionally, it gives insufficient attention to whether people have access to assistance, which may be an important component of challenging power asymmetries. Moreover, as suggested in Chapter 3, perceptions of process fairness may be a better choice of proxy for outcome quality than perceptions of outcomes themselves, not least as many processes can be addressed through policy.

Thus, a simple reformulation of this proposed headline civil justice indicator developed from legal needs surveys could be:

> *The proportion of disputes experienced in the past 24 months resolved through a process considered fair by the disputants.*

This construction would provide policymakers with an overall snapshot of civil justice in a particular country. It might not, however, be particularly well suited to advance innovations in the ways in which countries deliver access to justice. General experiences of dispute resolution do not necessarily tell policymakers whether justice institutions are advancing core goals. Moreover, people's assessment of fairness of process could depend significantly on expectations, which may vary greatly between populations and perhaps conspire against a transformative vision of access to justice.

A more meaningful and operational global indicator would endeavour to capture the adequacy of support, particularly for specific marginalised groups who need assistance in understanding, using and shaping the law. An alternative indicator focused on adequacy of support could be:

The proportion of disputes experienced in the past 24 months resolved through a fair process where the disputants received adequate support.

Drawing on the logic tree for proxy measurement of legal need and unmet legal need set out in Chapter 2. , adequate support could be defined broadly (e.g. from defined sources: column 6 of Figure 2.1) or narrowly (e.g. from defined sources and considered adequate by recipients: columns 6 and 7), and could also refer to problem seriousness (columns 1 and 2) and legal capability (columns 3 and 4). However, the addition of each additional aspect of measurement increases the complexity and ultimately the cost of an indicator. If all the above aspects of measurement are included, the resulting indicator would be more appropriately framed as a compound and multidimensional indicator:

The proportion of non-trivial disputes experienced in the past 24 months resolved through a fair process and in respect of which the disputants received adequate support to make informed decisions and pursue a fair outcome.

The components and illustrative questionnaire questions that could be used to construct this indicator are set out in Table 4.2.

Table 4.2. Compound indicator dimensions & corresponding questionnaire numbers

Access to Justice Dimension	Sub-dimension	Illustrative questionnaire question number	Example coding
Incidence	Volume of issues / problems	Q1 – Problem identification / category Q11 – Whether problem is concluded	Problems included if in scope and concluded.
	Seriousness of issues / problems	Q3 – Problem seriousness	Problems included if seriousness exceeds defined threshold
Legal capability	Legal awareness / understanding	Q18a – Understanding of legal rights	Assistance required if legal rights not understood
	Legal confidence	Q18d – Confidence in ability to achieve fair outcome	Assistance required if no confidence
Legal assistance	Actual use of legal assistance services	Q6 – Sources of information, advice or representation	Assistance obtained if help obtained from specified sources
	Adequacy of legal assistance services (overall)	Q18c – Adequacy of help	Assistance adequate if all help needed was obtained
Process	Procedural justice / fairness	Q14 – Process fairness	Process fair if 'fair to everybody concerned'
Outcome	Timeliness	Q22 – Problem start date Q23 – Problem end date	Timely outcome if problem duration less than defined threshold

Other factors, such as cost, could also be incorporated into such an indicator.

As described in Chapter 1. , inequality in access to civil justice exacerbates disadvantage and disproportionally affects marginalised groups. Thus, as noted above and as with other SDG indicators, global access to civil justice indicators need to be capable of disaggregation in order to highlight the experience of different groups, on the basis of income, gender, age, ethnicity, geographic differences, among others. The SDG framework includes a specific target on building capacity for specific forms of disaggregation:

> *By 2020, enhance capacity-building support to developing countries ... to increase significantly the availability of high-quality, timely and reliable data disaggregated by income, gender, age, race, ethnicity, migratory status, disability, geographic location and other characteristics relevant in national contexts*[9]

In practice, SDG indicators have taken two approaches to meeting this requirement: For some themes, SDG indicators specifically state what level of disaggregation is required in the indicator itself. For example, SDG indicator 1.4.2 on land tenure security calls for disaggregation by gender ("the proportion of total adult population with secure tenure rights to land, with legally recognised documentation and who perceive their rights to land as secure, by sex and by type of tenure"). Indicator 2.3.2 on productivity of small holders calls for disaggregation by both gender and indigenous status ("Average income of small-scale food producers, by sex and indigenous status").[10]

Other SDG indicators adopt a broad approach and do not include specific reference to particular populations in the indicator. These indicators instead rely on the SDG framework's commitment to disaggregation across population groups.[11]

In constructing a global indicator for access to civil justice, policymakers should consider whether the global indicator ought to be constructed to specifically explore the experiences of marginalised groups or pursue disaggregation across those domains articulated by the IAEG. For example, a disaggregation-specific indicator could be framed as "the proportion of A, B or C disputes experienced by X, Y or Z population in the past 24 months resolved through a process considered fair by the disputants where the disputants received adequate support." While this would ensure headline data highlighted the experiences of particular groups, there could be a risk that it ignores groups relevant in particular national or subnational contexts or fails to highlight emerging inequalities of experience. Despite these questions of scope, legal needs-based indicators nonetheless offer the potential for holistic measures of access to civil justice not capable of being generated by other sources.

Because of low levels of legal literacy, the greatest challenge to the economy of a legal needs survey is efficiency in defining the range and establishing the incidence of justiciable problems within a survey's scope. This was discussed in Chapter 2. A "relatively straightforward" line of questioning in the context of indicators of access to health care is "direct questioning of individuals as to whether there was a time when they needed health care but did not receive it" (Allin and Masseria, 2012, p. 114). For example, the model question for "unmet need for medical examination or treatment" that appears in the *EU Income and Living Conditions Survey* asks, "Was there any time during the past 12 months when you really needed medical examination or treatment (excluding dental) for yourself?"[12] If the response is positive, the following question is asked: "Did you have a medical examination or treatment each time you really needed?" Such an approach might be trialled in the legal domain, with people asked whether they were unable to secure needed advice or assistance concerning a dispute (with some examples of dispute types provided to indicate scope[13]). However, for the reasons discussed in Chapter 2, the lack of specificity is likely to be problematic, unless the question follows on from the identification of specific types of problems. Further experimental investigation into the impact of different approaches to justiciable problem identification/definition would be of great value. Beyond problem identification, further Table 4.1 prioritisation will also often be necessary.

Limits of legal needs surveys revisited

As described in Chapter 1, while legal needs surveys provide a unique insight into the experience of justiciable problems across populations, they have their limitations, as do all surveys. General population legal needs surveys are excellent for establishing levels of justiciable problem experience, levels of legal need, and the relative use of legal services and processes. However, without large sample sizes, they are limited in what they tell us about the experience of particular populations, as is important in the context of SDG indicators. As explored in Chapter 2, oversampling or additional surveys are often necessary to enable the experience of particular populations to be reliably compared to that of the general population.

General population legal needs surveys are also ill-suited to capturing details of the experience of formal processes, particular legal services and rarer problem types. Again, without large sample sizes, their utility is limited. General population surveys are inherently inefficient at capturing data concerning phenomena experienced by a relatively small proportion of the population. Thus, the great ability of general population legal needs surveys to expose the peripheral nature of justice institutions to most disputes also points to their weakness. If detailed information about particular legal institutions is required, it is usually better sourced from user surveys or, if technical or beyond the purview of users (as discussed in Chapter 2), from administrative data.

Evidently, the measurement of different dimensions of access to justice, and capture of different perspectives, requires the use of diverse data sources. As illustrated in Table 4.1 – which sets out the data sources most appropriate to investigating each of the broad range of dimensions of access to justice suggested in the text above – some aspects of access to justice are best measured using administrative data, geospatial data, expert review and user surveys. However, when it comes to problem incidence (a common denominator for indicators), legal capability, legal need, problem resolving behaviour, adequacy of support and overall processes fairness, it is best to use legal needs survey methodologies to get the big picture.

Moreover, the combination of measures from different data sources can yield the most valuable insights. For example, the limited knowledge of lay individuals means they are unable to provide much insight into the technical aspects of access to justice, such as the location or availability of legal assistance services. If people are unaware they live in close proximity to a legal aid office, or are unaware of or mistakenly believe they are ineligible for legal aid, then they cannot attest to its availability. In this case, geospatial data, administrative data or expert review of legal aid eligibility would be better sources of information. But the combination of measures of population awareness and availability/eligibility may be most telling for policymakers, highlighting the disconnection between provision and uptake.

An example of the above approach is the Colombian *Index of Effective Access to Justice.* Of the 24 indicators used, 13 rely exclusively on survey data, nine of which use legal needs data, nine administrative data and two geospatial data.[14] One uses both administrative and survey data, as numerator and denominator respectively. And elsewhere, the *Justice Index*[15] and *Rule of Law Index*[16] utilise expert review – typically a specialised form of survey of expert stakeholders in the justice system to gauge, for example, the nature of procedural rules and the presence or absence of best practices for ensuring access to justice.

The path ahead

Many jurisdictions in which legal need surveys have been used have undergone a paradigm shift in the orientation of justice policy. Legal needs surveys have contributed to a shift away from an institutional to an individual and collective perspective, because they show that disputes occur and are resolved mostly outside the purview of both courts and lawyers. Legal needs surveys are unique in their ability to give an overview of civil justice, providing overarching, individually focussed, system-wide indicators, and exposing the reach of support services and institutions. New comparative datasets like the World Justice Project and HiiL will provide policymakers with new opportunities to experiment with different indicator formulations. However, legal needs surveys are not ideally suited to monitoring details of specific service provision and formal dispute resolution processes. Such complementary data can be gathered from other sources. In the access to justice field, there are many options to draw from when it comes to defining both headline indicators and the combination of supplementary and complementary indicators in order to complete a comprehensive and balanced picture. The inclusion of an access to civil justice indicator using legal needs survey methodologies would prove a tremendous asset to the current SDG global indicator framework. This global headline indicator should supplement and catalyse national level operationalisation of legal needs indicators.

Notes

[1] Sustainable Development Goals contains target 16.3 http://www.un.org/en/development/desa/what-we-do/rule-of-law.html.

[2] UN Resolution 70/1, adopted by the General Assembly on 25th September 2015 paragraph 74(g).

[3] https://www.theglobalfund.org/en/key-populations.

[4] Handbook of Democracy and Governance Program Indicators (Washington, DC: U.S. Agency for International Development, 1998), referenced by Vera Institute (2003, p. 2), available at https://www.vera.org/publications/measuring-progress-toward-safety-and-justice-a-global-guide-to-the-design-of-performance-indicators-across-the-justice-sector.

[5] Barendrecht et al. (2008) and Pleasence et al. (2009) discuss various methods that can be used to establish the most urgent types of justiciable problem.

[6] The Virtual Network for the Development of Indicators on Peaceful, Just and Inclusive Societies for Goal 16 defined complementary indicators as "those that are necessary to complete measurement of a complex concept," and supplementary indicators as those that "round out" measurement, to allow countries to "adapt the universal goals to their own contexts and identify other dimensions of the target that are important to them" (Virtual Network for the Development of Indicators on Peaceful, Just and Inclusive Societies for Goal 16 2015, p. 22).

[7] The original target called for a 5% increase by 2004.

[8] Access to civil justice is detailed as a "possible additional indicator to address" in Annex V of the *Report of the Inter-agency and Expert Group on Sustainable Development Goal Indicators,* 7-10 March 2017.

[9] Target 17.18.

[10] See https://unstats.un.org/sdgs/indicators/indicators-list/.

[11] Interagency and Expert Group Working Group on Data Disaggregation, https://unstats.un.org/sdgs/files/meetings/iaeg-sdgs-meeting-06/20170607_updated%20version-overview%20of%20standards%20of%20data%20disaggregation.pdf.

[12] Methodological guidelines and description of EU-SILC primary target variables in the health domain are set out at http://ec.europa.eu/eurostat/documents/1012329/8655367/PERSONAL+DATA_Health.pdf/0a942278-dd03-47f6-9af6-3f3000f678ce.

[13] The approach of indicating disputant types, employed in the disputes module of the 2017-2018 pilot of the dispute module of the South African *Governance, Public Safety and Justice Survey*, would seem to most naturally fit the form of this question.

[14] Ibid.

[15] http://justiceindex.org/methodology.

[16] See World Justice Project (2018).

References

Allin, S. and C. Masseria (2012) "Measuring access to health care in Europe", in A. McGuire and J. Costa-Font (eds.), *The LSE Companion to Health Policy*, Edward Elgar, Cheltenham.

Barendrecht, M., M. Gramatikov, I. Giesen, M. Laxminarayan, P. Kamminga, L. Klaming, J.H. Verdonschot and C. van Zeeland (2010), *Measuring Access to Justice in a Globalising World,* HiiL, The Hague.

Barendrecht, M., Y.P. Kamminga and J.H. Verdonschot (2008), "Priorities for the justice system: Responding to the most urgent legal problems of individuals", TILEC Discussion Paper No. 2008/011, TISCO Working Paper No. 001/2008), Tilburg University Faculty of Law, Tilburg.

Columbia Law School and the National Center for Access to Justice (2016), *Recommended Access to Justice Indicators for Implementation of Goal 16 of the UN 2030 Sustainable Development Agenda in the United States*, Columbia Law School Human Rights Institute and the National Center for Access to Justice, Fordham University, New York.

Her Majesty's Treasury (2000), *2000 Spending Review: Public Service Agreements*, HMSO, Norwich.

Legal Services Research Centre (2003), *Baseline Measures for the Lord Chancellor's Department's PSA Targets 3 and 6*, Legal Services Research Centre, London.

Pleasence, P., N.J. Balmer, T. Tam (2009), "Failure to recall," in R.L. Sandefur (ed.), *Access to Justice,* Emerald, Bingley.

Sarantakos, S. (1993), *Social Research*, Macmillan, Basingstoke.

Vera Institute (2003), *Measuring Progress Toward Safety and Justice*, Vera Institute, New York.

Virtual Network for the Development of Indicators on Peaceful, Just and Inclusive Societies for Goal 16 (2015), *The Indicators We Want*, Federal Ministry for Economic Development and Development, Berlin and United Nations Development Programme.

World Justice Project (2018), *World Justice Project Rule of Law Index 2017*, World Justice Project, Washington, DC.

Yuthayotin, S. (2015), Access to Justice in Transnational B2C E-Commerce, Springer, Cham.

Annex A. Annotated Model Core Legal Needs Survey Questions

Figure A.1. Model problem identification question

An open question is ill suited to problem identification, and separate lists (often presented on show-cards) for different problem categories are too time consuming. Here, a single list of problem categories is presented, with examples provided to improve clarity.

References to 'legal' problems should be avoided. Here, problems are contextualised as 'everyday' to improve the reporting rate.

'Problems and disputes' has been the most common terminology used to date.

A dichotomous question presents the simplest task for respondents, promoting reliability. If necessary, the number of problems experienced can be ascertained through immediate follow-up.

I am going to read you a list of problems and disputes that people commonly experience in everyday life. In each case, can you tell me whether you have personally experienced such a problem in the past two years; by which I mean a problem that started since [DATE] or started before then, but continued afterwards.

(Please only include problems that you have had yourself, not problems experienced by a business you run, in the course of self-employment or by an employer, and not situations where you represented or helped somebody else with their problem. And please only mention problems once)

Clarity on which problems to report is essential. Here, it is made clear that all problems existing within the reference period should be included, regardless of when they started.

Business related problems can be a significant aspect of the lives of the self-employed. This is particularly relevant in low income countries. However, they are conceptually (and often legally) distinct from personal problems, so should ideally be asked about separately. Approaches to doing so are detailed in Section 3.

Data accuracy is promoted by explicit reference to causes of reporting errors known to present a particular risk.

This is to prevent double counting.

Surveying individuals, rather than households, etc., promotes data accuracy.

A 2-year reference period provides a balance between maximising problems reported and enabling contemporaneous monitoring.

Figure A.2. Model problem seriousness question

Emphasis is placed on the words 'as a whole', to indicate that the circumstances and impact of a problem should be considered.

Thinking about the problem as a whole, consider a scale of 0 to 10, where 1 represents the least serious type of problem you could face and 10 represents the most serious.

To provide some examples, a score of 8 might be [ANCHOR 1] and a score of 2 might be [ANCHOR 2].

What number best represents the seriousness of your problem?

The two anchors should comprise an example of a very serious and relatively trivial problem. The examples need not be justiciable problems. Anchors must be appropriate for the population surveyed.

Figure A.3. Model problem impact question

> Use of this phrasing removes ambiguity around whether impact that constitutes an element of a problem should, or should not, be included.

Did you experience any of the following as part of or as a result of this problem?

a) ill-health or injury

b) high levels of stress

c) damage to a family relationship

d) being harassed, threatened or assaulted

e) damage to your property

f) loss of employment

g) having to move home

h) financial loss

i) fear or loss of confidence

> Financial loss is included in preference to loss of income, which is narrower.

> As loss of employment/moving home do not equate to becoming unemployed/becoming homeless, some surveys have separately asked about the latter.

Figure A.4. Model media information question

Inclusion of information sought on behalf of respondents allows a more comprehensive assessment of help seeking behaviour.

'Information' is the term that has been used to define the scope of questions of this type. More tailored Internet or app based help will be captured, though not detailed.

Use of the term 'obtain' limits scope to information seeking that is (at least partially) successful.

References to 'legal' information, advice, etc., should be avoided; as respondents may not recognise legal dimensions of help received.

Did you, or somebody acting on your behalf, obtain information from any of the following sources, to help you better understand, resolve or prepare to resolve [the problem]?

a) A website or 'app'

b) A leaflet, book or self-help guide

c) Newspapers or magazines

d) Television, video or radio

Items (a) to (d) include all modes of mass communication asked about in surveys to date. In the future, the items may need to be updated to accommodate technological change.

'To help you better understand, resolve or prepare to resolve' is broader than commonly used phrases such as 'to try to resolve'. It more clearly includes preliminary information and help seeking directed towards, for example, understanding the nature of a problem or dispute resolution options.

Figure A.5. Model sources of help question

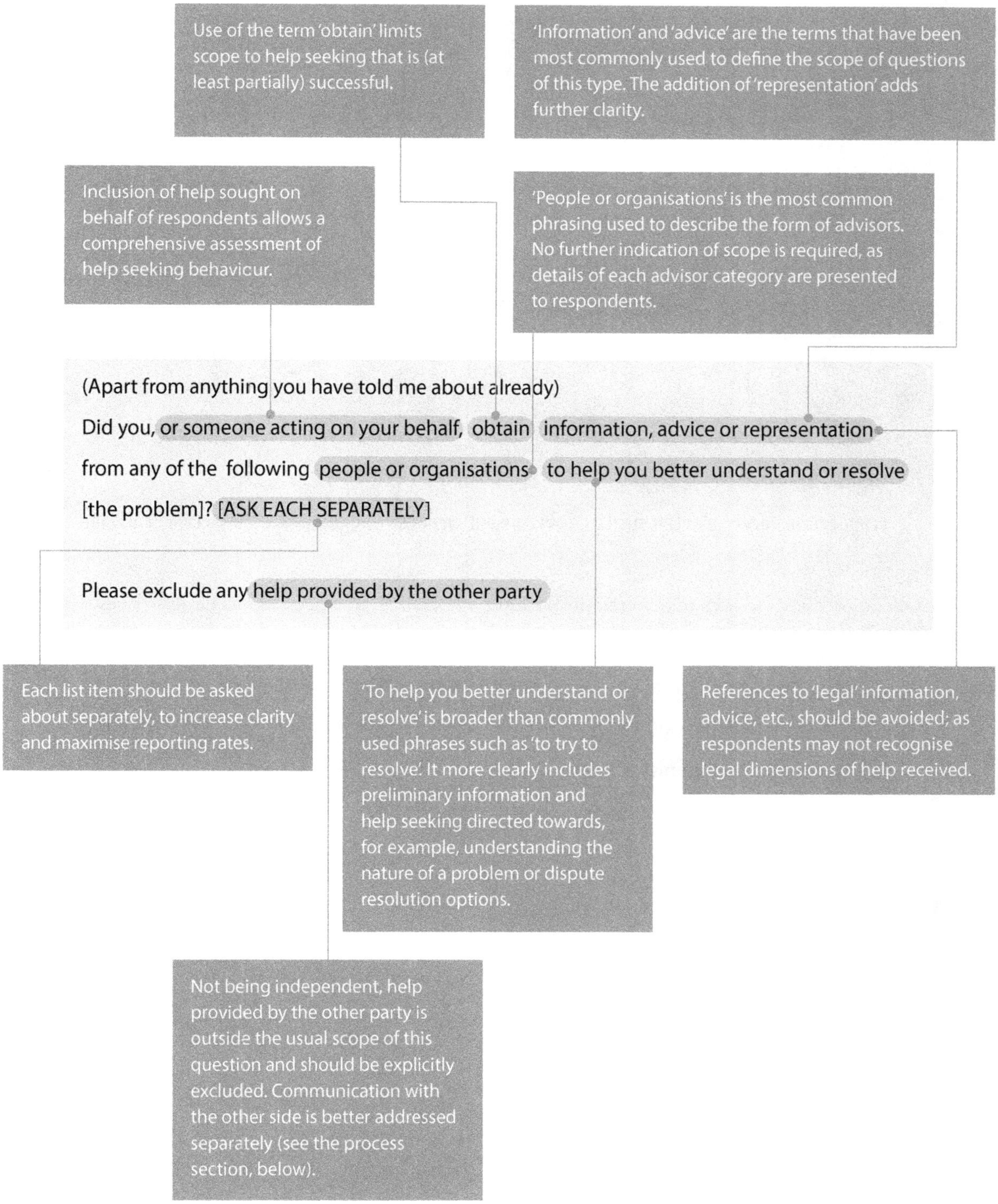

Figure A.6. Model list of sources of help

This first category is designed to capture only non-expert informal help from family, friends and acquaintances. It therefore excludes help from those whose job involves providing advice on relevant issues. Their help should be recorded within the other categories.

Providing examples in relation to sources described using relatively technical language should assist clarity and recall.

a) Family, friends or acquaintances (excluding people whose job is to advise on problems such as these; please mention these people in their professional capacity)
b) A lawyer, professional advisor, advice service or advice helpline; such as [examples] (specify)
c) A court [or tribunal] or other dispute resolution organisation (such as [examples]) or the police (specify)
d) A national, regional or municipal government department, agency, council or a politician (specify)
e) Your employer, a trade union or professional association, or a trade association (such as [examples]) (specify)
f) A health, welfare, financial services or other professional (specify)
g) A community or religious leader or organisation, an [civil society organisation/ charity], or trusted person or organisation (specify)
h) Any other person or organisation

Include if appropriate

The most appropriate term to describe the non-government, non-commercial sector should be used.

Box A.1. Model process question

(Apart from anything you have told me about already) Did any of the following things happen as part of [the problem] or sorting it out? When I say ""you"" here, I mean you or somebody acting on your behalf.

a) You communicated with the other party.

b) You or the other party made a claim to, or made use of, a court (or tribunal).

c) [If applicable] You or the other party made a claim to, or made use of, an [Indigenous/ customary] dispute resolution process (e.g. [examples]).

d) [The problem] was reported to the police (or other prosecution authority).

e) You or the other party turned to, or action was taken by, a formal designated authority. or agency, such as [examples, e.g. Ombudsman, regulator (e.g. [example]) or enforcement authority (e.g. consumer protection authority)].

f) You or the other party turned to, or action was taken by, another state authority (e.g. [examples]).

g) You or the other party turned to, or action was taken by, a religious authority.

h) You or the other party turned to, or action was taken by, a community leader or organisation (e.g. [example]).

i) You participated in formal mediation, conciliation or arbitration (e.g. [examples]).

j) You or the other party made use of a formal appeals process operated by the other party or independently.

k) You, the other party or somebody else turned to, or action was taken by, another third party for adjudication, mediation or intervention.

l) There was no negotiation or third party involvement.

[For each positive response from a to k]

Who initiated this action?

[If the respondent did not initiate processes b to h or j and k]

Did you respond to this action?

Figure A.7. Model residual activity question

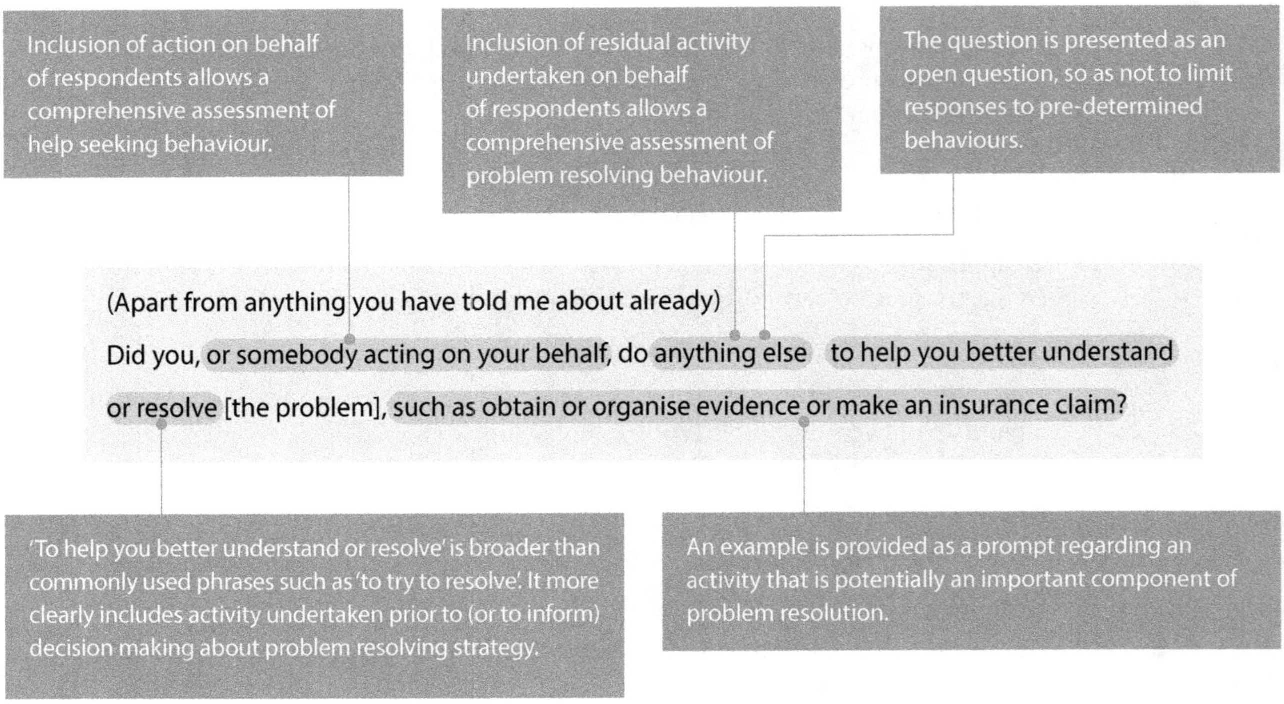

Figure A.8. Model fact of outcome question

The phrase 'done with' is preferred to other previously used wording – notably 'over or resolved' – as it suggests no change in the future, rather than non-existence.

As 'done with' is intended to encompass two distinct forms of problem conclusion (problems being completely resolved *and* the resolution of persisting problems being abandoned by all parties), its definition must be made explicit.

Is [the problem] ongoing or done with? By 'done with' I mean that the problem is either completely resolved or that it persists, but you and everybody else have permanently given up all efforts to resolve it further. [PROBE FULLY]

a) Ongoing

b) Too early to say

c) Done with, but problem persists

d) Done with, problem fully resolved

There may be a period of time in which it is unclear whether a problem has been resolved, or all attempts to resolve it have been abandoned. Thus, a response option reflecting this uncertainty is necessary.

Given the centrality and complexity of this question, particular effort should be made to ensure accuracy.

The definition of 'done with' is the most important element of the question, so should not be shortened or removed in the interest of survey efficiency. It is important, for example, that it refers to the intentions of both the respondent and the other party.

Figure A.9. Model manner of outcome question

The question is presented in a closed form, as the data sought is particular and the question, if open, is quite broad.

Being concerned with manner of outcome, the question emphasises that the correct response should reflect how the outcome was 'ultimately' brought about.

Which of the following statements best reflects how the problem outcome was ultimately brought about?

The problem outcome was ultimately brought about by …

a) … a court (or tribunal) judgment

b) … a decision or intervention by another formal authority

c) … mediation, conciliation or arbitration

d) … action by another third party

e) … agreement between you and the other party

f) … the other party independently doing what you wanted

g) … you independently doing what the other party wanted

h) … you moving away from the problem (e.g. moving home, changing job)

i) … the problem sorting itself out

j) … you and/or all other parties giving up trying to resolve the problem

As problem conclusion can involve problems persisting, but the parties giving up on their resolution, this must be reflected in the manner of outcome categories.

Figure A.10. Model reasons for not obtaining help question

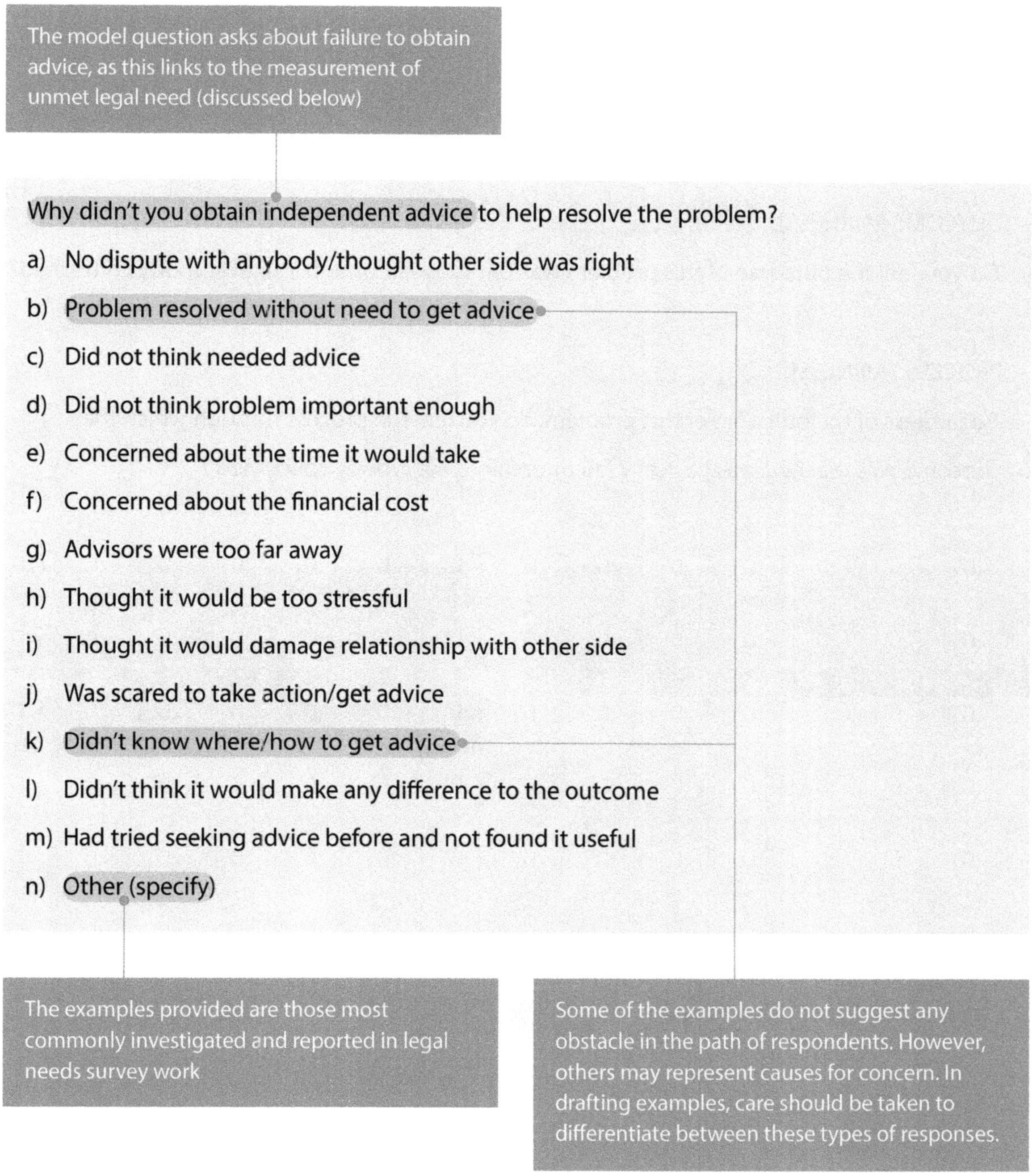

Figure A.11. Model process and outcome fairness questions

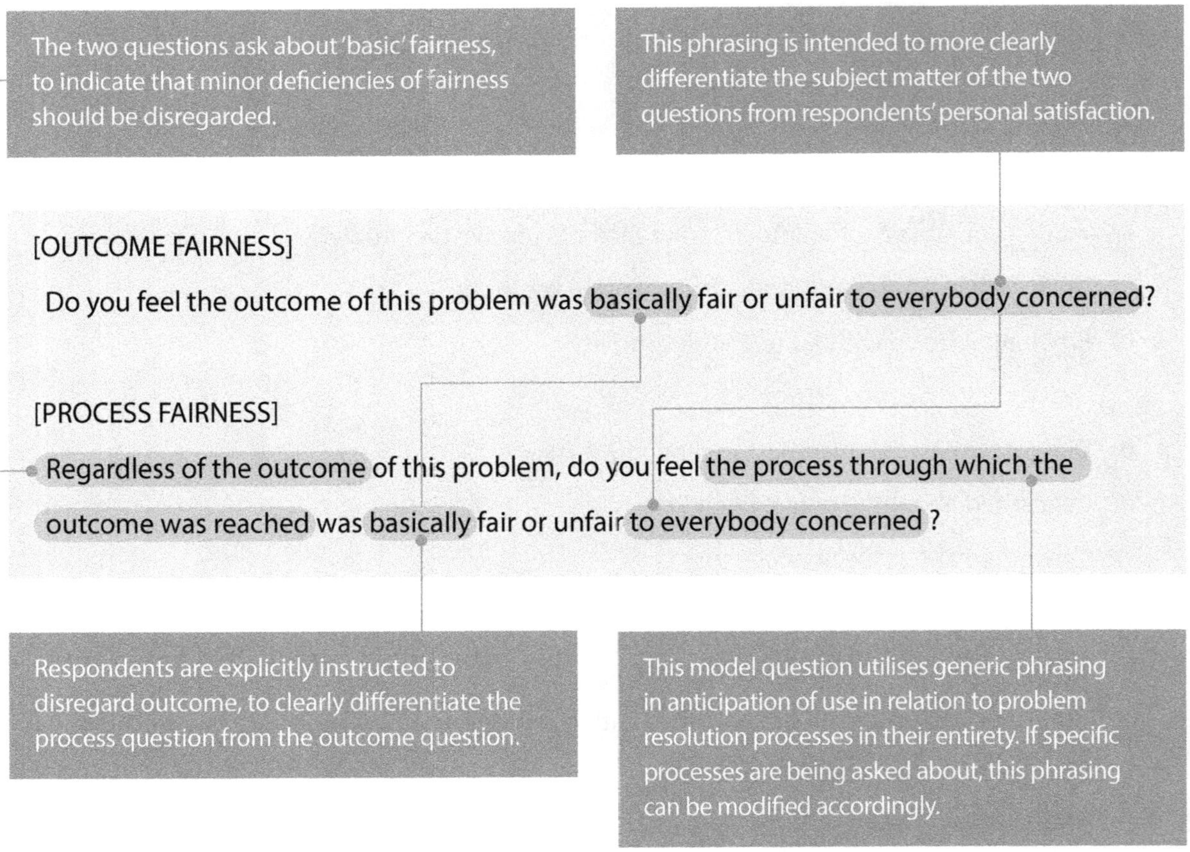

Figure A.12. Model problem resolution cost question

To remove ambiguity, it is necessary to specify whether or not indirect forms of payment are included in the scope of this question.

To remove ambiguity, costs explicitly include those borne by respondents' family and friendship groups; being distinct from forms of third party financial support.

While not constituting a definition of indirect payments, insurance premiums and membership subscriptions are the most common pooled resources from which indirect payments may be made.

Excluding indirect payments, such as insurance premiums or membership subscriptions, but including payments made by family members and friends

Did you, personally, have to pay for any of the following in order to resolve the problem :

(a) Lawyer and other advisor fees

(b) Court, mediation or other administrative fees

(c) Telephone calls and correspondence

(d) Collecting information or obtaining evidence (incl. reimbursement of witnesses' costs)

(e) Travel (e.g. bus fares or petrol to visit an advisor)

(f) Lost business or salary, from taking time off work (e.g. to obtain advice)

(g) Bribes / kick-backs (Remember, your answer is confidential)

(h) Incidental domestic costs (e.g. childcare)

Although in tension with the inclusion of payments by family and friends, the word 'personally' emphasises that the question concerns costs met, rather than the full cost of services.

The use of an example reminds respondents that the questions concerns the costs of problem resolution, not of problems themselves.

Listing cost elements clarifies the scope of the question and assists recall.

This clarifies the question concerns problem resolution, not problem impact.

Following the practice in HiiL's *Justice Needs and Satisfaction Surveys*, respondents concerns about reporting bribes can be allayed by reiterating that responses are confidential.

Figure A.13. Model legal capability questions (identified problem)

> By mixing the 'legal' response category with other potential descriptions, the question avoids leading respondents.

> Allowing more than one response avoids the risk of legal characterisation going unreported because it is not the dominant characterisation. Multiple responses also provide insight into broader perceptions of problems.

Which of the following describe the problem? You can choose more than one option, or none.

a) Bad luck / part of life
b) Bureaucratic
c) A family or private matter
d) Legal
e) Political
f) A social or community matter
g) Economic
h) None of these

To what extent do you agree or disagree with the following statements about the problem?

a) I understood or came to understand my legal rights and responsibilities.
b) I knew where to get good information and advice about resolving the problem.
c) I was able to get all the expert help I needed.
d) I was confident I could achieve a fair outcome.

> These items relate to the three aspects of legal capability: awareness of legal rights and responsibilities, awareness of services and legal confidence.

> This phrasing captures instances in which respondents come to their understanding as problems progress.

> A common stem is used for speed. and efficiency.

Annex B. Illustrative Longer-Form Legal Needs Survey Questionnaire

This annex sets out an illustrative longer-form legal needs survey questionnaire. The questionnaire is not intended to be prescriptive or ideal for a particular implementation but rather provides an example of a legal needs survey questionnaire that addresses the topics set out in earlier sections.

The overall structure is of the broad type discussed in Chapter 2. The questionnaire builds upon the core questions set out in Table 3.3, adopting those questions as an initial core question loop for administration to a reasonable sample of identified problems. Follow-up and further questions are then asked concerning a (sub-) sample of problems included in the initial loop. The (maximum) number of problems to be asked about at the core and follow-up level is not specified. In practice, these numbers reflect the priorities of survey stakeholders. The follow-up questions also include further loops of questions concerning sources of help and processes. For the reason just stated, numbers are again not specified.

While primarily designed for CAPI based face-to-face administration scripts, routing has been minimised to facilitate conversion to pen and paper delivery if necessary. Nevertheless, the questionnaire does contain a significant amount of routing, and paper and pen delivery in its current form would be challenging. The questionnaire could also be easily modified for telephone and online delivery.

To simplify its presentation, not all coding options are included, notably "don't know" and "refused" options.

The form of problem identification questions is not specified, but a longer questionnaire provides opportunity to pose questions covering a greater range of problems. Surveys such as the original *Paths to Justice* survey used show-cards to present respondents with the details of problem types. As noted above, just over half of past national legal needs surveys posed questions concerning 70 or more problem types. Asking about detailed problem types individually is also possible and the best option for telephone surveys. However, if this approach leaves insufficient time to address issues of central importance to survey stakeholders, then it may be necessary to take the expedited approach adopted by the two most recent New Zealand surveys and 2017 Sierra Leone survey.

Most of the questions concerning justiciable problems are drafted to be appropriate for concluded problems. Some questions are asked only of concluded problems, while others may need to be phrased differently for ongoing problems. Indications of alternate phrasing are included in the text. A small number of questions are asked only of ongoing problems.

The longer-form questionnaire draws upon a significant number of past surveys, particularly repeated and larger-scale surveys. In doing so it includes questions that provide an introduction into the broad range of topics covered. Surveys referenced in this guide can also be a source of reference for measurement planners.

In broad terms, the original *Paths to Justice* survey questionnaire is a source of detailed questions on technical aspects of support and formal process. However, the technical nature of its questions has been criticised. The 2012 Colombian survey also included a significant number of questions focused on formal process. The *English and Welsh Civil and Social Justice Survey* and the later *English and Welsh Civil and Social Justice Panel Survey* are a source of detailed questions on the nature, impact and cost of problems, the nature of advice obtained as part of problem resolution, awareness of law and legal services, and reasons for decisions. The 2015 English and Welsh survey (not an iteration of the *English and Welsh Civil and Social Justice Survey*) developed substantially upon the last of these in relation to the choice of advisor. The 2014 Canadian survey also included a substantial set of questions focused on the impact and cost of problems. HiiL's *Justice Needs and Satisfaction Survey* includes an extensive set of questions focused on the cost and quality of process.

Table B.1. Illustrative longer-form legal needs survey questionnaire

Content	Explanatory notes
Introduction	
Good morning/afternoon/evening. My name is ... and I am with ... who have been commissioned by ... to conduct a survey to find out how people deal with a range of issues people can face in everyday life, such as with housing, work, or within families, and the types of help that are needed and used to do this. Your [address/telephone number] has been randomly selected for inclusion in the survey, as one of an intended sample of *x* [addresses/ telephone numbers across the country], as it is important that we collect information about the experience of a representative group of people. The questions should take about ... minutes, and to achieve a fully random sample I would like to ask them of the person at this address who will be the next to have a birthday and is currently *y* years old or above. Would that be you, and if not, could I speak to that person? [Repeat if necessary] Any answers you give are confidential, and participation in the survey is entirely voluntary. If you agree to participate, you may choose to skip a question or end the interview if you so wish. No information that identifies you will be shared or used in any report of the survey's findings [Additional text to meet ethical requirements, as required] Do you agree to participate?	An introduction serves to frame a survey, and to ensure that the ethical requirements for personal interviews and collection of personal data are met. An introduction should also engage respondents, motivating them to complete a questionnaire. Thus, text should be added to explain the importance of the survey in a manner likely to resonate with potential respondents. As discussed in Chapter 2, reference to law and the use of technical language should be avoided in the introduction to a legal needs survey, and justiciable problems should be described in lay terms. If incentives are offered for participation in a survey, details should also be included in the introduction.
Initial demographics	
[Basic demographics and demographics for routing]	For efficiency, some legal needs survey questions can be filtered by demographics. For example, if business related problems are asked about following Q3, then an initial demographic question could be used to identify who is to be asked.

Content	Explanatory notes
Problem identification	
1. I am going to read you a list of problems and disputes that people commonly experience in everyday life. In each case, can you tell me whether or not you have personally experienced any such problem in the past two years, by which I mean a problem that started since [REFERENCE DATE] or started before then, but continued afterwards? (Please only include problems that you have had yourself, in a private capacity, not problems experienced by a business you run, in the course of self-employment or by your employer, and not situations where you represented or helped somebody else with their problem. Please only mention problems once. Since [DATE] have you had any problems or disputes to do with … [Detailed problem types presented on show-cards or individually, grouped by Table 3.1 categories]	This is the most important question in the questionnaire. It determines the scope of the survey. If the question is poorly worded, then out-of-scope problems will be followed-up and/or in-scope problems will be missed. The greater and more accurate the detail of problem descriptions, the more effective the question will be. The question is the first asked, as all other questions rely upon data obtained from it. If respondents have experienced problems in a category, then Q2 and Q3 should be asked immediately, for efficiency purposes. If Q2 > 1, then Q3 should be looped for up to *x* number of problems.
2. [For each Q1 problem category reported, ASK IMMEDIATELY (i.e. do not wait until all Q1 categories have been asked about)] How many such problems have you experienced in the past two years? Please count problems of the same type, where the other party remains the same, as one problem.	
3. [For each Q1 problem category reported, ASK IMMEDIATELY for all / up to *x* number of problems. If Q2 > 1 ask about problems in order of recency, starting with the most recent] Thinking about the problem as a whole, consider a scale of 1 to 10, where 1 represents the least serious type of problem you could face and 10 represents the most serious. To provide some examples, a score of 9 might be [ANCHOR 1] and a score of 2 might be [ANCHOR 2]. What number best represents the seriousness of your problem?	This question is asked at this early point in the questionnaire as the data it generates will be used to identify the pool of problems sufficiently serious for follow-up. Data generated by this question is also of broader interest. It can contribute to measuring unmet legal need using the framework set out in Figure 2.1, enable the relative seriousness of problems to be investigated, and explored as a predictor of strategy choices, etc.
Core question loop	
[Randomly select *y* number of problems from the pool of identified problems with seriousness scores of 3 or more. For each selected problem, ask Q4 to Q23. If there are no such problems, go to Q81]	If there is interest in including business related problems, then one of the strategies outlined in Chapter 2 should be adopted. Either business problems can be asked about separately, following completion of initial problem identification, or the text excluding business problems can be removed (or modified, along the lines of the 2017-18 Nepalese survey, to include "problems experienced through a business that provides you with self-employment (but not an enterprise providing employment to others)") and respondents asked whether problems were faced in a personal or business capacity during follow-up.

Content	Explanatory notes
I am now going to ask you some questions about [PROBLEM 1, etc.] 4a. What was the problem about? [Code to detailed Table 2.1 categories] 4b. Did you share this particular problem with other people, neighbours, or other members of your community (as in the case of some problems concerning, for example, the environment or communal land)? 4c. [If 4(b) = Yes] Who did you share it with? a) Household member(s) b) Other friend(s) or family member(s) c) Work colleague(s) d) Neighbour(s) e) Community f) Other	Question 4(a), (b) and (c) check Q3 data, provide examples of problem detail for reporting, and further define the nature of the problems reported. Questions 4(b) and 4(c) identify whether problems are shared. They provide indication of the extent to which justiciable problems are experienced across populations.
5. Did you obtain any information from the Internet, an app, a video, printed material or the media to help you better understand or resolve the problem? a) A website or "app" b) A leaflet, book or self-help guide c) Newspapers or magazines d) Television, video or radio	
6. (Apart from anything you have told me about already) Did you, or someone acting on your behalf, obtain information, advice or representation from any of the following people or organisations to help you better understand or resolve the problem? Please exclude any help provided by the other party. [ASK EACH SEPARATELY] a) Family, friends or acquaintances (excluding people whose job is to advise on problems such as these; please mention these people in their professional capacity) b) A lawyer, professional advisor, advice service or advice helpline, such as [examples] (SPECIFY) c) A court [or tribunal] or other dispute resolution organisation (such as [examples]) or the police (SPECIFY) d) A national, regional or municipal government department, agency, council or a politician (SPECIFY) e) Your employer, a trade union or professional association, or a trade association (such as [examples]) (SPECIFY) f) A health, welfare, financial services or other professional (SPECIFY) g) A community or religious leader or organisation, an [NGO/charity], or trusted person or organisation (SPECIFY) h) Any other person or organisation (SPECIFY)	Further specification is included in the question to enable coding to a detailed set of categories based on the Table 2.2 taxonomy. An open form of this question could also be used here: Apart from anything you have told me about already) did you or someone acting on your behalf obtain information, advice or representation from any person or organisation to help you better understand or resolve the problem? For example, from family or friends; a lawyer, professional advisor or advice service; a court, government body, or the police; a health or welfare professional; a trade union or employer; a religious or community leader or organisation; an [NGO/charity], a trusted person or organisation or anybody else? [PROBE] If Q6 (particularly in its open form) is asked ahead of Q5, there is a risk that information obtained via mass communication channels will be reported in Q6, preventing a clear distinction between this and help received personally.

Content	Explanatory notes
7. (Apart from anything you have told me about already) Did any of the following things happen as part of [PROBLEM 1, etc.] or sorting it out? When I say "you" here, I mean you or somebody acting on your behalf. [ASK EACH SEPARATELY] a) You communicated with the other party b) You or the other party made a claim to, or made use of, a court (or tribunal) c) [If applicable] You or the other party made a claim to, or made use of, an [Indigenous/ customary] dispute resolution process (e.g. [examples]) d) [PROBLEM 1, etc.] was reported to the police (or other prosecution authority) e) You or the other party turned to, or action was taken by, a formal designated authority or agency, such as [examples, e.g. Ombudsman, regulator (e.g. [example]) or enforcement authority (e.g. consumer protection authority)] f) You or the other party turned to, or action was taken by, another state authority (e.g. [examples]) g) You or the other party turned to, or action was taken by, a religious authority h) You or the other party turned to, or action was taken by, a community leader or organisation (e.g. [example]) i) You participated in formal mediation, conciliation or arbitration (e.g. [examples]) j) You or the other party made use of a formal appeals process operated by the other party or independently k) You, the other party or somebody else turned to, or action was taken by, another third party for adjudication, mediation or intervention l) There was no negotiation or third party involvement	As with Q6, an open form of this question could also be used here: Did you, somebody acting on your behalf, the other party or anybody else, make a claim to a court (or tribunal), or turn to any other third-party individual or organisation such as [institutional examples] or to a community or religious leader [or respected family member] to adjudicate, mediate or intervene to help resolve [PROBLEM 1, etc.]? [PROBE] Process is asked about separately to help, as respondents will not necessarily choose, or even engage with, processes. Thus, it is distinct from help seeking and other problem-solving behaviours.
8. [For each positive Q7 response for *a* to *k*] Who initiated this action? [READ OUT ONLY IF NECESSARY] a) The respondent b) The other party c) The third party responsible for the process d) Another third party.	For efficiency, Q8 should be asked of each process type the moment it is reported. Likewise, Q9 should immediately follow all instances of Q8.
9. [If the respondent did not initiate processes *b* to *h* or *j* and *k*] Did you respond to this action?	
10. Did you, or somebody acting on your behalf, do anything else to help you better understand or resolve the problem, such as communicate with the other party, obtain or organise evidence, or make an insurance claim? [OPEN] a) Communicated with the other party b) Obtained or organised evidence c) Made an insurance claim d) Other (SPECIFY)	Without this "catch-all" question, it is not possible to be certain whether respondents took no action to try to understand or resolve reported problems.
11. Is the problem ongoing or done with? By "done with" I mean that the problem is either resolved or that it persists, but you and everybody else have given up all efforts to resolve it further. [PROBE]	This is an essential question for enabling coherent data analysis. Problems that are ongoing and problems that are concluded are not equivalent. For example, unmet needs within ongoing problems may go on to be met.

Content	Explanatory notes
a) Ongoing b) Too early to say c) Done with - problem persists, but all have given up trying to resolve it further d) Done with - problem resolved	The wording used here is careful to suggest finality.
12. [If Q11 = *c* OR *d*, otherwise go to Q17] Which of the following statements best reflects how the problem outcome was ultimately brought about? The problem outcome was ultimately brought about by … [ASK EACH SEPARATELY] a) a court (or tribunal) judgment b) a decision or intervention by another formal authority c) mediation, conciliation or arbitration d) action by another third party e) agreement between you and the other party f) the other party independently doing what you wanted g) you independently doing what the other party wanted h) the problem sorting itself out i) your moving away from the problem (e.g. moving home, changing job) j) [Only if Q10 = c] … you and/or all other parties giving up trying to resolve the problem	It is important not to conflate process (as asked about in previous questions) with the manner in which problems conclude. They are linked, but distinct.
13. Do you feel the outcome of this problem was basically fair to everybody concerned? a) Fair to everybody concerned b) Not fair to everybody concerned	Q13 and Q14 concern quality of process and outcome. Q14 can also contribute to measurement of unmet legal need using the framework set out Figure 2.1
14. Regardless of the outcome of this problem, do you feel the process through which the outcome was reached was basically fair or unfair to everybody concerned? a) Fair to everybody concerned b) Not fair to everybody concerned	
15. Excluding indirect payments – such as insurance premiums or membership subscriptions – but including payments made by family members and friends, [did you/have you], personally [have/had] to pay for any of the following in order to resolve the problem: [ASK EACH SEPARATELY] a) Lawyer and other advisor fees b) Court, mediation or other administrative fees c) Telephone calls and correspondence d) Collecting information or obtaining evidence (incl. reimbursement of witnesses' costs) e) Travel (e.g. bus fares or petrol to visit an advisor) f) Lost business or salary, from taking time off work (e.g. to obtain advice) g) Bribes / kick-backs (Remember, your answer is confidential)	If interest is limited to legal service costs and process fees, then a shorter Q15 is appropriate, although it will not provide the same insight in benefit-cost analysis: "Excluding indirect payments – such as insurance premiums or membership subscriptions – but including payments made by family members and friends, [did you/have you], personally [have/had] to pay for [the help you received from [advisor]/[process] fees]?" If respondents report costs for a category, then Q16 should be asked immediately, for efficiency purposes. Q15 can be shortened by not asking about each cost item separately, but with fewer items the data will be ambiguous.

Content	Explanatory notes
h) Incidental domestic costs (e.g. childcare)	
16. "Approximately how much [did you have/have you had] to pay for [cost item]?"	If a shorter version of Q15 is used, then Q16 should be phrased as follows: "Approximately how much in total did it cost you to deal with this problem?" This phrasing is inappropriate if individual cost items have been identified, as respondents will in any event need to add the cost of the items. Another approach is to ask the following: "How difficult was it to find the money to pay for this/these things?"
17. Which of the following describe the problem? You can choose more than one option, or none. [ASK EACH SEPARATELY] a) Bad luck / part of life b) Bureaucratic c) A family or private matter d) Legal e) Political f) A social or community matter g) Economic h) None of these	Q17 and Q18 together address the four broad aspects of legal capability discussed in Chapter 2. The two questions also provide data that can be used as part of the process of measuring unmet legal need using the framework set out in Figure 2.1.
18. To what extent do you agree or disagree with the following statements about the problem? [strongly agree, mainly agree, mainly disagree, strongly disagree] a) I understood or [came/have come] to understand my legal rights and responsibilities b) I [knew/know] where to get good information and advice about resolving the problem c) I [was able/have been able] to get all the expert help I needed d) I [was/am] confident I [could/can] achieve a fair outcome	
19. Did you experience any of the following as part of or as a result of this problem? [ASK EACH SEPARATELY] a) ill-health or injury b) stress c) damage to a family relationship d) being harassed, threatened or assaulted e) damage to your property f) loss of employment	

Content	Explanatory notes
g) having to move home h) financial loss i) loss of confidence or fear j) problems to do with your education k) problems with alcohol or drugs	
20. [If 6 = NO to all items] Why didn't you obtain independent advice to help resolve [PROBLEM 1, etc.]? [PROBE] [DO NOT READ] [CODE ALL THAT APPLY] a) No dispute with anybody/thought other party was right b) Problem resolved without need to get advice c) Did not think needed advice d) Did not think problem important enough e) Concerned about the time it would take f) Concerned about the financial cost g) Advisers were too far away h) Thought it would be too stressful i) Thought it would damage relationship with other party j) Was scared to take action/get advice k) Didn't know where/how to get advice l) Didn't think it would make any difference to the outcome m) Had tried seeking advice before and not found it useful n) Other (SPECIFY)	As well as providing valuable strategic information concerning obstacles to advice, this question also provides data that can be used as part of the process of measuring unmet legal need using the framework set out at in Table 2.1. If interest is primarily in legal advice, then the routing for this question can be amended to ask about only this.
21. Finally, can you tell me roughly what month and year the problem started?	Establishing problem start and end dates provides greater flexibility in using ongoing problems within analyses.
22. [If Q11=c] And when did you and everybody else give up all actions to resolve the problem?	
23. [If Q11=d] And when did it conclude?	
[End of core question loop]	
Detailed problem loop: Nature	
[Randomly select *z* number of problems from those asked about in the core question loop. For each selected problem, ask Q24 to Q80. If there are no such problems, go to Q81]	The number of problems asked about in the core question loop and in this detailed problem loop will often be the same. However, the cap in number may vary between the sections to reflect different stakeholder priorities. If the cap is the same, then the questionnaire could be restructured to include one, rather than two, main loops.
I am now going to ask you some more detailed questions about different aspects of [PROBLEM 1, PROBLEM 2, etc.]. First some questions about the nature of [PROBLEM 1, etc.].	
Detailed problem loop: Nature	

Content	Explanatory notes
24. Which of the following [was/is] being sought? [READ OUT] [CODE ALL THAT APPLY] a) Money or property b) Something being restored to how it was c) Somebody recognising rights or meeting responsibilities d) Change to the nature of a relationship d) Change to a decision f) An apology g) Something else (Other)	To simplify routing, this question follows the approach of the Justice Needs and Satisfaction Survey and asks about the subject matter of the problem rather than ask about objectives.
25. Who was the problem with? [DO NOT READ] [CODE ONE ONLY (most relevant to problem)] a) Family member b) Friend c) Colleague d) Employer e) Neighbour f) Other individual g) Community organisation h) Commercial organisation i) Police j) Other public servant or authority k) Other (SPECIFY)	The codes set out are broadly framed and suitable for use across problem categories. Some surveys have adopted different codes for different problem categories to reflect the nature of the categories and in the interest in greater distinction.
26. Thinking about the time the problem first started, would you say … [READ OUT] [CODE ONE ONLY] a) You thought the other party had done something wrong or were at fault b) The other party thought you had done something wrong c) Or were at fault d) Both thought the other had done something wrong or were at fault e) Or neither thought the other had done anything wrong or were at fault	This question aims to ascertain, in lay language, whether survey respondents were claimants or defendants. The question has been used extensively. It originated in the *English and Welsh Civil and Social Justice Survey*.
27. Was there ever any disagreement between you and the other side about what you or they should do in response to the problem?	Disagreement is relevant when choosing a problem resolving strategy. It has been asked about in a number of surveys. It is also possible to ask about the level of disagreement.
28. Did any party resort to physical violence or threats of violence during the disagreement or in the process of settling the disagreement?	This question is adapted from one in the World Justice Project's *General Population Poll*.
29. Thinking about [PROBLEM 1, etc.] as a whole, which of you or the other side would you say had more resources to address the problem? By resources I mean money, access to specialist help, etc. a) The other party had more resources b) The survey respondent had more resources	Resource imbalance is theorised to affect both resolution strategy and outcomes.

Content	Explanatory notes
c) The parties had equal resources d) Don't know	
30. Excluding the other party, was the problem shared with other people, such as members of your family, friends, colleagues, neighbours or other members of your community? [CODE ONE ONLY] a) No, only me b) Family or friends c) Colleagues d) Neighbours or community	This question is adapted from the Argentina survey and World Justice Project's *General Population Poll* (GPP). The GPP also included a follow-up, asking whether, "to achieve a solution, did you require that these people agree with your position or that they took collective action?" Surveys in which members of households are interviewed separately have also asked about problem sharing, to ascertain if problems are reported on multiple occasions.
31. Do you think [PROBLEM 1, etc.] was due to you being discriminated against on the basis of any of the following? [READ OUT] [CODE ALL THAT APPLY] a) Age b) Gender c) Disability/ill-health d) Ethnicity e) Caste/economic class f) Religion g) Political affiliation h) Sexual orientation	In some surveys, discrimination has been asked about as a discrete problem category. However, here the approach of the *English and Welsh Civil and Social Justice Survey* has been adopted, with discrimination asked about as an attribute of problems of any category. The forms of discrimination asked about should be appropriate for the jurisdiction concerned.
32. [If Q19a=Yes] You said earlier that the problem resulted in ill-health or injury. Did this cause you to visit a health professional or spend time in hospital? a) No b) Visited health professional c) Spent time in hospital	This and the following questions can be used to build up a picture of the overall cost of justiciable problems. Surveys including detailed questions on problem impact include the 2004 *English and Welsh Civil and Social Justice Survey* and the 2014 Canadian survey. Potentially, all types of impact asked about in Q19 could be followed-up.
33. [If Q32b=Yes] How many visits did you make?	Additional questions on health impact could, for example, the cost of medication, etc.
34. [If Q32c=Yes] How long did you stay in hospital?	
35. [If Q19b=Yes] You said earlier that the problem resulted in your suffering from stress. Did this cause you to visit a health professional?	
36. [If Q35=Yes] How many visits did you make?	
37. [If Q19a=Yes OR Q19b=Yes]	

Content	Explanatory notes
How much did you personally have to pay for medical treatment?	
38. [If Q19e=Yes] You said earlier that the problem resulted in your property being damaged. How much did it cost to repair or replace the property (or how much would repair cost)?	
39. [If Q19f=Yes] You said earlier that the problem resulted in you losing your job. How long were you without a job? Months/Weeks/Days	
40.[If Q19f=Yes] How much, if any, income did you lose as a result of losing your job?	
41. [If Q19f=Yes] Did you receive [welfare payments] as a result of losing your job?	
42. [If Q41=Yes] How long did you receive [welfare payments] for?	
43. [If Q41=Yes] How much did you receive in [welfare payments] per month?	
44. [If Q19g=Yes] You said earlier that the problem resulted in you having to move home. How long were you without a permanent home? Months/Weeks/Days	
45. [If Q44>0] a) Relatives or friends b) Emergency housing paid for by government or another organisation c) Emergency housing that you had to pay for yourself d) Other (SPECIFY)	
46. [If Q19h=Yes] You said earlier that the problem resulted in you suffering financial loss. How much money did you lose?	
Detailed problem loop: Information and advice	
[If Q5a=Yes OR any advisor identified at Q6] Now, some questions about support you obtained.	

Content	Explanatory notes
47. [If Q5a=Yes] You mentioned earlier that you obtained information from the Internet or "app" to help better understand or resolve the problem. Which of the following did you obtain? [ASK EACH SEPARATELY] a) Information about your rights and/or the law b) Information about ways to resolve the problem c) Forms or other documents d) The identity of an online dispute resolution process e) The identity of an offline source of help, dispute resolution process or relevant authority f) Contact details for an offline source of help, dispute resolution process or relevant authority g) Something else (SPECIFY)	Relatively few surveys have asked follow-up questions about digital information seeking, although the practice has been common in recent surveys in England and Wales. As with the nature of help obtained from advisors (Q49 et seq., below), establishing the nature of digital information obtained gives insight into levels of support. This and later advisor focused questions can also be used to generate an overall picture of digital service use, along with its social and other stratification. Other information sources could also be followed-up in similar fashion.
48. [If Q5a=Yes] How useful did you find the Internet in trying to resolve the problem? a) Very useful b) Somewhat useful c) Not very useful d) Not useful at all	This question contributes to assessments of digital service delivery and the relative value of different forms of support. If the former is of particular interest, then examples of additional questions include: "How much of what you were looking for did you find?" "Excluding search engines (such as Google), what was the most useful website that you visited, or app that you used to obtain information from the Internet?"
Information and advice sub-loop	
[If advisors identified in Q6, go to Q49. Otherwise go to Q65] [[If advisors identified in Q6, questions Q49 to Q64 should be asked in a loop until no further advisors are detailed at Q50c or a maximum number of *y* advisors has been asked about, with *y* being determined with reference to interview length and the results of piloting]	Many respondents will obtain help from only one advisor. However, help can be – and often is – obtained from multiple advisors. Following-up only a single advisor in this case can be problematic. First, advice is relatively uncommon across typical samples, which may result in unviable advisor sample sizes (especially in relation to particular advisor types). Also, there can be a difference in what is sought from first, lest, etc., advisors. This means selection of advisors for follow-up must be carefully considered. Following-up all advisors can also be problematic, yielding lengthy "outlier" interviews. A sensible compromise, adopted in the 2017-2018 Nepal survey, is to follow-up three or four advisors, so only rarely excluding advisors from follow-up. Many of the questions in this section can be easily adapted to be asked of advisors as a whole.
49. [If exactly one advisor type identified at Q6] You (also) mentioned that you, or someone acting on your behalf, obtained help from [Q6 ADVISOR] to better understand or resolve the problem. Can I just check, [did you obtain/have you obtained] help from more than one [Q6 ADVISOR]? [If Q49=No, go to Q51]	The term "help" can be used here, as the distinction between information/advice/ representation and process has already been established.

Content	Explanatory notes
50a. [If Q49 = Yes] From whom did you first obtain help? [Record non-identifying description to distinguish advisors within this section] [Go to Q51]	This simple approach to ordering advisors, used previously in (for example) the 2014 Canadian survey, avoids the need to identify the number of advisors of each type at Q6.
50b. [If more than one advisor type identified at Q6] You (also) mentioned that you, or someone acting on your behalf, obtained help from [LIST OF ADVISOR TYPES IDENTIFIED AT Q6] to better understand or resolve the problem. From whom did you first obtain help? Do not give their name, just indicate the type of person or organisation. [Go to Q51]	
50c. [If 50a or 50b asked previously] [OPEN: Use for inserts] [Simultaneously code to Q6 codes] After [ADVISOR 1, etc.], who did you obtain help from next? Do not give their name, just indicate the type of person or organisation. [Go to Q52 if If ADVISOR 2 (etc.) if Q6 category (a), otherwise go to Q53, or, if 50c=Nobody else, go to Q65]	
51. [ADVISOR 1 ONLY] What was the trigger for you getting help from [ADVISOR 1]?	
52. [If ADVISOR 1, etc. is Q6 category (a)] Can I just check, does [ADVISOR 1, etc.] have professional experience of helping people with problems of the type you faced?	This question confirms coding at Q6 and ensures that a distinction can be drawn between friends, etc., who are advisors and friends who are not. It is relevant in relation to whether legal need is met or unmet.
53. [If ADVISOR 1, etc. is NOT Q6 category (a)] How did you find out about [ADVISOR 1, etc.]? [PROBE] [DO NOT READ] [CODE ALL THAT APPLY] a) Previous use b) Referral from another advisor c) Friend, family or colleague d) Online e) Yellow pages, or similar offline directory f) Newspaper/magazine/radio g) Other (SPECIFY)	This question relates to advice seeking decision making. It can be included if there is interest in understanding more about how advisors are identified and chosen. This was a particular focus of the 2015 English and Welsh survey.
54. In which of the following ways did [or do] you communicate with [ADVISOR 1, etc.]? [ASK EACH SEPARATELY]	This and the following questions provide information concerning, for example, how support is accessed, the use of digital services and the reach of different service channels. Previous surveys have indicated that channels vary because of distances to advisors and demography.

Content	Explanatory notes
a) Saw the advisor in person b) By telephone c) By email d) Through a website or app e) By post f) Some other way (specify)	
55. And what was [or is] the most common way you communicated with [ADVISOR 1, etc.]? [ASK EACH SEPARATELY] a) Saw the advisor in person b) By telephone c) By email d) Through a website or app e) By post f) Some other way (specify)	
56. [If Q55=a] When you met [or meet] [ADVISOR 1, etc.] in person, how did [or do] you usually get there? a) By car/van/motorcycle b) By public transport c) Walked/cycled	
57. Approximately how long did [or does] it take you to reach [ADVISOR 1, etc.]? Days/Hours/Minutes	Some surveys – such as those in Nepal, Poland and the *Justice Needs and Satisfaction Survey* – have focused on time, while others – such as the 2010 Ukraine survey and the *English and Welsh Civil and Social Justice Survey* – have focused on distance. Here, time is used, acknowledging that the impact of distance may vary considerably across jurisdictions. If there is interest in calculating the total time respondents spent travelling to advisors (e.g. in relation to cost-benefit analyses), a further follow-on question can ask, "…and how many times did you travel to see the advisor?" This question was asked in the Polish survey. The cost of travel is separately captured in Q15. The most comprehensive treatment of mode of contact, duration, distance, etc., was in the 2006-2009 *English and Welsh Civil and Social Justice Survey.*
58. Which of the following did [or has] [ADVISOR 1, etc.] [do/done] to help you? [ASK EACH SEPARATELY] a) Provided pre-packaged information, such as a leaflet b) Provided information about your rights and/or the law	This question gives insight into levels of support and the types of support provided by different advisors. To provide a more detailed picture of the success of help-seeking, the *English and Welsh Civil and Social Justice Panel Survey* also asked what types of help were sought from advisers, as well as further questions concerning the nature of the help obtained.

Content	Explanatory notes
c) Provided information about ways to resolve the problem d) Provided information about types of financial support available to help you resolve the problem e) Recommended what you should do f) Helped with paperwork g) Communicated with the other party on your behalf h) Communicated with relevant authorities i) Managed the problem resolution process on your behalf j) [IF Q7=b-k] Represented you in [PROCESSES] k) Suggested where to go for further information, advice or representation l) Something else (specify)	The question could be asked as an open question, although this could impact on coding consistency.
59. [If Q58=k] Did you go on to get further help from the source suggested by [ADVISER 1, etc.]?	
60. Would you describe the help that [ADVISOR 1, etc.] provided as mostly legal in nature?	Past surveys indicate that people facing justiciable problems seek help from a broad array of sources, many of which provide help that is not legal in nature. The type of help obtained can be relevant in determining whether legal need is met or unmet.
61. [If Q6b=Yes] Did you receive funding (for example, through legal aid), or have insurance, to help to pay for the assistance you received from [ADVISOR 1, etc.]? a) No b) Yes, legal aid c) Yes, insurance d) Yes, other funding (SPECIFY)	If the cost of help from specific advisors is of interest, then it should be asked about ahead of Q61.
62. How useful was [ADVISER 1, etc.] in resolving the problem? a) Very useful b) Somewhat useful c) Not very useful d) Not useful at all	This question corresponds with Q48.
63. Would you recommend other people in your situation to consult [ADVISOR 1, etc.]?	While similar to the previous question, this question combines satisfaction and utility. It also provides a broader base for Q64.
64. [If Q63 = No] Why is that? [DO NOT READ] [CODE ALL THAT APPLY] a) Made no difference or made problem worse b) Inadequate, poor or badly explained advice c) Not the kind or level of support sought d) Too far away or hard to get to e) Inconvenient opening hours	

Content	Explanatory notes
f) Too expensive g) Language barrier h) Other (SPECIFY) [If Q49=No, go to Q65, otherwise go to Q50c]	
[End of information and advice sub-loop]	
65. [If any advisors identified at Q6: "In addition to the sources of help you have told me about"] Did you try unsuccessfully to obtain information, advice or representation from anywhere [else]?	Unsuccessful attempts to obtain help indicate structural obstacles to access.
66. [If QX=Yes] Where did you try unsuccessfully to obtain information, advice or representation from? [CODE TO Q6 CODES]	This question corresponds to Q6, although is closed in form. A form more similar to Q6 could be used if there are concerns about recall accuracy.
67. [If Q65=Yes OR Any advisor identified at Q6 (excluding category (a)] [If Q65=Yes AND Any advisor identified at Q6: "Including sources you did get help from"] Did you experience any of the following difficulties when trying to get help from the sources you have mentioned? [ASK EACH SEPARATELY] a) Too far away or hard to get to b) Inconvenient opening hours c) Difficulty getting through on the phone d) Difficulty getting an appointment e) Too long to get a response f) Too expensive g) Language barrier h) Poor adaptation for disabilities i) Inadequate, poor or badly explained advice j) Source not able or willing to help k) Any other difficulty (SPECIFY)	This question could be linked exclusively to the previous question but can also – as here and in Mongolia and Nepal, for example – provide a more general indication of obstacles faced. Though an open form could also be used, this question adopts the approach of surveys in, for example, Argentina, Mongolia and Nepal, to stimulate recollection in relation to convenience, access and quality.
68. [If Q15a=Yes] You mentioned earlier that you had to pay for lawyer or other advisor fees. How difficult was it to find the money to meet these costs?	
69. [If Q11=a] Do you intend to get advice about the problem in the future?	This question is asked about ongoing problems to give a fuller picture of problem resolution strategy.
Detailed problem loop: Process and outcome	
Now, some questions about the problem resolution process and outcome.	
[If processes identified in Q6 (excluding a and d), go to Q70. Otherwise go to Q73] [For all respondents who answer QX, questions QX to QZ should be asked in a loop	No questions concerning the details of Q6 processes are included, as processes tend to be rare and understanding of technical aspects of process limited. If

Content	Explanatory notes
until no further advisors are detailed at QX or a maximum number of *y* advisors has been asked about, with *y* being determined with reference to interview length and the results of piloting]	there is interest in such questions, the original *Paths to Justice* survey contained a significant number of detailed questions.
70. Thinking about [PROCESS 1, etc.] why did you choose this way of trying to resolve the problem? [PROBE] [DO NOT READ] [CODE ALL THAT APPLY] a) Appropriate authority/process b) Advisor chose or recommended c) Previous use d) Cost e) Convenience I didn't choose	This question is adapted from the Colombia 2012 survey.
71. Thinking about [PROCESS 1, etc.], to what extent do you agree or disagree with the following statements. For each statement, please tell me whether you strongly agree, mainly agree, mainly disagree or strongly disagree. a) The process was fair and I had opportunity to explain my position b) I was treated with respect c) The process and decisions were clearly explained d) The outcome of the process was much the same as for other people in similar situations The process concluded in a timely matter	This question includes single items for each of procedural, interpersonal and informational justice and outcome transparency (discussed in Chapter 2). There is also an item concerning timeliness. If there is interest in additional questions, the *Justice Needs and Satisfaction Survey* includes many further examples, based on the extensive *Measuring Access to Justice in a Globalising World* project.
72. Was any part of [PROCESS 1, etc.] conducted online, incorporate online submission of forms or evidence?	
[End of process sub-loop]	
73. Thinking about the problem resolution process as a whole, how stressful did you find it? Very stressful, fairly stressful or not very stressful?	While the problem resolution process may bring about benefits, it also involves economic and other costs.
74. Again, thinking about the problem resolution process as a whole, [were you/have you been] asked to (or did you need to) pay a bribe or incentive as a part of the process of resolving a problem?	
75. And do you feel that at any point in the problem resolution process you [were/have been] discriminated against, in how the problem [was/has been] dealt with, on the basis of any of the following? [READ OUT] [CODE ALL THAT APPLY] a) Age b) Gender c) Disability/ill-health d) Ethnicity e) Caste/economic class f) Religion g) Political affiliation h) Sexual orientation	Questions concerning discrimination have generally related to the nature of problems. However, the Mongolia survey also asked about discrimination in the context of the problem resolution process.

Content	Explanatory notes
76. [If Q11=c OR d] Thinking about the problem outcome, to what extent do you agree or disagree with the following statements. For each statement, please tell me whether you strongly agree, mainly agree, mainly disagree or strongly disagree. a) The outcome involved a fair distribution of benefits and burdens b) Any loss or harm arising from the problem (e.g. financial or concerning relationships) has been made good c) [ONLY IF Q11=d] The problem was solved in a timely manner and is unlikely to reoccur [ONLY IF Q12=a to e] The [decision of the [Q12 process]/agreement] was fulfilled]	This question includes single items for each of distributive and restorative justice and outcome functionality (discussed in Chapter 2). If there is interest in additional questions, the *Justice Needs and Satisfaction Survey* includes many further examples, based on the extensive *Measuring Access to Justice in a Globalising World* project.
77. Was the outcome better or worse than you had hoped for?	
78. [If Q13=Yes] Did resolving the problem fairly lead to improvements in any of the following? [INCLUDE PREVIOUSLY REPORTED Q13 ITEMS] a) Your health b) Levels of stress c) Family relationships d) Levels of harassment or violence e) Your employment situation f) Your housing situation g) Your finances h) Your confidence i) Your education situation j) Your alcohol or drug problems	This question could also be routed from Q76 or a combination of Q13 and Q67. Or Q11=c OR d
79. Is there anything that you wish you had done differently to try to sort out the problem? [PROBE] [DO NOT READ] [CODE ALL THAT APPLY] a) Got (more) information or advice b) Got information or advice sooner c) Acted sooner d) Been more resolved e) Not get advice f) Taken no action g) Avoided the problem h) Other (SPECIFY)	
80. And, looking back on this problem and [how things turned out/how it is progressing], do you feel the situation might [have worked out better/be progressing better] if you had obtained [more] information, advice or other support? a) Yes, definitely	

Content	Explanatory notes
b) Yes, probably c) Not sure d) No, probably not e) No, definitely not	
[End of detailed problem loop]	
Legal capability	
General legal capability questions can be placed either following initial demographics questions (at the start of the questionnaire) or ahead of the additional demographics section (at the end of the questionnaire). If capability questions are placed at the start they must be formulated to avoid drawing attention to the 'legal' focus of the questionnaire. A benefit of including general legal capability questions at the start is that they can help to engage respondents; particularly those who go on to report no justiciable problems. Placing questions at the start also means that respondents will not have been exposed to questions providing names of sources of help, processes, etc. However, if access to justice related attitude questions are included in a questionnaire, they should appear here; as they will then benefit from respondents' reflections on their own experience of justiciable issues.	
Finally, some questions about your confidence in being able to resolve problems such as those I have been asking you about, and your perceptions of the justice system in [JURISDICTION]	Questions concerning legal capability have generally been drafted on an ad hoc basis, with measures developed without use of modern psychometric methods. If survey stakeholders have particular interest in, say, perceptions of a specific aspect of the justice system, appropriately developed questions may not be available. If this is the case, there may be little scope for appropriate development. The following questions incorporate three sets of questions that can be used as scales found to have acceptable psychometric properties (see Chapter 2 above), along with further theoretically grounded questions in a commonly used form. Particularly in this section, questions are illustrative, and a very different approach may sometimes be necessary in practice. However, if untested questions are used, their limitations should be acknowledged.
81. Thinking about significant legal problems – such as being unreasonably sacked by your employer, injured as a result of someone else's negligence, involved in a dispute over money as part of a divorce, or facing eviction from your home. To what extent do the following statements describe you? For each statement say whether it is not at all true, hardly true, moderately true or exactly true. a) I can always manage to solve difficult problems if I try hard enough. b) If someone opposes me, I can find the means and ways to get what I want. c) It is easy for me to stick to my aims and accomplish my goals. d) I can remain calm when facing difficulties because I can rely on my coping abilities. e) When I am confronted with a problem, I can usually find several solutions. f) I am good at finding information to help resolve problems. g) I am afraid to speak to people directly to press my rights h) Worry that I don't express myself clearly can stop me from acting. i) I avoid pressing my rights because I am not confident that I will be successful. j) I do not always get the best outcome for myself because I try to avoid conflict.	This first question, incorporating ten items, includes both the Legal Self-Efficacy Scale (LEF) and the Legal Anxiety Scale (discussed in Chapter 2). Both scales were developed using modern psychometric methods and have acceptable psychometric properties. Scoring guidance is available. The example problems that are included are those detailed in the user guidance. However, it may occasionally be necessary to adapt these to be jurisdictionally appropriate. Placement of the scales towards the end of the questionnaire allows reference to the range of justiciable problems already discussed. This will strengthen contextual understanding.

Content	Explanatory notes
82. If you had a dispute with an official authority regarding, for example, an application to get vital registration, how confident are you that you could achieve a fair outcome, one you would be happy with? Very confident, quite confident, not very confident or not confident at all? [Prompt if necessary: "This outcome might be achieved by you individually, or through use of an outside person, organisation, or formal dispute resolution process."]	This question is adapted from the "subjective legal empowerment" questions discussed in Chapter 2, and draws on implementations in the *Justice Needs and Satisfaction Survey*, Nepal and England and Wales. As in the 2011 Moldova survey, two additional similar questions are included, rather than (the more traditional) five, as recent testing suggests they do not readily combine as a scale. Problems can be adapted to reference local interests.
83. And if you were unable to resolve such a dispute on your own, where might you get expert help to assist you in resolving the problem? [OPEN]	Appropriate coding will vary substantially between jurisdictions and geographical regions.
84. If you had a dispute with an employer over, for example, your dismissal, how confident are you that you could achieve fair outcome, one you would be happy with? Very confident, quite confident, not very confident or not confident at all? [Prompt if necessary: "This outcome might be achieved by you individually, or through use of an outside person, organisation, or formal dispute resolution process."]	
85. And if you were unable to resolve such a dispute on your own, where might you get expert help to assist you in resolving the problem? [OPEN]	
86. If you became a victim of domestic violence, and were physically assaulted by a family member, how confident are you that you could achieve fair outcome, one you would be happy with? Very confident, quite confident, not very confident or not confident at all? [Prompt if necessary: "This outcome might be achieved by you individually, or through use of an outside person, organisation, or formal dispute resolution process."]	
87. And if you were unable to resolve such a dispute on your own, where might you get expert help to assist you in resolving the problem? [OPEN]	
88. Do you know any places where you can get free legal advice, if you need it? [OPEN]	A simple question asking about awareness of free legal advice services, or legal aid, can be effective in ascertaining the visibility of public legal assistance services. This question is adapted from the Argentina survey.
Now some questions about your perceptions of the justice system. **[Individual attitude questions]**	Previous legal need surveys have included a very broad range of attitude questions, varying in focus (e.g. police, legal system, lawyers, courts, etc.), themes/domains (e.g. fairness, bribery, cost, speed, utility, inequality, access, corruption, etc.), coherence and number.
89. Finally, some questions about your general impression and experience of the justice system. We are not concerned with the "criminal" justice system. We are concerned with the justice system that deals with the sort of issues we have been talking about, such as being unreasonably sacked by your employer, injured as a	Finally, this section includes a third standardised scale, this time of perceived accessibility of justice (the Inaccessibility of Justice (IoJ) scale discussed in Chapter 2). Again, it has acceptable psychometric properties.

Content	Explanatory notes
result of someone else's negligence, involved in a dispute over money as part of a divorce, or facing eviction from your home. Thinking about issues like this, to what extent do you agree or disagree with the following statements: (For each statement, please tell me whether you strongly agree, mainly agree, mainly disagree or strongly disagree.) a) Issues like these are usually resolved promptly and efficiently b) People with less money generally get a worse outcome c) For issues like these, law is like a game in which the skillful and resourceful are more likely to get what they want d) It is easy to take issues like these to court if needed e) For issues like these, lawyers are too expensive for most people to use f) The justice system provides good value for money g) For issues like these, people like me can afford help from a lawyer h) Rich people's lawyers are no better than poor people's lawyers i) Taking a case to court is generally more trouble than it is worth	Scoring guidance is available.
Additional demographics	
[Sensitive and additional demographics]	e.g. health status, poverty proxies, etc.
Concluding remarks	
[If there is interest in recontacting respondents, consent should be obtained at this point.]	

Annex C. Topics included in Legal Needs Surveys to date

This annex sets out the full range of topics included in the more than 50 surveys set out in Table 1.1 and Table 1.2. Some surveys addressed only a few topics, others many. No survey has addressed or could be expected to address all the topics detailed.

Attitudes (general)

- Attitude towards justice system (lawyers, courts, traditional dispute resolution, etc.)
    - Accessibility (including cost, etc.)
    - "Interpersonal justice" (including respect, etc.)
    - "Procedural justice"/fairness (including neutrality, manipulability, etc.)
    - "Informational justice" (including transparency, clarity, etc.)
    - Effectiveness (including timeliness, whether solves problems, etc.)
    - What is most effective means to solve problems today
    - What is most common means to solve problems today

Attitudes (to processes used)

- Fairness of process
    - In general
    - "Interpersonal justice"
    - "Procedural justice"
    - "Informational justice"
- Whether costs reasonable
- Influence on process
- Emotional response to process
- Physical state of institutions (accessibility, location, cleanliness, facilities, etc.)

Capability/empowerment

- Awareness of law – Reported problem
    - at time problem commenced
    - at later date
    - reasons for change
    - Hypothetical (see "Hypothetical scenarios")
- Awareness of legal services - General (open question/list)
    - Reported problem (open question/list)
    - Defined problem (see "Hypothetical scenarios")
    - Proximity
    - Most accessible
    - Legal aid/free legal services (general/specific services/specific problems)

    - Legal aid eligibility
    - Legal Aid reform
    - Cost of legal services
- Awareness of processes/institutions
- Subjective legal empowerment
- Perceived character of reported problem (including whether seen as "legal" / whether considered a problem that should be dealt with using legal mechanisms)
- Whether aware of legal implications of problem
- Whether equipped to deal with experienced problem at outset (general, understanding, knowledge, etc.)
- Ability to meet cost, time, etc., of acting (see also "Cost of problem resolution")

Causes and consequences (of identified justiciable problems)

- Links between reported problems
- Whether reported problems contributed to or followed on from one another
- General impact on life
- Details of broader causes of problems
    - Personal
    - Social
    - Economic
    - Health
    - Environmental
- Details of broader impact of problems
    - Personal (fear, loss of confidence, substance abuse, etc.)
    - Social (damage to relationships, child behaviour, etc.)
    - Economic (lost employment, income, home, etc.)
    - Health (mental, physical, etc.)
    - Environmental (property damage, etc.)
- Duration/cost of period of lost income
- Duration/value of period of welfare receipt
- Use (and type/extent of use) of public services (e.g. health services)
- Other costs of problem impact
- Was any of loss insured/how much recovered through insurance

Choice of advisor

- How found out about advisor
- Whether (in seeking assistance) information sought on:
  - Available services
  - Recommendations
  - Expertise/timeliness
  - Costs of services
  - Regulation of services (and if not, why not)
- Difficulty of obtaining advice
- Whether respondent knew what sort of assistance required
- Factors in choice (e.g. distance, cost, reputation, ethnicity, etc.)

Cost of problem resolution

- Fees paid by respondent
  - Information/documentation/advice/representation
  - Courts and other processes
- Fees met by third parties
  - Information/documentation/advice/representation
  - Courts and other processes
- Itemisation of fees
  - Global
  - Itemised (to whom, for what, etc.)
- Where payments made by respondent, source of funds (e.g. savings, loan, etc.)
- Form of fees (fixed, hourly billing, etc.)
- If not fixed fees, whether and what estimate provided at outset (and form of communication)
- Explanation of higher fee than estimate
- Whether any negotiation on fees, and if successful
- Legal aid
  - Whether Legal Aid applied for
  - Whether Legal Aid received
  - If refused Legal Aid, why
  - What Legal Aid covered

- Details of other third parties meeting fees (e.g. Legal Aid, insurance company, etc.)
- Other monetary costs borne by respondent (e.g. travel, communication, evidence gathering, babysitting etc.) (global, itemised)
- Whether bribes required to be paid as part of problem resolution process, how much and to who
- Other monetary impacts (e.g. lost income (associated with time needed to resolve problem), etc.)
- Proportionality of costs
- What would be an acceptable amount to pay
- How much would have been willing to pay
- Time spent resolving problem (globally/by activity)
- Other (non-money/time) impact *of resolution* (e.g. stress, damage to relationships)
- Cost as an obstacle to action (see also "Reasons")
    - Whether
    - Which aspect of dispute resolution
    - Whether/where information about costs obtained
    - Why information about costs not obtained

Courts/tribunals (see also "Processes used")

- Whether court/tribunal contacted
- Whether formal process issued
- Which court/tribunal
- Whether hearing occurred
- Whether respondent attended
- Tasks undertaken by respondent
- Whether referred to mediation/conciliation
- Whether pressed to give particular testimony
- Whether respondent (and other party) represented, and by who
- Attitude/nature of experience (see "Attitude to processes used")
- Outcome (see also "Outcome")

Demographics

- Household characteristics
- Personal characteristics

Experience of justiciable problems

(open question/presentation of categories/ presentation of detailed problem types) (single or multiple reference periods)

- Number of problems experienced
- Nature of problems experienced (see "Nature of identified justiciable problems")

Formal assistance (from independent "advisors")

- Details of advisor(s)
- Whether friend/relative
- Whether advisor(s) were trained lawyer(s)
- Independence of advisor(s)
- Who appointed/chose lawyer(s)
- Demographics of advisor(s)
- Number of advisors
- Ordering of advisors
- Date of first contact with advisor(s)
- Links between use of different advisors (e.g. signposting, referral, etc.)
- Why particular advisor(s) chosen (see "Choice of advisor")
- Nature of assistance (see "Nature of assistance provided by advisors")
- Form of communication/mode of contact (see "Mode of contact")
- Distance of advisor(s)
- Mode/duration of travel (see "Cost of problem resolution")
- Number of times advisor(s) contacted
- Duration of contact (see "Cost of problem resolution")
- Obstacles/barriers to access (e.g. opening hours, distance, cost, language, etc.)
- Whether assistance obtained through an intermediary
- Whether respondent had to pay (see "Cost of problem resolution")
- Satisfaction with assistance obtained
    - Global
    - Communication
    - Honesty
    - Timeliness
    - Action

- Reasons for satisfaction/dissatisfaction
- Response to being dissatisfied (complaint, advice, etc.)
- Use/satisfaction with response of regulator
- Consequences of response (apology, fee reduction, etc.)
- Utility of assistance obtained
- Relative utility (where multiple advisors) of advisors
- Timeliness of assistance
- Which was "main" advisor (or most useful)
- Impact of assistance from advisors on social, health, and economic circumstances

Historical use of legal services/processes

- Whether/when services used
- Whether/when processes used

Hypothetical scenarios

- Vignettes
    - Awareness of law (see "Capability/empowerment")
    - Awareness of legal services (see "Capability/ empowerment")
    - Predicted problem resolution strategy (global and elements (e.g. use of advisors))
    - Reasons for choice
- Future experience of similar problems (to those reported)
    - Whether different problem resolution strategy likely (global and elements (e.g. use of advisors))
    - Predicted problem resolution strategy (global and elements (e.g. use of advisors))
    - Reasons for choice
- If somebody else experienced same problem
    - Would recommend same strategy/advisor(s)
- Generic
    - Predicted problem resolution strategy (global and elements (e.g. use of advisors, processes, etc.))
    - Who would *not* discuss with

Information (excluding information about advisors)

- What type of information sought

- What type of information obtained
- Where information obtained from (see also "Use of Internet")
- Reason for obtaining information from identified source(s)
- Utility of information

Mediation, conciliation and arbitration (see also "Processes used")

- Whether mediation, conciliation or arbitration organised (and which)
- How many
- What role respondent had
- Whether respondent (and other party) represented
- Attitude/nature of experience (see "Attitude to processes used")
- Outcome (see also "Outcome")

Mode of contact (with advisors)

- Global/individual
- Ever
- First
- Predominant
- Preferred
- Available

Nature of assistance provided by advisors

- What assistance was wanted (general)
- What assistance was sought (e.g. moral support, information/advice, practical support)
- What assistance was obtained
- What information was provided about assistance to be given (on instruction, first meeting)
- Degree of delegation
- Whether prior agreement on what assistance was to be provided
- Whether respondent got all assistance needed
- Character of assistance obtained (e.g. emotional support, legal, practical, etc.)
- Whether advisor provided other services to respondent also
- Whether advisor tried to sell respondent other services

Nature of identified justiciable problems

- Brief description (open text)
- Perceived character of problem (see "Capability/empowerment")
- What problem about (e.g. money, property, changing behaviour, apology, etc.)(see also "Objectives")
- Whether personal or business
- Whether shared (within household)
- Nature of other party/parties (including demographics)
- Relationship with other party/parties
- Whether claimant or defendant / Who considered to be in the right/responsible
- Existence and extent of disagreement
- Problem duration (see "Problem duration")
- Whether ongoing (see 'Problem duration')
- Seriousness (see "Problem seriousness")
- Links to other identified justiciable problems (see "Causes and consequences")
- Whether problem involved discrimination

Objectives (in trying to resolve problem)

- Nature of objective (monetary, non-monetary, etc.)
- Value (of matter problem concerned)
- Relative importance (where multiple objectives)
- Whether objectives achieved (e.g. fully, in part, etc.)

Outcome

- Brief description (open text)
- Whether concluded (see "Problem duration")
- Means disagreement/problem concluded (e.g., through a court decision, negotiation, etc., including "putting up with" problem)
- Satisfaction/happiness with outcome (all parties)
- Favourableness of outcome
- Fairness of outcome (all parties)
    - In general
    - "Distributive justice"
    - "Restorative justice"

- Timeliness of outcome
- Finality of outcome/whether outcome implemented
    - Whether respondent complied
    - Whether other party complied
    - Enforcement mechanisms
- Sufficiency of explanations provided for outcome/"Transparency" of outcome
- Understanding of outcome

Problem duration

- How long problem lasted/has lasted to date
- Problem start date
- Problem end date
- Whether problem ongoing
    - Whether disagreement ongoing
    - Whether problem ongoing
- Whether ongoing problem will conclude
- When ongoing problem will conclude

Problem seriousness

- Relative seriousness
    - Most serious
    - Scaled seriousness (seriousness, importance of resolution, etc.)
    - Impact on life (time spent worrying, ability to live normally, etc.)
- Impact (specific) (see "Causes and consequences")
- Has situation improved/deteriorated
- Seriousness to others

Problem resolution strategy

- Brief description (open text)
- Overall strategy (single questions for determining basic approach)
- Whether thought problem would be sorted out without action
- How difficult it was thought it would be/it turned out to be to sort out problem
- Relative difficulty of resolving (multiple) problems
- Capability to resolve problem (see "Capability")

- Whether any action taken
- Obstacles to action (cost, time, social implications, etc.) (see also "Capability")
- When first action taken
- Whether previous experience influenced strategy
- Whether information obtained (see "Information")
- Whether any information/advice suggested respondent would not obtain objectives (in seeking to resolve problem)
- Contact/negotiation with other party
    - Whether
    - Form of communication
    - What aiming to achieve
    - What achieved
    - Obstacles to contact
    - Unsuccessful attempts to communicate (either way)
    - Contact through an intermediary
- Use of Internet (see "Use of Internet")
- Use of written materials
    - Whether
    - About what
    - Produced by
    - How helpful
- Whether assistance sought/obtained from family/friends ("informal assistance")
    - Whether
    - Who
    - Why
    - What sought
    - What obtained
    - How useful
    - Whether expert
- Sources of formal assistance (see "Formal assistance'"
- Unsuccessful attempts to obtain information (see "Unsuccessful attempts to obtain information/assistance")
- Unsuccessful attempts to obtain formal assistance (see "Unsuccessful attempts to obtain information/assistance")
- Consideration of formal assistance

- Processes used (see "Processes used")
- Consideration of processes
- Third party involvement in sorting out problem (see also "Processes used")
    - Whether/by who solicited
    - Type of involvement
- Other actions to try to resolve problem (e.g. thinking about options, collecting evidence, etc.)
- Whether withdrew claim/defence
- Ordering of elements of strategy
- Reasons for strategy choices (see "Reasons")

Processes used

- Formal processes used
    - Nature
    - Court/tribunal (see "Court/tribunal proceedings")
    - Formal mediation, conciliation or arbitration (see "Mediation, conciliation and arbitration")
    - Ombudsman
    - Police
    - Tribal/social
    - Religious
    - Other
- Informal processes used
    - Nature (e.g. negotiation, use of intermediaries)
- Party initiating process(es)
- Cost of process(es) (see "Cost of problem resolution")
- Whether process(es) concluded problem (see "Outcome")
- Reason for choice of process
- Duration of process(es)
- Ordering of processes
- Whether any documentation needed to be signed, and whether documentation understood
- Language process used
- Availability of interpreter
- Ability to monitor/communication concerning progress of process

- Whether suffered any abuse/discrimination as part of process (including bribes) (see also "Cost of problem resolution")
- Whether suffered any threats or physical violence
- Details of any detention experienced
- Satisfaction with process(es) used
- Utility of processes
- Relative utility (where multiple processes) of processes
- Attitude to processes used (see "Attitude to Processes used")

Reasons

- For inaction
- For not doing more
- For handling a problem alone
- For not obtaining independent advice or other assistance
- For not obtaining legal advice
- For not obtaining help from lawyer
- For obtaining (or considering) help from lawyer
- For obtaining (or considering) help from other source
- For not using formal process
- For withdrawing claim/defence

Regrets (regarding how problem handled)

- Whether regrets about how problem handled
- What wish had done
- What wish had known
- Would assistance have led to a better outcome
- What assistance would have improved outcome

Traditional dispute resolution mechanisms (see also "Processes used")

- Whether traditional dispute resolution mechanism used
- Which traditional dispute resolution mechanism
- Attitude/nature of experience (see "Attitude to processes used")
- Outcome (see also "Outcome")

Unsuccessful attempts to obtain information/formal assistance (from independent "advisors")

- Details of advisor(s)
- Why unable to obtain information
- Why unable to obtain assistance

Use of Internet

(general use/access dealt with separately through demographic questions)

- Whether used
- What looked for/hoped to achieve (e.g. locate help, obtain information, etc.)
- What found/achieved
- Websites visited
- How websites identified/located
- Utility of Internet

OECD PUBLISHING, 2, rue André-Pascal, 75775 PARIS CEDEX 16
(42 2018 55 1 P) ISBN 978-92-64-30952-4 – 2019

www.ingramcontent.com/pod-product-compliance
Lightning Source LLC
Chambersburg PA
CBHW061210240926
51846CB00006B/1178
9789264309524